CONCIERGE
Confidential

MICHAEL FAZIO

with MICHAEL MALICE

The Gloves Come Off—
and the Secrets Come Out!
Tales from the Man Who Serves
Millionaires, Moguls, and
Madmen

ST. MARTIN'S PRESS ✺ NEW YORK

CONCIERGE CONFIDENTIAL. Copyright © 2011 by Michael Fazio with Michael Malice. All rights reserved. Printed in the United States of America. For information, address St. Martin's Press, 175 Fifth Avenue, New York, N.Y. 10010.

www.stmartins.com

Book design by Jonathan Bennett

Library of Congress Cataloging-in-Publication Data

Fazio, Michael.
  Concierge confidential / Michael Fazio with Michael Malice.
     p. cm.
  ISBN 978-0-312-64376-8
  1. Fazio, Michael. 2. Personal concierges. 3. New York (N.Y.) I. Malice, Michael. II. Title.
  HD9999.P3942F39 2011
  640—dc22

                                                             2010039287

First Edition: February 2011

10   9   8   7   6   5   4   3   2   1

This is a true story, though some names have been changed.

Contents

Preface

There's service, and then there are servants.

The nobleman reclining on a chaise lounge and snapping his fingers is the picture of absurdity. Service is much more of a business-to-business transaction. Both parties come to the table with something that the other wants. And much like other business transactions, a little strategy—and simple human consideration—will yield the best possible outcome.

Recently, one of my clients needed help planning a big date. Jordan was contacted to be on the show *The Millionaire Matchmaker* and he wanted his television appearance to reflect his personality and who he was as a person. For a long time, I had been getting Jordan into all the hippest and coolest places in Manhattan. I was glad to do it. He did all the things that one would expect of a young millionaire and yet he wasn't afraid to admit that it was all new to him. He didn't feign indifference, as if everything was expected to happen as if by magic. He was grateful and he was appreciative. The result was a trail of good will and great energy that he left behind wherever he went. Jordan doesn't have any servants, but he doesn't need them. Instead, he has people delighted to give him good service wherever he goes.

We discussed what the ideal date would be. After eliminating his ideas of skydiving, throwing the opening pitch at a Yankee game, and hiring Shaq for a private game of 2-on-1, I helped convince him that a day trip to the Hamptons would be a more solid choice for a reality show date. His budget would accommodate just about anything.

I realized that a forty-minute helicopter ride to East Hampton would be much more fun than the usual two-and-a-half-hour drive from New York City. I also realized a brand-new helicopter would be even more impressive. I made it a point to hit the phones until I found a charter company who had a shiny Bell 407. They were based at Teterboro, forty-five minutes away. Jordan wouldn't think to ask them to transport the helicopter to the Wall Street Heliport—and he didn't need to. I took care of it. All he had to be aware of was that they would be departing from Wall Street at noon.

The helicopter interior could have been designed for James Bond himself. Jordan's date looked to him for cues to what her reaction should be. She worried that she was supposed to act as if she was accustomed to being shuttled in a private helicopter. But Jordan made no attempt to stifle his ecstatic reaction, which made it okay for her to be awestruck, too.

When the couple landed in East Hampton they were picked up by limousine. They were then taken to the most picturesque vineyard in Long Island, Wolffer Estateö, where I'd planned a wine tasting right in between the rows of vines. I convinced East Hampton Gourmet that they should amend their no-delivery policy for Jordan, and he got a gorgeous lunch hand-delivered to the vineyard. Every piece was perfectly orchestrated.

The price tag for his day exceeded $10,000—but I made it feel like a million. That's the difference between good service and *outstanding* service: you get more than you pay for. I didn't need to make sure that the helicopter was the newest one in the fleet. It wasn't necessary for me to personally go over the directions with the limo driver from the heliport to Wölffer. I made it a point to meet with the general manager of the vineyard to see *exactly* where Jordan's table would be, and I personally supervised the packing of their lunch. Throughout the date, I took time out of my day and kept tabs on everything with the vineyard marketing director.

Jordan would never have thought of this level of attention to detail. People in service are better at providing it than clients are at asking for it. The best service means delivering what you wanted—and then delivering what you didn't even *know* you wanted.

During the date, Jordan sent me a simple text: "It's like a movie." Turning a reality show into something out of Hollywood romance is a form of magic, and one I was more than happy to perform.

They say a good magician never reveals his secrets. But I'm about too. . . .

I.
Almondgeddon

You sell the sizzle, and not the steak.

There's no apartment building more sizzling than The Setai Wall Street, which has the chutzpah to describe itself as "the world's most privileged condominium"—and the reputation to back it up.

It's as dark as a nightclub in the lobby, with Buddha Bar music playing in the background. It smells very exotic, too. You can't really tell if it's fresh gardenias, or if they have scented candles, but it definitely smells very nice—and very, very *rich*. The floor is covered with beautiful silk rugs, and the walls are adorned with gigantic tribal jewelry pieces framed in boxes that protrude almost a foot off the wall. You'd expect there to be some Playboy Playmate in a gorgeous nightgown, smoking a cigarette and dipping into caviar, lounging on the sofa in the lobby.

My concierge company had long since taken concierging outside of the hotel context and into luxury buildings, but there's luxury and then there's *luxury*. When it came to our relationships with buildings, we always got the "nice girl," the Betty. We never got the fancy, sexy Veronica—and The Setai was *definitely* Veronica. Being a concierge is often about trying to get behind the velvet rope. Getting The Setai would be like jumping over the rope and parking ourselves there, so that we're not on the other side constantly trying to push our way in. We'd be in a position to decide who gains access.

I wanted to send in a proposal when The Setai was first going to open, but it was hard to sit down and focus. Concierges do more before nine o'clock than most people do in a day. As my staff and I had our meeting, the discussions settled around:

Do organic tampons only come in one absorbency? (They do? Order a crate, then.)

Ms. Strauss wanted Ciao Bella to deliver a salad with grilled chicken to her apartment on Tuesdays and Fridays at noon—but Ciao Bella isn't open for lunch, and they don't deliver. Her "second choice" restaurant, Jacques, is also not open for lunch. Plan C?

Mr. Jaiswal was just inoculated when he climbed Kilimanjaro in Tanzania. Are there inoculations specific to Rwanda for his next trip? (Yes—and *how*.)

Ms. Sheehan needs to be called. Someone needs to remind her that she can't tell anyone where she got her $5,500 ticket for the premiere party for the new Sarah Jessica Parker movie. She also wants to get private typing lessons.

"I don't remember the brand name," Daria reads from a client email, "but I just returned from Moscow and I saw an air purifier in the window of an electronics store. It was really sleek looking and modern. Can you get one of those for me?"

Car service is a must for Robin, our jeweler, who will be carrying $100,000 worth of diamonds to Mr. Stadtmiller's office. He's "too busy" to go into the store; maybe the diamond studs *aren't* for his wife? He also wants a second-hand television for $75 or less delivered to his office—*today*.

There is a pop-up restaurant in Paris sponsored by Electrolux. You can only make reservations online, they are only open for a year—and they are *totally* booked. *Does anyone have a vacuum cleaner connection?* (Action item: make contact with the director of corporate communications for Electrolux in Milan.)

Who knows the best Jewish bakery in the Marais area of Paris?

Any ideas for a fifty-eight-year-old's bachelorette party? Anyone?

But if my mind was in the countless requests we were working our way through, my heart was focused on finding time to write that business proposal for The Setai. It was the days of yore—2007—when Soho House still mattered and people fought for reservations at Spice Market. The market had yet to crash, and The Setai was going to be the new playground for all the hedge funders sick of Core Club.

I met countless times with their marketing people over the following months, and presented every possible scenario to get the account. I tried the deluxe plan: Four people on duty at all times! White gloves! International coverage for members! Then I suggested the economy plan: Two people covering fourteen hours a day between them, gloves optional.

No matter what I said, they weren't biting. But apparently someone in the company thought enough about me to add me to their email list, and I kept track of everything that was going on in The Setai. I knew when the south elevator would be closed. I learned about March's spa schedule. Regardless of the subject line of the email, I made sure to read the thing. One day I noticed that the emails had a new footer:

Enjoy,
Crystal Springs
Director of concierge services, Setai Club, Wall Street

Crystal Springs? *Crystal Springs?* I thought they would have had some really hot Scandinavian model or a real-life Bond Girl. But Crystal Springs sounded like an off-brand bottled water, or some teenage deodorant. I printed out the email and brought it over to my partner, Abbie Newman. She's the "Abigail" in Abigail Michaels Concierge (except her full name isn't *really* Abigail, but who cares). "Look at this!" I said. "Someone named *Crystal Springs* is the concierge at The Setai!"

"That name sounds familiar," Abbie said. Abbie knew everyone and could out-schmooze anyone. I wouldn't be surprised if she told me she used to sit down on Sundays to watch *The Ed Sullivan Show* with Howard Hughes. "I've either met her or I just bought a candle with that scent."

"Let's look her up online," I suggested.

We found pictures of Ms. Springs, and I understood it immediately. She was pretty and she was only about thirty years old. I could laugh at her name, but at the end of the day she was doing The Setai—and I wasn't.

PEOPLE YOU'D ASSUME WOULD MAKE GREAT CONCIERGES—BUT WON'T

The Party Girl Who Hangs Out at All the Hotspots. She might forget to put your name ahead of hers on the "list." Hangovers can also hamper her service skills in the "early" morning hours before noon.

Out of the blue, I got a call from the club manager. He'd spent decades in the hotel industry; he wouldn't even glance at something that didn't bear five stars. "Michael? This is Toma Vaca." At least that's what his name sounded like, filtered through his thick French accent. "I want to know what is your idea on how you do Setai."

"What do you mean?"

"Do your people come here or we call you?"

"There's many ways we could do it," I said, trying to decipher his idiom (which is part of the job, anyway). "We could have an on-site person, or you could call into our office remotely and we could handle requests that way."

"Because Crystal, she tell me she is no more. She is gone!"

"Really?" She left The *Setai*?

"She done wonderful work, she taken really good care of the people, but she not happy and she got another job for a hedge fund company as their social director. I really, really want to do this, and can you give me a proposal?"

"Sure."

"Can you have it in an hour?"

"Uh . . . No." I hadn't sent him proposals for *months*; most of the data I had was no longer relevant. So I spent the entire weekend working on two new tentative proposals. Toma Vaca took them to the owner and we got approved immediately.

"We want to do one of these," Toma Vaca told me. "But I think it's going to be the smaller one. Let's have a meeting."

Toma Vaca should have been an artist, because the picture he painted of The Setai's clientele was exactly what I had suspected. Rock stars hobnobbing with hedge fund superstars—in other words, the kind of people who would suck the life out of you. The building was not only a luxe condo, but also a private membership club. It was clear that the residents would be using our services the most.

"So how many members do you have?" I asked him.

"Oh, we're doing very well on the membership. The members, they like to have very nice. Very nice Porsche, they drive. Celebrities, they like to come. Oh, the luxury!" He wasn't speaking English, and he wasn't speaking French. He was speaking Keyword.

He couldn't answer many basic questions, but it didn't really throw me. Part of a concierge's job is ascertaining what someone wants, even if they don't have the vocabulary to explain what that thing is. Besides, I had an entire week before they wanted us to take over. I was used to delivering things "now, now, *now!*"

"All right, look," I said. "I need Crystal to download everything to me. First, so I can understand if you're making the right choice with this skeleton crew that we're going to be putting in here. And second, I want to make sure for my own self that we didn't underbid this."

The next day, I had an appointment to see Crystal. I had seen her pictures online, and I had left the bathroom smelling like her, but I had yet to meet her. I brought along Daria, our VP of client services. She'd been in the concierge business even longer than I had.

The doorman pointed us to Crystal's office, and we sat down and waited for her. The room itself, like most back-of-the-house office spaces, was pretty industrial and not at all elegant. I slowly looked around at the mess that was everywhere. Peeking out from under her desk was a pair of really expensive shoes. The combination of those two things should have warned me about what was coming, but I wanted to give her the benefit of the doubt.

Fifteen minutes later, Crystal arrived in a complete flurry. She had on a short little jacket, a pair of really slim pencil pants, and some cute ballet flats—and everything was clearly designer. Her gigantic Marc Jacobs bag could have served as a suitcase.

There wasn't even a hello.

"I'm sorry!" she said, in a jittery voice. "I don't know if I'm a very good trainer. Okay, let me tell you about the residents here first. Mrs. Armstrong. She's just really, really nice, but her son's kinda weird. Like, don't look at him. Don't shake his hand, because he's got *really* weird boundary issues and stuff. I think he's got ADD, but I don't know. He's probably like twenty-eight years old. So anyway, he's really nice, but he doesn't live here, but he's a member."

I waited for her to pause, so I could slow her down. But not only did she not pause, she didn't seem to be breathing. *Holy crap,* I thought. *She's one of those people that can speak on both the exhale and the inhale!*

"Mrs. Armstrong owns a really, really famous film company in London. I guess it's kinda like Paramount Pictures, except it's London, you know, they're really, really big. And she has a handler and his name is Roger, and he's really, really nice. He's like the business manager, so when she starts to spend too much money, he'll call you and tell you that you have to tell her that it's time to stop, because he doesn't want to do it."

I didn't look Daria in the eye because we both would have burst out in hysterics. She was furiously scribbling notes as Crystal talked, flipping pages in her notepad faster and faster.

"Oh!" Crystal said, snapping her fingers. "Mrs. Armstrong gets a fresh-squeezed orange juice and an almond croissant every morning at eight, but she likes the kind that's *not* a rolled almond croissant, it's like a *pain au chocolat,* except it's like a flat croissant. It's got almond paste. It's different than a rolled almond croissant. At one time, I used to get them from room service at Cipriani Wall Street, but then they became very unreliable, because they found out the bellman was coming over to our property and he wasn't allowed to, so they put an end to it."

I watched Daria write down "Cipriani Wall Street," and I watched her cross it out just as quickly. I could see a little bit why Crystal was so frazzled. She hadn't been dealing with the Mrs. Armstrongs of the world for decades, like I had. That echelon of client is a bit out of touch with how things actually get done. Mrs. Armstrong is surely picturing the Ritz-Carlton or the Four Seasons, delivering to her an almond croissant on a silver platter with, literally, hand-squeezed orange juice in a crystal goblet. And none of those gauche Valencia oranges, either.

It doesn't mean Mrs. Armstrong is *evil*. She is the kind of woman who would call my company and say, "Oh, hello, dear. It would just be *wonderful* if every morning, by eight o'clock, I could have my almond croissant." There's nothing threatening about that. But that same person inevitably calls at 8:01, wondering, "Oh, darling, now you *know* that I did ask for it at eight." In other words: It's not really a request, it's a command.

Now I started wondering where I was going to find these almond croissants for Mrs. Armstrong. It's not like there was a Korean deli around the corner, and that wouldn't have been good enough anyway. Was I going to have to pay somebody extra to go out and make sure that Mrs. Armstrong got her croissant, the flat kind (not the rolled kind!) with the almond paste?

The almond croissant was becoming an emergency. This was almondgeddon.

"Let me tell you a bit about our members and the parties," Crystal continued. "Renée Zellweger's a member and Molly Sims is a member, and they like are most likely to show up at the fashion events, or anything design oriented. But really the parties that have the biggest draws are when we do swimsuit and lingerie parties. Agent Provocateur is one of the companies that loves to throw parties here, and all the football players come for that. But of course you have to watch the lingerie models, because they will throw themselves at the football players. If people get drunk and they want to have sex in the bar, call the Ritz-Carlton to send a car for them and reserve them a room."

After two hours, Daria and I had enough. We went back to our office and started to decipher her notes. They were just words, and we had to try and remember if the stories had ever gone anywhere: "Football player, lingerie, ADD, fresh-squeezed." It was like she was playing Password. Maybe that's why Toma Vaca spoke Keyword; he'd been around Crystal all day. Everything was so disorganized I thought that Crystal had been flat-out messing with us.

To cover my bases, I sent her an email reiterating the information she gave us in a clear, concise format and asking for some basic info.

No response.

It was T-minus two days. I didn't have time to wait for her to get back to me. I forwarded the letter to Toma Vaca, in the hopes that he could fill in some blanks. "Oops! I forgot send this to you before, but this is what I sent to Crystal."

No response.

I waited a couple of hours and then I called him. I decided that there were just a few things that were vitally important: Who are the members? How are they identified? Who lives in the building, and who has any kind of request happening between now and when we start on Friday? What are residents told as far as our hours and our obligations?

"I'll email you all these things," he assured me.

"Oh, and what's the phone number directly to the concierge desk?" I asked.

"I'll find out! Right away!"

He doesn't even know the number? I thought. *Oh, this is bad.*

I waited and waited—no response. I had meetings. My day continued—and I was starting to flip out. I wrote an email to the owner, asking him the same very basic questions that I had asked Toma Vaca. The owner then called up Toma Vaca and tore him a new one.

I found this out when Toma Vaca called me that night. "I don't know what to say to you," he began. I expected the next words out of his mouth to be an apology; they were not. "I am so disappointed that you have a relationship with me, but you go over my back. I give you everything you ask for!"

"I didn't go behind your back or over your head, whichever you mean, to complain about you. I need to get the names of the people who are going to be calling my office in two days! Not to mention, I don't know what's going on with the NFL draft party that's happening tonight that you're hosting for Calvin Pace, and has two hundred and fifty people on the list, including Fox News who's coming to broadcast it. Is he going to be calling me because fifty of his closest friends couldn't get in? I don't have Mrs. Armstrong's phone number. I don't have anybody's credit card. So I'm supposed to just start paying for things for them out of my own pocket?"

"I don't know how you work, and we don't know each other very well, but this is not the way to get a good relationship with me. If you ever have a problem, you need to just come to me."

"Well, I *do* have a problem. You have created an absolute catastrophe at that property. You have no command over your staff. You let this girl operate completely autonomously. You don't know what's going on. You're in over your head and you know it, and you're bluffing. I'm not going to be your fall guy when things go wrong—which they will if I don't get this information!"

Toma Vaca took a deep breath. "Okay, we start new, pretend. I want this to be successful. You will see that I am very direct and whatever I feel I have to express it. I am glad we talk and explain each other." It was like he was shaking the Etch A Sketch of our relationship, and it made me respect him a bit more. "We need to have a meeting tomorrow morning, and I will get you everything that you need."

The next morning—one day before my company was taking the reins—we all had a big meeting at The Setai. The superintendent was there, the engineer was there, the marketing director, the membership sales director, the condo sales director, the spa manager—and Toma Vaca and Crystal Springs. Each person gave their piece, and between everyone I figured out the puzzle that was how The Setai actually worked. The final thing I needed was access to the building database and email. Fortunately, the IT guy had conferenced in on the meeting. Unfortunately, the speakerphone was so full of static that he sounded like a subway announcement.

"I just need to be able to go to the files on that server," I told him.

"What? I can't hear you."

"I need to get into your share drive," I reiterated.

"Sorry, you're driving *where*?"

"Pick up the phone," I told Toma Vaca. "Just tell him what I need."

Tentatively, Toma Vaca reached for the phone, pressed a button—and disconnected the call. He sat there, staring at the screen, wondering what to do and making little mumbling sounds.

PEOPLE YOU'D ASSUME WOULD MAKE GREAT CONCIERGES—BUT WON'T

The Charming Foreigner with the Ritzy Accent: Yes, he's cosmopolitan and can speak to any guest in their native language. But his charm is compensating for the fact that he's probably never really had to get down and dirty with the work.

I could tell Toma Vaca had no idea how to reach the IT guy, but I had been in touch with him before. I started reading Toma Vaca the guy's number. "Six-four-six . . . No, I think you have to dial a nine first to get an outside line."

After that was taken care of, we started discussing exactly what kind of concierge service they were looking for. "We really do believe we only need partial coverage," one of the managers said. "We just want somebody who's very visible when the members come in after work. It's a big gathering spot for after-work drinks. Someone presentable."

"So more like a prop?" I suggested. "I could get you some gorgeous models who are astute enough to know how to say hello to people."

"Perfect!"

I called a modeling agent that I knew, and basically set up a casting call in my office that afternoon. I saw a bunch of people, but I wasn't finding the person who was Wall Street smart and Setai pretty.

And in walked Peyton. I was immediately taken with her. Not only was Peyton *gorgeous,* but her résumé was all business—literally. She had been a personal assistant to corporate executives, people who managed $150 million funds. She had long, flowing red hair with bangs that were pushed to the side. She looked very J.Crew, naturally clean and beautiful—but I could tell that she had a chic side as well. I hired her on the spot.

PEOPLE YOU'D ASSUME WOULD MAKE GREAT CONCIERGES—BUT WON'T

The Gorgeous Model/Actor with the Magazine Hair: If they're dumb, they can't do their job. If they're smart, they're going to land a film role in two seconds and be out the door.

The next day, our official start date, I came by The Setai to see how Peyton was handling things. I was stunned, and not because she was stunning. She had makeup on, with big red lips. Her bangs were totally slicked with gel, and she had curled them so they were just barely over her eyes. Her hair was pulled back really tight in a barrette. She had a jacket with a little ruffle around it, and a shirt underneath that exposed a tiny bit of cleavage. Her skirt was so tight that she couldn't step more than six inches at a time. She was carrying a peach-colored miniature spiral notebook that looked like it came from the MoMA Store, and a fancy pen to write with. The best thing about her costume—because that *is* what it was—were her gigantic horn-rimmed glasses. I could tell that they were props, because when I looked at them closely I could see that there was no magnifying power to the lenses.

In other words, she looked *fantastic*. You sell the sizzle, but you eat the steak. She wasn't there to *be* a concierge. She was a trophy playing a part, just like The Setai wanted. While she was there, greeting members and taking requests, me and all the other concierges in my office would be working around the clock to make sure the work actually got done—which it did.

Calvin Pace had his party, and everyone who was supposed to got in. Mrs. Armstrong got her croissant every day, the flat kind (not the rolled kind) with the almond paste. I had them brought in from the Financier Patisserie on Cedar Street; as far as she was concerned, they simply continued to appear as if by magic. The members' requests were being taken care of: somebody wants to be invited to the *Playboy* table at a Kentucky Derby fund-raiser party that's completely sold out. *Done.* People constantly ask for reservations for Maialino, Kenmare, and Locanda Verde. *No problem. What time would you like a table?*

That's because when you want a concierge, you probably don't want Party Girl Who Hangs Out at All the Hotspots, or a Charming Foreigner with the Ritzy Accent, or a Gorgeous Model/Actor with the Magazine Hair. Your best bet might be the forty-five-year-old who looks more like a landlord than a doorman, who got his start thinking that he was going to be the next big Hollywood movie mogul.

2.
Lady Liberty

The door was locked, and I didn't have the key.

The Liberty Agency was a small office inside a quaint, exposed-brick building. But for the fact that it was in Westwood, California, it could have passed for a New York town house. I remembered it perfectly from the job interview; now if only I could get in. "Hi, I'm Glennis's assistant," I told them downstairs. "I think you have a key for me?"

The secretary nodded and passed it to me. "Is this your first day?"

"Yeah."

"Good luck!"

I went upstairs and let myself into the office. Even though it was a just a small boutique agency, and even though it felt very cozy and quaint, it was still Hollywood. There wasn't a lot of celebrity memorabilia, but it still had the *feel*. Scripts were stacked up on the desk. The wicker wall units looked like they were from some magical far-off place, like Bali. On the wall there were photos. Sheens—Charlie and Martin—smiled in every direction, and Estevezes, too.

Glennis had her own inner office, and there was a desk outside it for me. Or so I gathered. I walked around, practically on tiptoe. Crime scenes didn't get as much as reverence as I gave to the clutter.

Then the phone rang. I looked at it for one second, wondering if I should answer it. "Glennis Liberty's office," I said, not even bothering to say my own name.

"Hey there," she said.

"Hi!" I was ready for her to tell me which scripts to read so that I could help her decide what the next Sheen movie should be.

"I need you to go into my office. The third shelf down, on the bottom. I need you to take my curlers out. Put a half a cup of water in them and plug them in for me."

Before I could say anything, there was a dial tone.

Okay, I could do this. I found the curlers and took them off the shelf. *Water. Where's the water?* I didn't even have a cup. There was a mug on Glennis's desk. *Can I use it? Would it be all right to get the mug wet?* I took the mug to the bathroom, filled it up with a half cup of water, poured it into the curlers, and then plugged them in. They started steaming and churning.

I sat down, being careful not to touch anything else, while I waited for her to show up. A few minutes later, the phone rang again. "Glennis Liberty's office?" I said, still tentative.

"Hey, who's this?" It was Charlie Sheen. *I am on the phone with Charlie Sheen.*

"This is Glennis's assistant, Michael Fazio."

"Cool. Are you new?"

"Yeah."

"Glennis there?" he—*Charlie Sheen*—said.

"No, she's not."

"All right. Well, I'll try her later."

I hung up the phone. *Oh my God,* I thought to myself. *I'm so in the* biz!

Soon Glennis arrived. She looked like an older Ralph Lauren model, tall and slim with aviator frame glasses and shoulder-length blond hair. She had the momentum of a Tasmanian devil, all frantic energy and bags everywhere. "Hey there," she said, as she passed me to go into her office. She went inside and shut her door. She wasn't mean, but I expected that there was going to be a *little* love.

I sat. I waited.

Twenty minutes later she buzzed me on the intercom. "I need you to come to my office." I opened the door. I don't know why I was surprised that she was sitting at her desk with gigantic electric steam rollers in her hair.

"These are the breakdowns," she said, handing me an envelope. "Go through these every morning and look for projects that you can submit our clients on.

"Get familiar with everyone we have on file in this cabinet. we've got a DP, an editor, a sound guy, and see what you can do with Ivan Kane or Pamela London. We need to get them in front of more casting directors."

What about Charlie and Martin? I wondered. *What are we doing with them?*

"Okay," I said, excited. I opened up the envelope and went through it. The breakdowns were like want ads for TV shows, listing whatever creative and technical positions were needed at the time. I began fishing through the files, trying to figure out what the hell a "DP" was.

"I've got a ten o'clock appointment," Glennis soon told me. "I'll be back!" Her hair ready to go, she left the office in the same kind of fury in which she'd come.

Then, Charlie called again. "Hey, is Glennis there?"

"Oh, you just missed her. Sorry!"

"Oh, damn. So, going to be an agent?"

"I'm keeping the options open, but yeah, I think it's the right place to start before moving into production one day."

"Cool," he said, hanging up.

I went back to learning the breakdowns, trying to put two and two together. After a couple of hours Glennis came back. "You didn't put my curlers away," she said.

"I'm sorry. I didn't realize you wanted them put away," I told her, just wanting everything to be okay.

She brushed away my apology. "I need you to get me lunch at Hamburger Hamlet. I want you to get a cheeseburger, have it cut into quarters, and have each of those pieces put on its own bun. Medium rare."

"Sure," I said. I could feel them rolling their eyes over the phone when I gave them the order. They knew Glennis well at that point and knew exactly what she wanted. They used to have their version of sliders called "baby cheeseburgers" on the menu, but they had long since discontinued them. Glennis didn't need to know that little detail. The mission was four baby burgers, no matter how it happened. It was the '80s and it was Hollywood, and everybody had their own food quirks—especially at such an industry-frequented place.

I brought the burger back to the office and stood there, not really knowing what to do with it. It was four buns with little pieces of meat, just like she wanted. Glennis was on the phone, but vaguely gestured at me to get her a plate. I brought in the food and put it down in front of her. She vaguely gestured for me again, this time for me to sit down. For fifteen minutes I sat and watched her on the phone. "Why didn't you tell me Charlie called?" she immediately said when the call was over.

"Uh . . ." He hadn't *specified* to tell her that he had called. I'd thought that we were all part of this big happy machine here, and he was just content to check in to see if she was there. That's when I realized that maybe I wasn't in the biz, that this wasn't a tea party— and I had to figure out how to take better care of Glennis.

Glennis gave me a look that said *"Hello,* is anyone home up there?"

Suddenly, Charlie didn't matter. From that point forward, I did everything I could to avoid ever ever *ever* getting that look again. I was a quick learner, and my new goal was clear. As long as she was tended to, my instinct told me, everything else would fall into place.

Now the service bug was in me.

The curlers became a morning ritual. I always plugged them in first thing when I got there in the morning. One day she was late, and the curlers turned off. I went, got the water and restarted them. *I get it,* I thought to myself with pride. *I get how to make this lady tick. She's going to be so happy now.*

Every day, I busied myself with the breakdowns and submitted candidates. I started to get good at understanding the roles. I'd tell Glennis how many people I submitted and give her all the phone numbers. She had what she needed, and she had it because of me.

Whenever Charlie came in, he'd go into her office and shut the door. I could hear them talking and I could smell him smoking. I just sat behind my desk with my electric typewriter, dying to know what was going on in there.

As he left one day, Charlie pulled me aside. "I've been putting out my cigarettes in her coffee mug," he told me. I knew that, of course. I was the one who had to clean them out. "Do me a favor. Get some joke ashtray, something really tacky. I want an ashtray in that office tomorrow." He handed me a twenty-dollar bill and left.

I stared at the money and thought about what to do. I could have gone to the drug store and gotten any old ashtray. But the service bug that I had discovered in me had only grown stronger. *What can I do that will just blow him away?* I wondered. *What will make him see— make them both see—that I'm creative and fun?*

After work I went up and down Melrose, for hours. I went to thrift stores. I went to supermarkets. I went to disgusting old antique stores. I went all over, trying to find the exact right ashtray. Forty dollars later, I wound up buying four different ones so I could make the right choice.

The winning selection was a plastic snow globe with a little Hollywood mountain in it and everything—and in 3-D! I waited for Charlie to come in, glancing at the door whenever I heard the slightest sound. Finally, he arrived. "Here you go," I said, handing the ashtray to him.

"*Cool.*"

But from the way that he looked at me, I knew that I had gotten him the right one. Yes, I had spent my own money. Yes, I had wasted my own time. But I showed him that I'd go the extra mile and I showed him that he could count on me.

Now that he knew that he could rely on me, Charlie took it up a notch.

Many Monday mornings, the phone would ring. "The Liberty Company. This is Michael."

"Oh," said the girl on the line. "Oh, I'm sorry. I think I have the wrong number."

"No problem." I hung up and waited for three seconds, until she called back. They always called right back.

"Is *Charlie* there?" she said.

"No, he's not. Can I take a message?"

"Can you tell him that Susan called?"

"Of course," I told her.

"Thanks!"

He walked in not long after. "Susan called," I told him.

He stared at me blankly.

"You know. *Susan.*"

He tried to remember what and who he did over the weekend. "Oh yeah!" he said, laughing. "Right. Oh, I forgot my bag at Hamlet. Could you go get it?"

It was five minutes away, so I just ran it. "Has Charlie Sheen left something here?" I asked the host.

"I don't know. I don't have anything."

"Where was he sitting?"

"Over there."

There were people in the booth he had been in, with a small paper bag scrunched in the corner. "I just need to grab that," I said to them. As I left the Hamlet I couldn't help but notice that the bag was unusually heavy. I opened it up. Inside there was something wrapped in packing paper, like it was going to be shipped. I gasped.

Charlie Sheen had left his gun at Hamburger Hamlet.

I carried it back by my fingertips, scared that it was going to spontaneously discharge. *Is he weird?* I asked myself. *Where has this gun been?* I had gone through a million questions by the time I had returned to the office—but I asked Charlie none of them. Good service means that you don't ask why, even when someone tells you to go get their gun.

THE MASTER MENTALITY

A friend of mine who worked for Martha Stewart had an experience that illustrated our plight. His name is Robert. Nobody calls him Bob—except Martha does, always. He was frantically running out to grab lunch one day—frantically, because he could never leave his desk. Without an umbrella, he sped down the street in the pouring rain. "Bob!" he heard. He turned around and saw that it was Martha in her town car.

Martha motioned him to come over. "Hold on," she said, "I just need to finish a call." She finished her conversation while he stood there in the torrential downpour. She wasn't being mean. She wasn't enjoying watching him get wet, while he was on the street

continued

and she was inside her car. She didn't think lowly of him. Quite the opposite: he was her everything. It was just like, "I need you . . . but in a second." Any healthy person with self-esteem would've said, "Lady, open your fucking door and let me in! I'm getting soaked here."

But Robert had the service bug. And part of the bug meant standing there, waiting until Martha was ready for him. There wasn't any need for her to apologize. After all, she didn't really do anything wrong. Robert's position wasn't even in service. But he, too, had the service bug and he wasn't afraid to serve.

Back during the Dark Ages, sending faxes to a hotel was not a given. They often had only one fax machine in the entire building. First you had to call and ask if you could send a fax to a guest. Then you had to call and tell them you were sending it. Finally, just to be sure, you called to find out if they received it and how many pages they actually got.

Martin Sheen was staying at the Mayflower Hotel in New York. Every day we were getting script pages in the office, fifteen sheets on that horrible thermal paper. Every day I had to call his hotel and do the whole song and dance to fax those pages over.

Maybe they got sick of doing it for me. One day I couldn't get a hold of anyone over there. I had always told Glennis when the fax had gone through; when I didn't tell her anything she knew something was up.

"It's impossible," I told her. "The guy at the front desk never calls me back."

"Why didn't you just call the concierge?"

I didn't even know that word. I'd heard of it but I didn't really know what it was.

When I called the concierge about Martin's fax, it was instant synergy. Everything was just as important to him as it was to me. I could ask him to go outside and tell me what color flag was across the street. If he needed to call me back, he would give me an exact time frame to expect the call, and he always followed through. He made me feel like I was doing *him* a favor by needing his help.

"Oh, I have a great idea," I finally told one. "Instead of me bothering you every hour, do you have a fax machine in one of the offices that we can just borrow for Martin Sheen?"

"Not a problem."

Nothing I asked for seemed presumptuous to the concierge. Everything seemed like a logical request and completely possible.

The concierge got someone to take a fax machine from one of the hotel offices, bring it into Martin's room, and plug it in. The concierge even tested it to make sure it was working. Every time Martin was due to stay at the hotel, I would connect with the concierge first. I knew I would be in good hands.

HOW TO DEAL WITH CONCIERGES

It's not pronounced *con-SEERS* or *con-see-air-GEE*. The worst is the pretentious *con-see-AIR*, which comes from people affecting a French accent—incorrectly. It's *con-see-AIRJ*.

In medieval times, the concierges were the keepers of the keys. They literally had the keys to the castle, and were on duty to open doors for people. In old hotels, the concierge held the guest room keys. With the advent of rail travel, the concierge met visitors at the station and took them to their destination. They were the ones who knew the route.

Nowadays, an on-site concierge is mandatory for a hotel to be certified as four stars. For five-star certification, the concierge desk has to be staffed twenty-four hours—with polyglots.

continued

A concierge is not the guy under the CONCIERGE sign at Home Depot or the person helping you with your credit card on the phone—despite their claims to the contrary. A real concierge is like your distant relative in whichever city you happen to be staying in. They get you to the hotel from the airport. They know you like ice cream, so they recommend the best ice cream place. They know where the best stores are, and where the best sales are. Their job is to get you where you want to go. If a travel book points you to three destinations, the concierge will tell you the best of the three—as well as let you know about the fourth destination that didn't make the book.

And because the concierge is like a distant relative, people feel comfortable making service requests they otherwise wouldn't. That can mean being an alibi, getting drugs—prescription or otherwise—or finding a place to keep the breast milk. The concierge might refuse you, but the one thing they'll never do is judge you. Odds are, they've gotten requests ten times stranger within the last ten minutes.

As the months passed, Glennis realized she could depend on me. I always remembered to keep those curlers steamed. I made sure that the burgers were done the way she liked them. It wasn't just the burgers, either; she never ordered from the menu. For her, every restaurant was like a buffet. If they had chicken over rice and steak over salad, she would want the chicken over the salad—with a side of rice. She was the menu designer, which was her way of asserting her position. I even tried to pick up her power habit of talking on the phone and chewing at the same time, but I could never pull it off without spitting my food onto the receiver.

Glennis was focused on Martin and Charlie, period. I was given Ramón Sheen and Renée Estevez (the secret Sheens) to look after. I really wanted something to happen with Renée, but every casting director had already seen her. They knew who she was and they just didn't want her.

I tried every little sales-pitchy thing I could think of. She wasn't that *Hollywood* pretty—so I described her as *mercurial*. "She could be anything," I insisted. "She's *not* ingénue. She's *not* leading lady. But she's so *mercurial!*"

As the months with Glennis became years with Glennis, I started to feel a bit lost. Yes, she gained more and more confidence in me and began referring to me as her *associate* rather than just her lowly *assistant*. Yes, she let me have my own little roster of actors, like one recurring guest on *Remington Steele*. For Beatrice Boepple, I landed her a role in a *Nightmare on Elm Street* sequel where she did a dramatic birthing scene giving birth to that adorable, razor-gloved infant Freddy Krueger.

But I didn't have a hot, commercially appealing actor who was easy to sell. One who wasn't mercurial, who could make my job a little easier and more rewarding. I was exploring possibilities with my career, and I was finding it pretty easy for me to make connections with people because of a strategy I had picked up. Whenever I saw an article in a newspaper that mentioned someone I hoped to connect with, I would clip out the article and send it to the person with a little note like, "Congratulations!" or "What an accomplishment!" It was a way to create virtually instant familiarity. Even thought they didn't know who I was, suddenly I was someone who was close enough to be clipping articles with personal congratulatory notes attached. At the very least, they paused for a moment to look at my note. If I would ever eventually contact them, I would be distantly recognizable at least to the extent that I could get past the receptionist.

I started going to showcases and acting classes, where the students performed these mini-recitals. I was talent scouting, but it was kind of fruitless. We constantly got photos in the mail; I was always opening envelopes looking for my own personal discovery. But that didn't pan out much, either.

One day there was mail addressed to Ramón Estévez, which is Martin Sheen's real name. *What a weird thing to put on the envelope,* I thought. *This is interesting.* Inside there was a letter to Martin and some stapled Xeroxes, crudely done. There wasn't even a headshot. There were pictures of an actress from *Cosmopolitan, Vogue,* and *Mademoiselle* and a VHS tape. The video was three hours of a Mexican soap opera named *Teresa,* and the production values were that of a horrendous school play.

But the star, Salma Hayek, was stunning and sexy. I took the color Xeroxes and went to talk to Glennis. "Please, oh please," I said. "Let me work with her. I think I can make something happen."

"Are you sure? Kiddo, how do you know she can act?" Glennis said.

"I *know.* I'm telling you, I know she can. I know I can do something with her."

"I'd like to see your energy focused more on helping me get some of our production projects up and running. But if you really want to take a shot at selling this girl, then let me meet her first."

"Great!" I went to my desk and gave Salma a ring. I was tickled to be making the call, if only to hear the excitement in the new actress's voice when an agent reached out to her.

"Hello?" Her accent was thick. *Really* thick.

"Hi, Salma. This is Michael Fazio, Glennis Liberty's *associate* from the Liberty Company. We received your pictures. Glennis wanted you to come in for a meeting."

"Oh, okay." She took down the information. She wasn't at all excited; if anything, she was kind of cold. (Or "professional," if I were selling her to someone.) When she came in a couple of days later, she was just as stunning in person as in the color Xeroxes. She didn't even look like an actress. She looked rich. She looked like a debutante.

I tried my best through assured small talk to let her know that I was a "real" agent. "That's a gorgeous ring," I said. "I *love* your bag." *Hi, I recognize the fancy stuff you're wearing. And since I recognize it, it should be obvious that I could be your best gay friend ever.* "You really pop on camera. You're so mercurial. The production values are really good on your show. What kind of below-the-line budget do they have?" *See, I know what I'm talking about! I'm going to be a movie mogul because I know about budgets and stuff.*

Mid-sentence, Glennis came into the waiting area, took Salma into the inner office, and shut the door. They talked for a bit and then Salma left. "If you want to do this, go for it," Glennis told me later. "But I don't know about her. She's going to be a handful."

"No, I'm telling you. I *know.* I know, I know, I know."

As usual, the breakdowns were always full of calls for characters described as "beautiful," "sexy," or "nicely built." Even if they were looking for a hobo, the character was somehow nothing short of a fashion model. Now, I had a new sense of confidence, because I was submitting an actress who was truly gorgeous. I had the luxury of simply saying, "She's *stunning,* and you need to read her."

After one day, I got a reading for Salma for *"It's Garry Shandling's Show."* I was excited; I had to be excited for the both of us. Salma never said that she was excited. She never said "thank you."

In fact, she never even went to the meeting.

"Oh yeah," she said, when I called her to find out what had happened. "I couldn't go. But I can go tomorrow. At three o'clock."

I felt humiliated. Still, I smoothed it over with the casting director. "She's new and she got lost," I fibbed. "She's so *busy.* But tomorrow she does have an opening at three."

This time, she went.

When I called for feedback, the reaction was really, really marginal. "Eh, she's not right for the part."

"Not right for the part?" I said. "The part is Rosa the maid."

"She's *too* Rosa. We need Rosa from L.A., not Rosa from Mexico who we can't understand."

But because her photos were so beautiful, I was always able to get her into auditions. "She's just here from Mexico," I said countless times, "and she's the star of one of the most acclaimed television shows *Teresa*. She *is* Teresa. Her accent's so exotic! I mean, it's real. It's *real*. You don't want someone faking this." I made her out to be a dignitary from a far-off magic land.

The feedback from casting directors was always lackluster. And the reaction from Salma was like ice. Everything was just *whatever* for her. Usually wannabe actresses are the complete opposite: "I'm sitting next to my mother. She's dying. I'll be right there." But if I told Salma that she was up for Martin Scorcese's new film, she'd say, "I can't be there at three. I'm busy. I'll do it tomorrow. At two."

Between the accent and the aloofness, after a couple of months she wasn't booking anything. "Have her back," I pleaded with one of the casting people. "Try her for this other role."

"No!" he told me. "Michael, you're sweet and I like you. So let me tell you something: I get what you're doing, but she can't act and you can't even understand her. You're wasting your time and you're probably bothering people. *Get over it.* You don't want to ruin your reputation because you're being so damn pushy about someone who is really difficult to cast."

"All right," I said. *Damn it.* I went into Glennis's office to tell her that it wasn't going to work with Salma.

"Are you sure now?" Glennis said.

"She's terrible. She's not reliable and people complain that she can't act. She's pretty, but big deal. I know I said I wanted someone pretty, but it really doesn't matter after all."

"It's your call. It's fine."

"Yeah. I don't want to do this anymore."

Glennis was trying to get into production and leave the agency behind anyway. It made for a perfect excuse. "You're really great," I told Salma, "but Glennis is giving up the agency franchise and we're going to start producing movies now. Glennis arranged for you to meet a few other agencies. So good luck to you."

"Okay," she said.

Less than a year later, she booked *Desperado*.

Maybe I wasn't up for being a Hollywood big shot after all.

3.
The Plane, the Plane

So what exactly *was* I good at? Sadly, I realized I was best at simply managing Glennis. I had an instinct for anticipating her needs and for getting them met no matter what. I figured if I was ever going to climb, I'd need to find a more powerful (and probably way more demanding) lady to work for. It was time to grow and try my hand in a higher-profile environment.

Dolores Robinson had a much bigger agency compared to Glennis's; it wasn't just about one family, an editor, and a few DPs. Not only that, but Dolores had more razzle-dazzle and worked with a broader spectrum of people. She networked, lunched, and partied with Hollywood's elite. Her call sheet was a list of every major studio head. She had people like Ron Howard and Larry David as neighbors of her Maple Drive office. She *had* a Maple Drive office, for God's sake! She had garnered Wesley Snipes his first major $8 million payout for *Demolition Man,* and her name was *always* in the trade publications. She knew everyone—and everyone knew *her.*

I knew who she was because a couple of months back I saw an article honoring her in the *Hollywood Reporter.* I had done my trick of cutting the article out and sending it to her with a little note: "Congratulations! What an amazing feature."

One day I saw an ad in the trades for an associate manager. The title was enough to grab my attention, but the Maple Drive address jogged my memory. When I confirmed that it was indeed Dolores Robinson who was looking for an associate manager, I called her right up. Even if my name wasn't instantly recognized, the flattering note I sent with the article a few weeks prior made it easy for me to talk my way past the nervous receptionist and Dolores took my call. The call led to an interview and the interview led to the new job. Now I was Dolores's new associate manager (read: assistant).

The thing with Dolores was that she was like a pet wolf. She was very smart and very warm—and you knew she could turn on you in a second. There was nobody I was more afraid of than her, but I knew enough to never let that show. Nor did I have an attitude about it. If you don't own your confidence, that pet wolf will growl and bite you. If you fake it and you come on really strong, it'll kill you. But if you really convince yourself in every fiber of your being that you can tame the wolf, you're cool, and everything's fine. With Dolores, being cool meant having business taken care of, making sure everything was in order, and being tuned in to her.

She never sensed my fear. She never growled and attacked me. I watched how the interns approached her. Dolores sat in her office with her chair turned around, facing away from the door. "Dolores?" the intern meekly asked. "Do you have a second?"

The chair spun around so fast she should have gotten whiplash. "Can't you see I'm busy?"

"I'm sorry . . ."

"Are you blind? I am trying to read! How am I ever going to finish this script?"

The next time it was a phone message. Instead of saying anything, the intern went into Dolores's office as unobtrusively as possible and gingerly placed a message on the desk.

Dolores wouldn't even touch it. "What is this?" she yelled.

"Uh . . . it's a phone message."

"From *whom*? What do they want?"

"Kevin Parker had a question for you. He was returning your call from this afternoon."

"So what did you tell him? Hello? I asked you a question! What am I supposed to do here?" The intern just stood there, because no matter what the girl said, it would just be adding fuel to the fire. I could tell that Dolores knew she was being mean, just like I could tell that her intention was to educate and encourage the intern to have more of a backbone. But the only thing that happened is that the poor girl sheepishly bowed her head and walked out of the office.

As the intern walked past my desk near tears—again—I pulled her aside. "Hey, watch me. Deal with her like I do."

The girl nodded, still terrified.

I strode right up to Dolores. "There's a call on line three and they wanted to make sure that you read the script. *I* read it. Here are the notes I made for you."

"Thanks," she said. "I'll take the call. Where are the notes?"

"Right here," I replied, handing them to her. "I'll put the call right through."

"Do me a favor," she said. "The television trade show for syndication is going to be in Vegas next week. Call Diane at Warner Bros. and see if you can get me on one of their morning planes."

"Sure."

She was testing me. Dolores had a way of seizing opportunities, and the Warner Bros. jet was an opportunity.

But still: The Warner Bros. jet? *Really?* I didn't even know Diane, but Dolores did. Shouldn't she be the one calling? Especially if she was kind of inviting herself. This was going to require stepping out of my comfort zone and letting go of my own personal hang-ups about pushing the envelope.

I went back to my desk and called up Diane. I had witnessed enough of Dolores in action that I was able to conjure up her warm, positive, and familiar delivery. "Hey Diane, it's Michael from Dolores's. You guys are sending planes on Thursday, aren't you?"

"It's looking that way, but I'm not sure who's confirmed," Diane said.

"*I'll* be taking the bus," I said, pausing for her little chuckle, "but Dolores was hoping to get out in the morning. Not sure when you do your seating plan, but Dolores will be traveling alone if you have a spare seat."

"I'm probably going to have space if she can leave pretty early. Give Ms. D a kiss from me."

"Thanks so much!" I said, writing down the info. How easy was that? My tone was upbeat and I kept the conversation short. I asked specifically for what I needed, and I got exactly what I had asked for without any emotional obstacles. Warner Bros. had a beautiful, comfortable private jet for entertainment industry big shots—like Dolores. Rather than wait for an invitation that might never come, why not simply ask?

I knew that she flew on the Warner Bros.' private jet all the time, even though she was simply a talent manager. What did she belong on the Warner Bros.' private jet for? I had thought it was because she was such a powerful person and because she was so feared. But now I wondered if she was just good at getting in there when she saw an opportunity. I hadn't been afraid to ask and I knew *how* to ask. Just like that, Dolores was on a flight.

When she was on those flights, she wasn't the Dolores I witnessed with the interns. She was upbeat, positive, and never overstayed her welcome. She abided by the rules and wasn't a bother. She didn't show up with a camera crew or eating smelly food on the plane. *She took up a seat but she didn't take up space.* Finding opportunities was a skill that she learned and perfected—and one that she taught me.

THE APPROACH

You have to have nerve to get people to do things for you. It doesn't mean you have to be obnoxious and pushy or assert some kind of authority. You do have to be bluntly honest and say exactly what you want. "Can I get a discount?" "What's the chance of getting to try a suite?" It's off-putting and people never do things like that. How do you respond to that sort of a question?

As a concierge I'm in a lucky position, because I'm on both the giving and the taking sides. People ask me and they usually ask me incorrectly. It's my job to get them what they want anyway—and I never ask on their behalf the way they've asked me. Otherwise, I'd never get what my clients want and I'd be out of a job.

Before you ask for what you want, you have to establish some commonality. "I'm in your world now; what's it look like? . . . What's the climate over there? . . . So can you do this for me?" It's set-up, and then the kill, and it's important to use just enough jargon to appear like an insider. At a hotel, for instance, the conversation would be something like, "What's your room rate? . . . What's your occupancy rate? . . . What's rack rate on a suite? . . . You know, I found it online for a hundred dollars less." That leads up to the point where I can simply ask if I can have the room for a hundred dollars less. "Is there any chance that you can do better?" is so vague that it won't work.

Be honest. Everybody can respect that. It's not about turning the tables and making the other person feel funny because of your bluntness. It's more like putting it out there and seeing what happens. Nine times out of ten you'll get *something* because you were honest. *Ten times out of ten* you'll get "let me see what I can do," because *nobody* in a service position wants to say no. It's all in the delivery. It's as simple as being in a department store and asking, "Is

continued

---

this going to go on sale tomorrow?" Ask verbatim but without an attitude of entitlement.

Being honest also means not trying to be everyone's best friend. You don't want to call a restaurant saying, "Hi, who's this?... How are you?... Oh, you know, Crystal is *such* a pretty name. Does your mother do meth?" It's completely irrelevant and palpably phony, especially to someone in a service position. But if you're like, "Hey Crystal, it's Michael. Are you guys slammed tonight?" it's a sense of familiarity and a respect for their position. Just because someone is serving you does not mean they are your servant. Quite the contrary.

You're not entitled to service; you *want* service. Fancy people often think that asking correctly is too much work. "Besides, isn't that just their job?" The funny thing is, that never translates. It's *your* job to win the case, Ms. Attorney. You don't win all of them, do you? Yes, it's the person's job to provide service. But there's a difference between them doing their job at the minimum and them going the extra mile—which is *not* their job. That's the definition of "extra": getting something you're not otherwise entitled to. But that extra mile *is* what you want out of them.

The only way to do that is to motivate. Money can be the motivator, as with tipping. It can also be pride, or acknowledgment. But you won't get it by asserting power and you won't get it by patronizing phony friendships. The waiter isn't there to be your friend; he's there to serve you food. He's busy and doesn't need the small talk. It doesn't matter that his name is cute or is the same as your brother's—he knows where you're going with that.

No matter what technique, remember that the mission isn't complete when they say yes. Once you get what you want, you have to let them know that you're glad they gave it to you. It's as simple as sending a note to let them know how great everything was. "Keep my contact information. I'd love the opportunity to return the favor if there's anything I can do for you."

And no, you can't have a discount.

As I started putting in fourteen-hour days with Dolores, I started to develop a comfort level with her. "Man," I said, "the snapshot thing is really powerful"

She giggled. "Yeah. It *is* a nice touch, isn't it?" It was in the days before MySpace.

Dolores would always carry a disposable camera around. She knew who the big players were even if she didn't really *know* them that well . . . yet. She would flash that warm smile and extend a confident handshake. "Look how handsome you are," she'd tell the target. "I don't have any pictures of us."

Before it felt weird, he'd have his arm around her and the picture was snapped. When she got the film developed, she would mail the picture of the two of them together. The little Post-it would say "How cute are you???"

"Does it ever *not* work?" I asked her.

"No, because I do it right. Remember to keep it short and keep it amusing, just like when you're talking to someone on the phone. Everyone is an egomaniac. No one wants to hear about *me*. It's always about you, you, you."

It was also always you, you, you at the agency. I was the one who Wesley Snipes called to pick him up from the courthouse when the cops impounded his motorcycle. I was the one who had to go to Jason Patric's house to pick up the mail—and let out his pet pig. When Dolores's contact lens rolled back in her eye, I was so methodical in getting it out that you would've thought that I was an optician or an ophthalmologist. (Whichever is the appropriate option, that's the one I had to pretend to be.)

I was so tuned in to all the Dolores cues that I learned nothing was said as an accident. If she said something like, "I'm going to start eating oatmeal in the mornings before I go to the gym," that meant I should make sure that there was a tray from room service waiting at her door by 7 A.M. To be safe, I would also need to make sure that a treadmill was reserved at 8 A.M. It didn't matter that she was in Cannes, which was a nine-hour time difference from Los Angeles. I woke up in the middle of the night to call her hotel to make sure that she got what she wanted. It wasn't as if she were being demanding. She couldn't be demanding, because I would never let it get to that point. For me it was about service, and to me service was about competency and taking cues.

Unfortunately, it wasn't my job to write and produce the movies that the client was going to be in, so I had to be good covering my piece of the process. If Wesley Snipes needed to be woken up at 6:00 A.M. in New York, which was 3:00 A.M. in L.A., I did it. In a way, I was more reliable than an alarm clock.

It worked both ways. I could've called the hotel and told them I needed a wake-up call for Wesley's room. But I honestly didn't trust them. I'd rather wake up at three and call Wesley myself, so I would be absolutely positive that it got taken care of.

And because I was so reliable, I was the poor soul who had to handle Rosie Perez.

Everything with her was an incident, and every day with her there was something.

Every. Single. Day.

"Hi, Michael," she said on the phone with her gilded accent. "Yeah, I didn't get my pages for tomorrow."

"Yes," I told her, "you did."

"No, I didn't!"

"Yes," I insisted, "you did. Susan signed for them an hour ago."

"Where are they?"

"I don't know, Rosie. I'm not with you."

"Well, they're not here."

"Hold on, let me find Susan." I put down the receiver and looked around the office. "Hey, Susan. Did you sign for Rosie's pages?"

"Yeah," Susan said. "I went and slid them under her door."

"Oh, there they are," Rosie said, looking in the place where Susan slipped them the day before, and the day before that.

If Rosie was staying at a hotel, the complaints changed a bit. "My car's not here," she called to let me know.

"It is."

"No, it's *not*."

"Where are you standing?" I asked her.

"I'm in front of the hotel. I told you he's not here. This is terrible! *I can't believe you did this!*"

Rosie the celebrity had her cell phone, but I of course did not. I called the dispatcher, who radioed to the driver for a description of the vehicle. "It's a black car with a seventeen in the license plate." That wasn't cutting it; it wasn't specific enough. "Do you see the car with the flashers on? Okay, the driver is holding his right arm up."

She wasn't even embarrassed; she was too busy thinking of herself as the next Jessica Lange. But me? I was exhausted. The next time she had a shoot, I called my best friend at every hotel: the concierge. "Can you do me a favor?" I asked. "Could you describe the front of the hotel?"

He didn't even ask me why. "There're six gray planters and they have little round boxwoods in them. Then there's one big planter with a pine. Would you like me to draw you a picture and fax it to you?"

With anyone else, it would have been sarcasm. With the concierge, it was simply good service. "That would be great. Thank you so much."

Sure enough, Rosie called again in the morning. "My car's not here!"

"Where are you standing?" I asked her.

"I'm in front of the hotel and he's not here."

"Are you in front of the round boxwoods or are you in front of the tall pine planter?"

"I'm in front of the pine tree thing."

"Is your back to the hotel?"

"Yes."

I knew from the dispatcher that there was a gray car, a maroon car, and then a black one—in that order. "Look to your right. It's the first one."

"No, that one is black. You said it was gray."

"Now look to your, uh, other direction." Silence. "You see it now? There it is." I hung up the phone with Rosie and sat there.

There had to be more to life than this.

GREAT MOMENTS IN HOLLYWOOD SERVICE HISTORY

Batman (1939)—Alfred the butler sits silently by whilst Bruce Wayne studies and exercises excessively, instead of seeing a therapist to deal with his parents' death. Wayne later grows up to lead Gotham City's nascent dom/furry community.

All About Eve (1950)—Eve Harrington moves into the upstairs bedroom to be the personal assistant to the famous Margo Channing, planning all the details of Margo's husband's homecoming—but making sure to get title credit.

What Ever Happened to Baby Jane? (1962)—Baby Jane Hudson, who grew old but didn't grow up, serves dinner in bed to her sister Blanche. The spoiled woman refuses the parakeet delicacy.

Family Affair (1967)—Butler Mr. French convinces his boss to tell the kids the truth about where babies come from—and creepily looks on as the man does so.

continued

The Brady Bunch (1969)—Alice helps Carol Brady (née Tyler) cover up the murder of her first husband; he is never mentioned again.

Return of the Jedi (1983)—Luke Skywalker uses an old Jedi mind trick on Bib Fortuna, Jabba the Hutt's "weak-minded fool" of a majordomo. Skywalker thereupon burns down Jabba's barge, while Jabba himself is strangled by Princess Leia.

Dynasty (1983)—Joseph the majordomo helpfully tries to lock the former Mrs. Carrington in a burning cabin, not realizing he had locked the current Mrs. Carrington inside as well.

The Golden Girls (1985)—Coco the gay houseboy is dismissed after one episode; the LGBTQ community instantly forgives and forgets the slight.

Small Wonder (1985)—Ted Lawson constructs a robot servant, and attempts to pass her off as his daughter by programming her with a monotone voice and dressing her in the same 1890s pinafore every day.

Mr. Belvedere (1988)—Butler Mr. Belvedere advises Wesley to go play in the woods so as not to disturb the Owens' party.

The Simpsons (1994)—A teary-eyed Smithers helps Mr. Burns write a mash note to his girlfriend.

Hotel Babylon (2006)—Tony Casemore, the hotel concierge, sacrifices time with his wife and family in hope of saving up enough in tips to retire at age forty-four.

4.
A Hell of a Town

I didn't *want* to leave L.A.

Even though I was just a go-to gopher for all these famous people, I felt like I was in with them. It was exciting, fun, and cozy—not like New York. New York was no bullshit. It was *real*. People weren't friendly for the sake of being congenial, like they were on the West Coast.

And yet I wanted to revisit my singing-songwriting aspirations and to do that I'd have to move. I was working with two girl rappers and it was making me crazy. Dolores had tried to throw me a bone by putting me in charge of them. I didn't know that their song "40 Dog" was about large male genitalia, so it's no wonder I wasn't exactly prepared. Working with them just made me want to sing again like I did during college, because they were doing it all and making a lot of money in the process.

My better half, Jeffrey, was originally from New York and we started traveling there more, visiting with his friends. "Maybe I could actually sing again," I said to him one day. "I think I do want to be Baby Jane, after all. At the very least, I could manage theater people as a job. Their creativity is much more my vibe than the film people's is."

"It's a big step," he said. "Think about it."

Of course he was right. It *was* a big step—too big probably. What if I couldn't get hired? Where would we live? I weighed the pluses and minuses in my head. "Let's meet halfway," I eventually told him.

"Halfway where?"

"Florida. We can stay with your mom or dad until we find a place, and I could go back to singing on cruise ships." Years before I had worked the cruise ship circuit, the fancy ones that held three hundred people. This time around, I could put together a CD. If I focused less on fancy and more on enormous, I could book myself on a ship with three thousand people. I felt confident I could capture 10 percent of them every week. If 20 percent of that audience bought a twenty-dollar CD, that would mean $1,200 a week—plus my salary. With those numbers moving didn't seem quite as big of a step.

"You should be singing, and I trust your plan," Jeffrey said. "I'm so over L.A."

I went to travel agencies and looked at the brochures for cruise lines, studying the system so I could figure out how it worked. Cunard Cruise Lines had the most prestige; it was the *Titanic* of cruise ships. I called them up and gave them my most name-dropping spiel. "Oh, I used to sing at the Mondrian where Michael Feinstein performed," I told them, "and I played at the Playboy Club. The Sportsman's Lodge, too. Let me send you my clippings."

I had made a collage with every little clip from the newspaper that had my name in it. Even if it just said, "Live on Saturday nights: Michael Fazio at the piano bar," I kept a photocopy. To emphasize my profile, I added pictures of my name in lights. Literally, there was a photograph of my name on the marquee at two clubs where I had performed. It was very twelfth grade, but it impressed them at Cunard enough that they offered me work on the *QE2* right away.

We packed Jeffrey's turquoise blue Honda Accord to the gills and then bought a cell phone because we were going to be driving across the country. It was 1993, and the damn thing was the size of a baguette. I was booked to start on the ship two days after we arrived at Jeffrey's mom's apartment in Aventura, Florida.

Cruise ships are the place once-big acts go when Hollywood stops answering their calls and their shows get farther and farther off the strip. But to me, a celebrity was a celebrity and there were a good number of them working the cruise. Thanks to working with Glennis and Dolores, I knew how to push myself into the inner sanctum. I quickly found out that Lou Rawls was a total gentleman, Nell Carter was simply brassy, and Susan Anton seemed like she had just stepped out of a beauty pageant.

The ship set me up at a bar named Raffles in the back, and every night I put on my white dinner jacket and sat down to play songs on a clear Lucite piano. At the start of the week there would be nobody there, but by Wednesday it would be packed with people listening to me sing campy Broadway standards. Straight people from all over the world couldn't get enough of me. I was like their little gay clown—"Gay people are so *fun!*"—and I sold CDs left and right.

Things were going well, but I found bad news waiting for me when I called Jeffrey back at home.

"My dad's really sick," he told me.

Oh no. "How bad is it?"

"It's melanoma, and it's stage III." He paused. "There is no treatment for stage IV."

I knew that I had to get back to Florida to be with him so I got on the phone and called whomever I could. The first guy I managed to contact was a sleazy old L.A. has-been you wouldn't buy a used car from. Vic had his own version of a twelfth-grade brochure complete with a collage of photos of him with a cavalcade of stars . . . from thirty years ago. To his credit, he managed to find me a really lucrative job singing at an upscale South Beach club. As quickly as I could, I got out of my contract on the *QE2*. Soon I was making $1,500 a week on salary at the nightclub, but I was also clearing a ton in tips— the scar-faced drug dealers came in and threw hundred-dollar bills at me all night. Things were once again good, but it wasn't long before Jeffrey's father passed on.

"We've got to get out of Florida," Jeffrey said. "I grew up here and now I'm remembering why I left."

"I can commute," I told him. "Let's move to New York, and I can fly down here to work. Airfare is only around two hundred dollars. I can do that for a while." True, I was making good money. But being in Aventura, Florida, I couldn't help feeling a little like Peggy Lee: "Is that all there is?" Everyone around me felt really fake, posturing like they were larger than life. And though I really enjoyed singing, now I was realistic about my future: I wasn't going to be a superstar and I didn't want to be a fifty-year-old lounge act singing for tips in a bar the rest of my life.

"What are you going to do once you stop commuting?" Jeffrey asked me.

"I'll figure it out." *But what else am I good at,* I wondered, *besides singing?* I knew how to look after people. I knew that I could make people feel cared for since it was what I had done during my time in Los Angeles. Maybe I could work in theater with classically trained actors who might not be as demanding to deal with as the Rosie Perezes of the world.

I called around Manhattan and got an interview with the president of a small talent agency. I was ecstatic. To me, not being a native New Yorker, he epitomized everything I thought a "New Yorker" was. He looked just like a professor, with the little reading half glasses and everything. His office was a mess, but with "smart" stuff; all theater. "Yeah, you have some potential," he said.

"Really?" I was thrilled.

"This is what I do for new agents. I'll pay you a thousand dollars a month. It's all commission, so you have to go get some clients."

A $1,000 a month? I was making *$1,000 a night* in Florida.

"Great. Let me get back to you." I went back to the apartment Jeffrey had found for us on East 10th Street. The place was so small I couldn't understand how humans were supposed to live in it. It was a one-bedroom—in the sense that the bedroom accommodated precisely one bed, and that was it.

I told Jeffrey about the whole agenting situation, but by this time he was getting fed up. "You'd better figure something out," he said. "You're all over the place. Do you want to sing, or do you want to be an agent? It's not cute anymore."

"I'll find some job I can work at night so that days can be free for interviews," I said. If I was a waiter or a bartender I knew I'd get completely fried, but if I worked the night shift at a hotel, checking people in at the desk, I thought I could manage. It would keep my days free and it would give me spending money—definitely more than $1,000 a month—and I could think and construct my next career move.

Within a day, I wrangled an interview at the InterContinental Hotel on 48th Street. When I walked in I was struck by how old-fashioned but opulent the lobby was. The people walking through it seemed to be arriving from far and distant lands; all the men were in suits and the women wore the Chanel equivalents with big gold buttons. It was clear that none of them was there simply for pleasure.

"I'm here to meet with Ian," I told one of the staff.

"He's right over there."

Ian, the resident manager, was a handsome light-skinned black guy who defined elegance. He was meticulously put together, down to the silk pochette sticking out of his breast pocket. "Right this way," he said. I followed him to his office in the hotel's executive suite. It looked like a gentlemen's smoking room, with big leather wingback chairs and a tufted chesterfield sofa. His huge desk even had clawed feet.

"So tell me a little bit about your background," Ian asked me. "Have you done any hotel work before?"

"I have not," I said. "What I *have* done is a lot of work in the entertainment industry in Los Angeles. I worked a great deal with celebrities, making sure that their accommodations were taken care of and that their needs were met. So I'm a hard worker with great attention to detail."

Ian cocked his head a little bit. Something had clicked. "A chap like you would be good as a concierge." He didn't call me a chap because he was British. He called me a chap because people who worked at places like the InterContinental used terms like that.

"Ah, that's it!" I said. Of course, the thought had never occurred to me, but as soon as Ian suggested it I knew it would be fun. If I'd often used concierges to do my job for me in Los Angeles, there was no reason I couldn't do theirs when I was in New York—aside from the fact that I knew practically nothing about the city. "That would be *perfect*."

"You need to meet Abbie. If you think this is something that you'd like to do, then let's move forward."

Two days later, I reported for orientation. I learned the rules of the hotel along with fifteen other new employees (mainly housekeepers and sanitation managers). I'd never been in a corporate environment, and I felt way out of my element. I had to learn arcane bits of trivia like that the hotel was founded in 1926—as if the guests would come up to the concierge desk and start to quiz me. There was no creativity or even *room* for creativity; if ambience were a color, this corporate world would be like a deep shade of beige—and on my first day I was scared out of my mind. It all started to hit me at once; I hadn't even thought about how I was going to have to wear a uniform. *Oh my God, I'm going to hate this job.*

Of course it didn't help that I was totally unqualified to pass as a New Yorker. I did background work on my own time, trying to guess what people would be asking for. I found the shoe repair, where the museums were and what their hours were, and what restaurants were right around the hotel. I tried to be as prepared as I could, because they were throwing me into the deep end of the pool.

The next day I went to sit in on the desk with Abbie. She had a gigantic smile and walked with a Bette Midler swagger, in addition to looking a bit like her, too. I knew we'd get along because Abbie wasn't just Jewish; she was New Jersey Jewish. And even though I was Catholic by birth, I was a Jewish boy at heart. I *loved* Yiddish words and I loved Jewish people. Hell, I even lived with a Jewish guy.

Abbie knew all the little nuances of New York and her enthusiasm was contagious. She taught me everything from the Rolodex to ordering cars to all the other minutiae which eventually wore on my attention span. That was until she said, "Let me tell you about theater tickets."

Finally, something I could sink my teeth into.

"We *could* use brokers," she said, "but if you're resourceful, you might do very well on your own. If we buy them from a broker, the tickets might be two hundred twenty-five dollars and they only give us a twenty-five-dollar commission. But if we buy them ourselves, then the tickets are eighty-five."

"So how much do we charge for them?"

"Two hundred, obviously. It's a win–win. The guests don't know where you got them from and they don't care. If you sell that ticket for two hundred twenty-five dollars with an eighty-five dollar cost, that's obviously a lot more money." She didn't make it sound scandalous because it was just how the system worked. If I worked the system then, with a little more effort, I could make a good deal more cash. In the same way that a store takes their product, marks it up, and makes a profit, I would be like other middlemen specializing in hard-to-get items.

I spent from three to five o'clock with Abbie, but after that I was on my own. I wasn't too worried, though. I had my little cheat sheet and had gotten used to the phone; eventually I stopped disconnecting people on accident. But by 7:00 P.M. the three phone lines were lighting up *constantly*. I made sure to be calm, so it *seemed* like I knew the answer to whatever the question was. I could guess from people's accents—and there were many—what kind of food they were looking for. I didn't know what "halal" meant, but I knew enough to look in Zagat's for Middle Eastern.

"Good evening, concierge. This is Michael. How may I be of assistance?"

"Hello, I'm calling from room 1212. Do you know where I can get some good chateaubriand?"

She didn't have an accent; therefore, I had no idea where to send her. "I'm pretty sure I know *exactly* where to send you. Let me look up the address and I'll call you right away."

Chateaubriand sounded French and it also sounded like a brand of wine. I got out the phone book to call the local liquor store. "Do you sell chateaubriand?" I asked them.

A pause. "No, we don't."

"Okay. Where do you think I can get chateaubriand?"

"I don't know. A steak restaurant?"

"Huh? Oh, it's a steak?"

"Yes, chateaubriand is a cut of steak," he said, not unkindly.

"Thank you very much." Smith & Wollensky was on my short list of places to send guests already. Why, I was practically a natural at my new job!

As my first shift was coming to an end, a man straight out of *The Sopranos* approached my concierge desk. He was a total cliché: shiny skin, shiny shoes, a little rotund, with his hair greased back and too much gold on his fingers. "Hello," he said, shaking my hand. "I'm Silvio. Welcome to the neighborhood!"

I felt the money cross from his palm to mine, and I put it away discreetly. I didn't know if it was wrong or not, so I felt kind of dirty for even taking it. "Thank you very much," I told him.

"I'm the owner of Cinquanta, two blocks away on Fiftieth. Everybody loves my restaurant, and I want you to know that I will always have a table for you. If you're ever in a bind with getting people seated somewhere, don't worry. Just ask for me."

"Thanks so much!" I said. *Wow,* I thought to myself. *So this is how it works. I never would have guessed that the owners would be making the rounds of new concierges.*

"All kinds of celebrities come to the restaurant," Silvio went on. "We're right across the street from the Palace Hotel."

As new to New York as I was, even I was aware that the Palace was first class. This Cinquanta restaurant must have been the same. And if the owner was telling me to ask for him personally, then it must also be really busy. As Silvio walked away, I looked at how much money he had actually given me. It was several hundred dollars; it was so much money that I didn't feel comfortable accepting it—but I couldn't exactly return it to him, either. I felt suddenly beholden to him.

Which, I guessed, was the point.

I had my short list of places where I would send guests of the hotel—and now I had one more name to add. I didn't even tell Abbie; Silvio was my first big city contact, and I was going to keep him my little secret. Every night, his hostess would call the desk when I was alone and ask for me by name. "Ciao, Michael!" she said, in her charming Italian accent. "How are you tonight? Come for a drink after work! Anything you need, call me."

They're so nice, I thought. *It's a really hot Midtown restaurant, yet they're trying to help me. And I was worried about leaving Los Angeles.*

I kept sending guests of the hotel to Cinquanta. "Ask for Silvio," I told them. "He'll take care of you."

And he did. Whenever the guests came back from dining there, they would always tell me how charming Silvio was and how special he made them feel. Finally, one night after work, I decided to go there myself and check out where I'd been referring everyone.

Walking toward Cinquanta, I could easily spot the restaurant from far away. It had an ultra-modern façade and visually stood out on the old-school block. The exterior of brushed stainless steel matched the décor of the restaurant inside. The cold metal was juxtaposed with bright colors, which brought to mind Miami. In fact, as I looked around the room and the diners, the place reminded too much of Miami. True, the place was full of people who had money, wore nice clothes, and enjoyed quality things. But it lacked a vibe, an atmosphere; the kind of thing that might attract a more exclusive, celebrity clientele.

I sat down at the bar and it wasn't long before Silvio appeared. He started offering plate after plate of food for me to sample. The whole staff came by and said hello, as if they knew me. I thought the place was pretty great—until I started eating.

The food was beautifully displayed, but *horrible.* It was like they got it at a deli and put it on a plate, the culinary proof that you can't put lipstick on a pig. When I saw the prices (thirty-five dollars for pasta!), I realized why it was possible for Silvio to be handing out hundred-dollar bills in exchange for recommending guests.

I was crestfallen. *How am I going to get out of this? I can't send people here.* That's when what Silvio was doing clicked. He wasn't being nice. He was being a businessman—and a good one. It was time for me to start doing the same.

The calls from Silvio didn't stop coming at the hotel. "No one's asking for Italian," I constantly had to tell him.

"We do steak!" he insisted. I couldn't tell him no. I knew he was a good guy, just trying to make a living. I'd try to throw Silvio a bone whenever I could. After all, a good restaurant experience isn't always predicated on the quality of the food. Some people want to be fawned over. Some people *want* to brag that they went to New York, and dropped thirty-five dollars for spaghetti; those people I'd send to Cinquanta. If they hated the food, at least they were never disappointed by the experience.

Now I was back to having just four restaurants that I could recommend to guests. Even if someone wanted to go to a different place every night, I was prepared.

Unless, of course, someone happened to be staying for five nights.

The guest was a middle-aged man, very well dressed, with brown hair in a conservative cut. "That restaurant was so great last time," he said. "Where would you suggest just like that?"

"Right." I had no idea what "last time" was, since I'd been making reservations all week. "Have you been to Le Cirque, and to Patroon?"

"You sent us there after Smith & Wollensky and Hatsuhana. We were thinking something along those lines, but downtown."

I had no idea that I'd be asked for reservations in other neighborhoods. I blinked at the guest. He blinked back at me. I smiled at the guest. He smiled back at me. *Just go back to your room for a minute and let me look through the Yellow Pages,* I thought at him, but he wasn't tele-pathic at all.

"So . . . do you have any suggestions?" he said.

"I know the *perfect* place," I told him. I struggled to remember the name of the restaurant down the block from my teeny apart-ment. It was a little eatery down the street, and it didn't even have a sign out front. If you walked by Il Cantinori, you'd miss it. I didn't know the place had a reputation, that Robert Mapplethorpe had often eaten there in denial of his advancing illness. I couldn't know that years later Carrie Bradshaw would have her birthday there and Victoria Gotti would have her book release party there. Hell, I wasn't even sure what it was *called*. "Il Contori," I said, desperately trying to remember its name from when Jeffrey had once mentioned it. "It's down on Tenth Street. It's great."

"Okay, we're going to need a table for six."

I picked up my copy of Zagat's, found the phone number (and the correct name!), and called the place. "Hi, this is the InterContinental Hotel. Can I get six people in, in about fifteen minutes?"

"Are you kidding?" the host said.

I lowered my voice so the guest wouldn't hear me. "Come on, you've got to help me out. I live right upstairs from you."

"You do?"

"Yes. I live right on Tenth Street." I *did* live upstairs—two build-ings over, but upstairs.

"Really? What apartment are you in?"

"I'm on the second floor."

"But what *apartment*?" the host asked.

"I overlook the street." I made it a point to chuckle in front of the hotel guest, as if this were my old buddy on the phone giving me a hard time.

"*Oh.* So then, do you know Kevin?" Kevin was the owner of the building. Kevin knew the host. Kevin happened to be in Il Cantinori at that exact moment, and he was looking at the host while we were on the phone.

"Of course I know him!" I said, hoping the host wouldn't ask me for a description of whoever Kevin was.

The host didn't say anything for a while. I think the bastard wanted to make sure that I was sweating. "All right, send them over," he finally told me. "And then come by and see me later. My name is Frank."

"Thank you," I said, hanging up the phone. I turned to the guest with my biggest smile. "You're all set for Il Cantinori in fifteen minutes."

"You're the best," he told me.

That night I made sure to swing by the restaurant on my way home. I had expected to be greeted by a prissy maître d' with a little mustache. Instead I got Frank, who looked like he could have been a former linebacker. "Hi," I said. "I'm Michael. I'm the concierge who called you earlier from the InterContinental."

He shook my hand and laughed immediately. "I'm Frank. Who you were trying to pull something over on?"

"What do you mean?"

"So who's Kevin?"

"I don't know," I admitted.

"Come here and have a glass of wine." Frank led me over to a table and I finally got a look at the place. I had often walked by, but had never actually walked in. Even though it was late, it still had a buzz about it. In a way, I felt like I'd walked into somebody's dinner party. It was like the people had been there all night, just sitting at their tables. *This* was the vibe absent at Cinquanta. "You can't really call a place like this and ask for a table for six people right away," Frank said. "You shouldn't do that. That was stupid."

It was obvious in retrospect but I hadn't even realized it. "I'm sorry. I'm new to the city."

"It doesn't matter," Frank said. "It's like that everywhere. You probably didn't think we were that popular because we don't have a sign out front, either. But that's the biggest clue that a place is usually packed."

I sipped my wine, and nodded. Frank clearly knew what he was talking about; he was speaking from years of experience. "I totally get what you're saying," I told him.

"Let me tell you a little bit about how the restaurant business works."

HOW TO GET A TABLE

A misconception people have is that restaurants are holding tables. They aren't. In fact, restaurants have (just like airlines) a virtual overbooking policy where there are more reservations than there are tables. With most of the better restaurants, you have to reconfirm your reservations. If you don't do so by the day before, they'll scrap your reservation.

Overbooking is quite a science, where the benefits outweigh the risks. The restaurateurs have it figured out: how many are typically no-shows as well as how long it takes for the appetizers, the drinks, and the whole thing—down to fifteen-minute increments. Some take things to the next level. RA Sushi on the Las Vegas strip overbooks to help ensure buzz and a sense of urgency. Style-makers and hipsters love intensity and drama, so a little bottleneck at the hostess's podium helps maintain the sense that you are in the "right" place.

Restaurants also have customer databases. If you're a really generous spender, or a big tipper, or a major pain in the ass, or sends things back, that's noted in the database. This works to a return-
continued

ing customer's advantage—*if* you're acting correctly. Instead of calling and asking for a table for Saturday night at 8:00, you can ask the hostess to look up someone's name. If the establishment likes that person—and they might tell you so if asked—then it's much easier to get a table.

Nine o'clock is the hardest time to get, then 8:00. Then it jumps to 7:15 and after that it's 10:15. In terms of size of party, it's hard to get twelve but it's not hard to get four. Just think of the logic. How many tables does a restaurant have that it can accommodate two people? Four? Six? Ironically, a reservation for four is usually easier than one for a couple. Most people go on dates, just two for dinner—leaving the establishment with more four-tops to fill.

Now, there's a wrong way and a right way to get a table. Tippee, the infamous hostess from Sen in Sag Harbor, taught me a very valuable technique to use when confronted with a mob scene and a mile-long wait. *Never* speak to the hostess at the podium. If you check in at the podium with the masses, you are visible and everyone keeping track will know exactly when you came and who "should" be seated before you. You're podium poison, and no one will feel safe doing you any favors. Even if you have to wait an extra few minutes, get the hostess's attention when they are away from the podium. When you corner them, compliment them on how amazing they are at handling the crowd. This sets you apart from the mob.

Let's suppose you call Faustina, or any such "it" spot, and want the four-top. The hostess then looks in the database, and they're probably all booked. If you're just a regular inexperienced guy, it's, "All right, thanks, never mind," and you're over.

But let's say you're really good on the phone. "Four at nine o'clock."

"I'm sorry, we're fully committed."

"Oh, what's your name again?"

"Joan."

"Oh, right, I was there two weeks ago. Were you there? Were you
continued

the one with blond hair in the front? I think we met. So listen, what about if—"

That's why it's a good idea to case the joint ahead of time. You don't even have to go there. You can just call a few days before you actually call for the reservation and just chat with somebody because you're not asking for anything. "Wow, I saw your review! Your restaurant looks amazing. What's your website? What's your name?"

So then, a few days later, it becomes, "Is this Joan? Hey, it's Michael. There are four of us for Thursday; can we come around nine?"

"No, I'm sorry, we're fully committed."

But because there's some sort of relationship established beforehand, you can keep the conversation going. "Oh, no. What's your schedule that night? What's the table before that? If we came at seven, do you need the table back by eight thirty? We can get out in an hour and a half." By acknowledging their system, you've established yourself as an insider—and they'll start to work with you. If you're a concierge who calls them all the time and sends them good people, then they kind of dig even deeper and look at the names on their reservation list. "Jeff Mullen, we know him. Terry Jacobs, we've never seen her name before. Lisa Ronson—no idea." Those last two could potentially cancel, since they don't have a history in the database. Often it's somebody's secretary that booked a reservation and doesn't even remember. The restaurant might be willing to double-book those tables—if you've established a relationship with them. They put you in as a cancellation for that hour, and tell you to call back that day. It's not like some secret table that they were holding is available, but it's just as good.

Even if you don't have a reservation, you can pull it off. My own personal strategy for when I don't have a reservation is sitting at the bar. I go to the hostess and start things out with something kind of funny. When it's a really, really hot restaurant, I'll say something like, "Do you guys accept reservations?" She'll kind of

continued

look at me like I'm an idiot, but then they realize that I'm being facetious. Then I'll say, "Great! Can I book a reservation for fourteen people in, like, five minutes?" It starts the whole thing right. Quickly, I go into, "Look, I know, I'm a loser. I didn't make a reservation. I'm going to go hang out at the bar. I'd love to come here. It looks so great. I'm just gonna play it by ear. I'm in your hands." I go and hang out at the bar and talk to the bartender, and have a drink, and sometimes order an appetizer. But I *always* get a table.

First of all, they want to accommodate me because I honored their system. But at the same time, I'm making light of how seriously people take the whole process. The hostess has to stand at a podium all night and watch the different postures that people take. She has to witness over and over the mistakes people make.

THE MISTAKES PEOPLE MAKE

Don't be totally clueless when you walk in, because you will immediately get blown off. There are people who read an article in a popular magazine or newspaper about a hot new restaurant. For some reason, they think that they're the only ones who've read the piece and now have some kind of secret information. They'll push past the doorman at Minetta's, thinking it's a little pub, and ask for a table for two because they read about it somewhere. They are clueless, and they're out. The hostess won't even look at them.

Another type is the guy who has no respect for the system. He thinks that he's going to get the table by just going in, and that there's no way the person at the front is going to stop him—except the person at the front *will* stop him, every time. His alpha male magic won't cut it.

Then there are the business card people. Just because you are the vice president of a department at some big company, you are not going to impress them at the door with your card. It doesn't matter how embossed your card is or how thick your card stock. Everyone might respect you at work because you're in charge of the system

continued

there, but that doesn't carry over like a bubble of entitlement. You need to respect the hostess, because she's in charge of the system there at the restaurant.

The one technique people use that sometimes works is the straight bribe. But because everyone knows about the straight bribe, it's a very hit-and-miss approach. Sometimes they will refuse you and treat you like dirt. Sometimes they'll take your money and, eventually, give you a seat. But even then you aren't really on the team— you've only bought your way onto the bench.

HOW TO TREAT THE STAFF

In New York, where the tax is over 8 percent, people have a habit of simply doubling their tax to approximate a 15 percent tip. *Don't.* Everyone thinks the tip on a meal is 15 percent, and it's not—and hasn't been for years. The tip is absolutely, without a doubt, 20 percent. The waiters all talk about how annoying doubling the tax is, because the difference is usually only a few dollars. When you're spending $200 on dinner, does it really matter? Waitstaff are exempt from minimum wage laws, since those tips are expected to be their salary. When you're giving them a small tip, you're really giving them a pay cut.

The biggest mistake most people make when they tip is when tipping on a credit card. Unlike when they're paid with cash, waiters get taxed on their credit card tips. A ten-dollar tip on a credit card becomes seven dollars. So if you've doubled the tax and then left a credit card tip, you've effectively only tipped about 12 percent.

A common misconception is that waiters don't have clout. They do. A lot of times there are employee meals in the afternoon, where the chef is trying something new or there's something left over. The waiter can go back and tell the chef that the guests at table 21 are friends of his. The chef will then send out the special on a little tray and you'll feel like a big movie star. The waiters can give you
continued

free drinks. They can send you dessert. They have a lot of pull—and they *will* remember you, for better or worse.

It's not just about the tipping, either. There are big tippers that are a pain in the ass. The waiters feel like whores because they definitely know that some tippers are good for a few hundred bucks—but they don't want to serve them. It's drudgery, and they rarely give those people extra anything. But a person who treats the waiter (or *anybody* in service) like it's a business-to-business transaction will get amazing results.

Most people don't realize this, but anybody can ask the waiter or the manager if they can meet the chef. That's usually a really good political move because it substantiates your position as somebody who appreciates being there. If you make it known that you love it so much that you want to see the kitchen, that's an excellent way to solidify a relationship with an establishment.

Chefs often feel unappreciated because people usually only want to talk to them if something was done wrong. That's why they love it when somebody comes in and tells them how beautifully the meal was done. Chefs are creative people. You should ask them where they worked before. You should ask them where they studied.

However, you should never tip them. That's rude. Instead, send them a thank-you card, or a great bottle of wine. The best trick is to mail them some crazy ingredient. It's cheaper and it's much more thoughtful—and it really gets to the core of their beings as chefs. If you have a chef's contact info, then you're *in*. It's even better than knowing the owner. If you ever want a table, *ever,* you call the chef.

Of course, a lot of this is easier to say than to do. It takes nerve to go to a restaurant and ask to go to the kitchen; you have to pull it off correctly. It's like when you're fifteen and want to buy beer with a fake ID. If you just get the beer and hand it up, it's easy. But if you start talking about how much you love beer, and how you've been drinking it for ten years, then you're getting carded.

continued

Don't try to validate yourself because it's extremely transparent. You're on *their* turf. Validate the *system* and validate the person. Validate them, and let them welcome you in. It's especially powerful in the service world because service people are often the least validated of employees.

HOW TO SEND FOOD BACK

When things go wrong, there's a right way to approach the situation.

One time I ate dinner at a little place on Manhattan's Upper East Side. The restaurant was very cute and sweet and simple. I hadn't eaten lunch and I was starving. I took a bite of the food, and it was delicious. But on my third taste, something wasn't chewing. There was kind of a funny texture. "Excuse me," I told my dining companion. "I'm sorry, but there's something in my food." I put my napkin up to my mouth, and I pulled out—a plastic bag. It was big but all scrunched up. I was *horrified*.

I didn't have a fit, but I also wasn't shy about it. I tucked it under my plate, and I very discreetly asked for the manager. "I was so loving this," I said to him. "This is so delicious, but we have a little problem. There's this bag in the food." I showed him the little bit of it that was still sticking out.

"Oh my God," he said. "I'm so sorry." He brought me another totally different entrée. Then he sent over a bottle of wine. Finally he sent over dessert. I sat there for two hours and had a great time. When I asked for the check, I was told that there wasn't one. (Yes, you still tip the waiter! Figure out exactly how much the bill would have been, and double the tip on that.)

He didn't have to do that. Most places would just take one entrée off the bill. I'm sure the manager was mortified; I was mortified. But neither of us *acted* mortified. Part of gracious service is to not be melodramatic. Because I respected his professionalism and the system, I got treated better than I otherwise would have. I validated the system.

5.
In Between the Sheets

Good evening," I said. "Concierge, this is Michael. How may I be of assistance?"

The guest on the phone had a thick Russian accent. "I vant you to get me a voman," he told me. He could have been asking me to find his girlfriend who was in the lobby or something. He could have been asking me to send him a maid to clean his room. But despite how hard it was to understand what he was saying, it wasn't hard at all to understand what he was asking.

"Do you prefer a certain type?" I asked him. "Blond or brunette?"

"I vant a very beautiful voman," he said.

Clearly my instincts were right. "I don't know anybody off the top of my head, but let me look into it and I'll make some phone calls." There was the notorious *Robin Byrd Show* on Channel 35, where hookers advertised their wares under the glare of bad studio lighting. But I needed an *escort,* not some trashy hustler. Where do the fancy escorts go? I asked myself. Would someone in the nightclub industry know? I picked up the phone and dialed AuBAR.

"AuBAR." They were coarse; exactly what you'd expect for a Eurotrash hangout.

"Hi," I said. "I'm calling from the InterContinental Hotel. I have a client who's asked for an escort. What do you think I should do? Do you know somebody?"

"*What?*"

It was loud in the background. Maybe she hadn't heard me. "*Do you know where I can get an escort? I'm calling from the InterContinental Hotel.*"

"I can't help you," she said as she hung up the phone.

There was a cabinet behind my desk, and all the way at the bottom were the Yellow Pages. It was in a big leather binder with those metal springs down the middle. I opened the cabinet and sat down on the floor, taking out the phone book. I flipped it open to the escort section.

The escort pictures in the Yellow Pages were huge. I was terrified that somebody was going to walk by the desk and see me, on the floor, looking at photos of prostitutes. I realized that I didn't even know where to start. I was looking for quality, and they could look gorgeous in the book and be trolls in person.

I flipped to the adult bookstore section, because there were no pictures there. I found one store that was close to the hotel and called them up.

A woman answered the phone. "Hello, Come Again?" It was the name of the establishment.

"Hi, I'm calling from the InterContinental Hotel. I have a client who's asked for an escort. Do you have some kind of a listing? I don't know what to do!"

"Oh honey, we'll figure this out for you." She was like this sweet, welcoming coach about to walk me through the game. "Well, we do have a swingers paper that comes out monthly, but that's not what you want. Did you look in the Yellow Pages?"

"Yes, but I don't know which one to pick. It has to be reputable and I don't want to get in trouble."

"Let me see if I can help you. What's your phone number?" She took down my information. "I'll call you back right away."

It had now been ten minutes, and the Russian guy probably thought that I was a loser because I couldn't get him a hooker. My service brain was freaking out. *Am I doing the right thing? Am I not doing the right thing?*

A few minutes later, the Come Again lady rang me back with a phone number for me to call. As a concierge, I was committed to the highest levels of professionalism and quality. I, of course, had to ensure that these hookers were, in fact, reputable. "I got your number from Come Again," I told the guy on the phone. "This is for a client of mine. He's a very high-powered businessman and needs a really reputable escort for the evening. How does this work?"

"Well, the rate is three hundred and sixty dollars."

"Oh, that's expensive." Sometimes when I said that they would come down on the price. This was not one of those times.

"I can assure you that we're a very professional agency."

"She has to be beautiful," I said. "That's what he's looking for."

"We will only send the best."

"Okay, I'll have him give you a phone call," I told them. "Thank you so much."

I told the Russian guy the contact information. "My associate called me back and gave me the number of a very high-quality agency. I called them and they're expecting your call, and they have someone available for you. But you have to do it between yourselves," I said, feeling very accomplished. "I can't get involved any further."

"Can I put it on a credit card?" he asked me.

"You'll have to ask the agency." I then got off the phone. Mission accomplished.

Things quieted down for a bit, so I took a deep breath and relaxed.

About twenty minutes later, I heard the sound that only really crappy shoes make. *Clack, clack, clack.* I looked up to see a young woman in a little spaghetti-strap shirt, whose big high heels were making the noise. She looked trashy, as though she had just left a nightclub—even though it was way too early in the evening for that. Just by looking at her, I could tell that she smelled of cheap perfume. *What a bimbo,* I thought to myself.

On one shoulder she had a huge bag. The bag slipped, fell on the hard marble floor, and everything inside of it went flying. The first thing I noticed was the little boom box with speakers on the side; it was very '80s. The big D batteries went rolling for a mile. *She's probably a stripper,* I thought to myself.

I got out from behind my desk and helped her pick up her things. Only then did I see the rest of the contents of her bag, and realized who she was.

The vibrator was not dick-shaped, though it was colorful and cylindrical. It wasn't really grotesque—if anything, the vibrator was the most appropriate thing about the girl. It was *elegant.* It was the kind of dildo you would hope someone would bring to the Inter-Continental Hotel, in the event that someone needed to bring a dildo to the InterContinental Hotel.

Come Again had come through for me.

"Here you go," I said to her.

"Oh, thanks so much," she said, not at all embarrassed.

I pointed her to the elevator and sent her on her way. That was easy. The man on the phone had been direct—as much as he was able—so I knew how to accommodate him. But when a female guest called the desk with a similar request, it took me some deciphering to figure out what she wanted.

"Good evening," I said. "Concierge, this is Michael. How may I be of assistance?"

"I think I'd like to book a massage," she said. "I want to book a massage, but I guess all of the spas are closed?"

It was dinnertime. The spas weren't closed; she was giving me a cue. I took it. "Well, I can get someone to come to your room."

"You *can*?"

"Of course."

"Oh my! What a great idea!"

"Is there any specific technique that you'd prefer? Swedish, deep tissue, cranial-sacral?"

"I think just Swedish?"

"Just like a rub?"

"Right, just for relaxation."

"No problem," I said. "I understand you'd probably prefer a female." Women always want female therapists. Men always want female therapists.

"Yes," she replied. ". . . Or a male."

"Okay, no problem. So do you prefer a male or a female?"

She started to stammer. "No, like, I . . . I prefer female, but a male is fine."

It got to the point where it was like herding cats. *The woman wants a guy,* I realized. *But does she want a "guy" or does she just want a male therapist?* "You know, there's a gentleman who comes here that works for a chiropractor and he's really, really good at adjustments."

I half expected her to say, "That's fine . . . or someone who's naked." "Okay," she said. "Just somebody who is strong."

Now I was going to have some fun with this.

One of the massage therapists who used to come to the hotel was named Sam Sundman. I knew that he was straight, but there was something male-stripperish about him. It was kind of like the way that some personal trainers seem like they could be bought. Sam was a good self-marketer. He'd come to the hotel in the evening and just say hello, but he was also a bit of a tease. At the end of the day, there was nothing in it for me. But maybe there was something in it for this lady guest. Maybe Sam really was trying to be a hustler.

It was time for my testing of Sam Sundman.

So living vicariously through this horny lady, I called Sam and I booked a massage. I wonder if my instincts about him were right. I had my little snicker, but it was short-lived because the concierge desk was so busy. Right away, it was on to the next three requests.

The next morning I get a call at home from Linda, the hotel's newest resident manager—and a very rigid woman. "What happened with Ms. Jamison, and a massage?

"She's a mess!" I immediately said. "If she's telling you that something inappropriate happened, then I'm telling you that that's what she wanted." I spelled out the whole story, like how she said ". . . or a man," ". . . or a man," ". . . or a man" around fifty times.

"Well," Linda explained, "she came down to the front desk and broke down."

"What?" The poor self-loathing woman!

"She was just crying hysterically, saying that she was touched inappropriately."

I started flipping out. I knew that I could be fired over this, easily. "You know what? He's a legitimate massage therapist, but I think that she was looking for massage and company. I know that he would never do anything if he wasn't invited to. Let me talk to him."

"Please do. This is quite serious. There might be charges pressed."

I called Sam right away. "What happened with Ms. Jamison last night?"

"Huh? I didn't do anything wrong."

"So what did you do?"

"Well," he explained, with all his masseuse articulateness, "she was, like, moaning and, like, gyrating around. Dude, I wasn't into it, but she kept pushing it. I'm sorry, but, y'know, she took my hand and, y'know, I wound up fooling around with her a little bit and she went down on me."

Holy shit, I thought. *Fuck, fuck, fuck, fuck.* It was eleven in the morning and I didn't have work until the afternoon, but I went right to the hotel as fast as I could to put out the fire. I sat Linda down and repeated what Sam had told me, in as clean and dignified a fashion as I could manage. What went down, and who went down.

The whole situation had escalated up to corporate. As I passed by the office window, I saw Ms. Jamison sitting there behind the glass. I couldn't believe it. In my mind's eye I had pictured Alexis Colby. In real life, she looked like a homely librarian—and I understood the whole thing right away. I just wanted to sit with her and tell her, "I know you feel dirty, I know you do, but I also know that you enjoyed it. You don't have to hate yourself."

Eventually, corporate took care of it and the whole situation went away. But the bigger environment of sex and hotels is something that will never go anywhere.

SEX AND HOTELS

I don't know what it is about hotels that generates bad sexual energy and shame. There's something at a hotel that just makes people porn out. The thing that *everyone* does in hotels is watch porn. The largest revenue generators in hotels are the minibar—and porn. The porn protocol for guests is very simple: Watch it, enjoy it, pay for it, and shut up.

continued

Virtually every single day, anybody that works in a hotel at night has the following phone call: "Uh, yeah, I was just trying to watch the in-room entertainment and I don't think it's working. I'm just gonna go to bed, so I just want to make sure that it's not on my bill." Or, "I'm trying to order a movie and it keeps turning on and off and I'm very upset. This is very distracting. This is terrible. Make sure that's not on my bill." Whatever euphemism they use, it's all porn—and the hotel employee knows it's porn. It can't *not* be porn, because the LodgeNet systems that are in all hotels reside on a whole separate computer from everything else. Yes, the employee could take it off the bill—but they'll also see it.

There are also the passive people who aren't going to fight to get the porn taken off the bill; they just want to make sure that it's not itemized. What they don't realize is that anything that's $9.50 is Disney—and anything that's $11.95 is porn. They'll say something like, "I'm going to order some in-room entertainment. Is that a separate bill?" They're hinting so that the hotel employee will assure them that, no, the title will not be on their bill.

But it's not just the guests who get their rocks off in hotels. It extends to the staff as well. Hotels, especially in the United States, are notorious for giving work visas to people from foreign countries. They bring them here and work their brains out for close to no pay. In Europe it's more of an honorable career to work in the hospitality industry, and they even have colleges for it. What happens, therefore, is that the American hotels get these wide-eyed little does from Berlin. You can come to New York! . . . *And work sixteen hours a day, and commute to Astoria, and live in a one-bedroom apartment with nine other people.* Their whole life revolves around the hotel, because they work all hours. Afterward, they go to the hotel bar (where they aren't supposed to be).

They're usually all roommates with one another. When one person goes back to Holland, somebody else comes in from Barcelona and lives in their room now. It becomes this whole incestuous community—and they always wind up sleeping with the same people.

continued

They also always wind up as easy prey for the sexual predators on the staff. We all knew that the food and beverage director was screwing around with the little girls. Then one day he just got sloppy.

The security guys called me over, laughing. "Hey, Michael. You need to come up here and look at this." They had him on tape, doing it on camera in one of the banquet rooms. It was him and some girl in a corner, looking like they were wrestling. Yes, he got fired. But I could understand his perspective. He was just a guy that ran the food and beverage department, and made sure that the water got charged out of the minibar. In the outside world he was nobody. But the hotel was his world. Here he had a bit of power, and he figured he might as well roll with that. Nobody got hurt.

Somebody only got hurt when it came to dealing with people with real power—the guests.

6.
The Bad, the Bad, and the Ugly

Lucinda Oskar worked at Deutsche Bank. She had a high position with the firm, and she was pure evil. She was the kind of person who was confrontational just for fun. She would complain about things like a fingerprint on the window. She would also tell us how long it took before we answered the phone. "Hello, it's Lucinda Oskar. It took you four rings to pick up."

I often fantasized about contacting people at Deutsche Bank and showing them what a monster she was. I wanted to record her phone calls and send the recordings to corporate communications or whatever, to let them know how their brand was being represented on the street.

Then I realized that she was probably generating billions in profits for them and they'd laugh in my face.

Every time she would check in, she would be exasperated immediately. She practically walked in sighing with impatience. "Hurry up!" she snapped at everyone, because to her everybody else was stupid. She was five feet of terror that I wanted to push in front of a taxi. Whenever I saw that she was coming into the hotel—which was quite often—I used to get a bit excited. She couldn't hurt me, no matter how much she tried. I'd dealt with bigger and badder than Lucinda Oskar before.

But Aneka wasn't like me. Aneka was one of the wide-eyed does from Europe, and in a much more tenuous position. One day she came up to the concierge desk in tears. "What happened? What's wrong?" I asked her.

"She's so upset with me!" Aneka sniffled, probably afraid of getting fired.

"Who?"

"Ms. Oskar."

"Tell me what happened."

"I picked up the phone and she wanted to know what the program was for the New York Philharmonic at Carnegie Hall. I didn't know. So she said, 'What are you, *stupid*? You don't have this information?'"

Aneka wasn't a concierge. There was no real reason for her to know what was going on at Carnegie Hall. There was no real reason for her to be speaking with Lucinda Oskar on the phone, either. What Lucinda liked to do was just dial phone extensions at the hotel until someone picked up. If no one answered the first number, she'd keep dialing until some random hotel employee answered a phone—in this case, poor Aneka.

"Come here," I told Aneka. "Don't worry." The hero in me took out the flyer, and I showed her how to find the information for future reference.

"Thanks." Aneka calmed down a bit, knowing she wouldn't be trapped the next time.

But I was going to make sure that there wasn't going to be a next time. Against all hotel protocol, I initiated a call to Lucinda Oskar in her room. "Hello," I said. "It's Michael from the concierge desk. I understand that you're interested in knowing the program for the

New York Philharmonic at Carnegie Hall." Then I just read her the program like I was a robot. "Is there anything else?"

"I don't know to *whom* I was speaking before," Lucinda said, "but she's so *stupid*. How difficult of a question was that?"

"I agree," I said, calm and steady, "that it's not a difficult question at all. What *is* difficult, however, is the concept of intentionally upsetting people. We can all agree that you were really seeking confrontation and *not* information."

"Who are you?" Lucinda snapped. "This is ridiculous! How can you talk to me this way?"

"Ms. Oskar, certainly we know that there is a difference between seeking assistance and seeking a confrontation. Asking Aneka if she is stupid, as you did, clearly indicates which one you were looking for." Lucinda tried to interrupt me, but I kept talking over her. "My name is Michael, and I think it would be best if you deal with me directly. It may be amusing to you to hurt others' feelings, but we are too busy for that." My tone was extremely professional, but I wanted her to understand that she was busted, and that it was time for her to stop the bullshit. I hung up the phone, feeling totally triumphant.

"Oh my God!" Aneka said, no longer feeling valueless and stupid. "I can't believe you did that!"

It's true that Lucinda Oskar was pure evil. It's also true that she was quite a smart lady, and she had stayed at the InterContinental chain religiously. She did what a smart lady who was pure evil would do: Instead of going to my manager, she went to someone in global corporate and repeated verbatim our conversation. That global corporate manager, whoever they were, then called my hotel's resident manager Ronald—who then called me.

I sat down in his big office. Its huge window faced the lobby; it was as if we were meeting in a see-through bank vault. I instantly realized what was going on. I also realized that even though it felt good for the moment, in hindsight I didn't really win. It felt good, but it was a waste of my energy because it didn't educate Lucinda at all. Still, I managed to redeem Aneka's sense of self-worth. Maybe it wasn't such a mistake.

Like a typical German hotelier robot, Ronald recited my conversation with Lucinda with exact precision. "Certainly we can't be treating our guests like this," he concluded.

"That is absolutely ridiculous," I insisted. "Look in the comments in her guest profile. Clearly the woman is out of her mind! Give me a break." It was true. If you looked in her profile you'd see, ad nauseum: complaint; complaint; room moved; complaint; room moved; rebate.

COMPLAINT KARMA

When you complain in a hotel, you leave a trail in the system. It's all logged through programs like Fidelio, Opera, or Hot Sauce. It's one of the big benefits of the industry-standard software. Staff often go out of their way to put *positive* comments in people's portfolios. When people act great, staff want that to trail them to other hotels in the chain.

The next time that a positive customer checks into a brand hotel in another city, whoever's checking them in will see the comments. Everyone *always* looks at the comments; it's an internal way for employees to warn one another or to encourage rewards for good behavior. When a customer I praised went to another Inter-Continental Hotel, I am positive that they received some perk upon checking in.

Being nice is free—and it gets you free things.

Ronald did not dispute my denial. I had too good of a reputation. As smart as Lucinda Oskar was, she was also quite stupid, because now I had a bug up my ass just waiting to get back at her.

The porter came down from her room and handed me her airline tickets, with a note of instructions. Apparently she didn't take me up on my offer to call me directly. Her instructions were asking for me to reconfirm her tickets. Reconfirming tickets is a very European, very old-fashioned thing to do, one which there's really no call for anymore.

Lucinda's tickets were for the 6:00 P.M. business-class flight back to London, wait-listed for first class. The 6:00 P.M. flight is the most popular flight; *everyone* wants to get out on that. With people as traveled as Lucinda, their ticket is usually not reflective of what they're actually doing. They've changed it many times, but because they're super-triple-platinum members they don't bother them with more tickets. It all comes down to the confirmation number.

I got on the phone and called British Airways—as she instructed. "Hi," I said, "this is John, Lucinda Oskar's assistant. I need to make some changes on her flight. Here's the confirmation number."

I read the guy the number from the ticket. "All right," he said. "How can I help you, John?"

"She wants to switch to the ten o'clock flight."

"Well, she's wait-listed for first class," he pointed out.

"Yeah, we're not gonna do that. We're gonna go with the ten o'clock flight."

"I'm sorry, but we don't have any first-class seats available. We don't even have any business available."

"That's okay, that's okay. Coach is fine."

"We'll wait-list her for business class. But there are a lot of people ahead of her for the upgrade, I'm afraid."

"Oh, darn! That's so unfortunate. All right, it's probably best for me to just take a confirmed seat for her in coach. She'll have to hope for the best. She just wants to get home, bless her heart."

From the sound of the seat number, she was practically in the back bathroom. "Is there anything else I can help you with?"

Should I? Shouldn't I? Ah, what the hell. "Yes. She would like a Hindu meal."

Now I had to send her ticket back to her room with the porter. I was very careful to make sure that I had clean hands and nothing could be traced back to me. All I did was write "okay" on her note, which she could have interpreted any way she wanted. She must have had a great flight, because I never heard from Lucinda Oskar again.

But even though Lucinda was a dreadful, horrible person, I didn't have to deal with her or think about her when she wasn't at the hotel. She wasn't some nemesis that haunted me day in and day out, an enemy I couldn't avoid dealing with no matter how much I tried.

In other words, she wasn't The Trough.

The Trough was, and still is, the most impossible restaurant to get into in New York City. It's been that way for over fifteen years, and it's kind of crazy. Other places are often very hard to get into—Per Se, Union Square Cafe, and Dorsia come to mind—but for it to go on for that long is kind of unprecedented. As the buzz trickled into their restaurant, the consequence became an air of total arrogance.

The whole idea of getting in somewhere fancy and important is to *feel* fancy and important. But when you go to The Trough restaurant, they make you feel like you're trespassing. You're taking a tour of Graceland, but all of the rooms are roped off. You're welcome to step inside—but you're not welcomed. Any restaurant-review website is full of scathing attacks on The Trough, simply because of their attitude. I absolutely loathe their whole condescending philosophy—and I eat my heart out because it's so impossible to get in.

Part of gaining access to a hot restaurant is knowing people on an individual basis. But you can't just call a restaurant of that caliber and ask who the manager is. It'll be like, "Um, *who's* calling? We can't give that out but I'll leave a message that you called." It's very much need-to-know information.

I used to case the place because it's not far from my house. The Trough seems like a pretty unassuming establishment from the outside, but the "no trespassing" energy it generates could not be any clearer. I was mastering the art of getting past the gate, but this place psyched everyone. One day, I saw an Italian Wine Merchants truck double-parked outside, delivering wine. I looked up their phone number and called them. "Hey, I was dining at The Trough and I think they mentioned that you do the wine? I *love* their wine list. If I wanted to get something from their list, how would I do it?"

"That's no problem. Was there anything in particular you were looking for?"

"Yes, I was just in there talking to the manager. To . . . uh . . . oh, man. I'm totally blanking on his name."

"It's Hal."

"Hal? Are you sure?"

"Yeah, it's Hal Druiter."

I chuckled at my "forgetfulness." "Of course," I continued, scribbling down the name while it was fresh in my mind. "I just love him. I'm going to ask *Hal* for his favorites and then call you back. Thanks so much! You've been a big help."

Now that I had his name, I called the restaurant asking for him specifically. I called over and over—and left messages over and over.

It was all for naught, but I still felt like I had gotten one step closer. I knew for a fact that The Trough had several tables specifically reserved for walk-ins. A lot of restaurants do hold literally a couple of tables for walk-ins (though not for reservations). They're designated just for that purpose, and they're usually at the bar or are side tables. If you put your ego in your pocket, walk in there, and say that you'll be happy to wait for a half hour, you *will* get a table.

One night I went into The Trough for dinner without a reservation, knowing that if I waited I'd get a table eventually—and get to meet Hal. When I saw him I was surprised, because he looked somewhat nondescript. He was about fifty years old, with a very precise blond hairstyle. But he was very charismatic and seemed like he recognized everyone. "Hi," I said to him when I walked in. "I'm Michael Fazio. You're so hard to get in touch with! You must see my name every day on your call list."

"Oh, yeah," he said. "I'm sorry."

"We're just going to try your walk-in policies tonight," I told him, using the right lingo.

"Great. It'll be just half an hour or forty-five minutes."

I had money to give him, but I wasn't sure when I should pass it along. Giving straight cash is always a tricky thing to gauge. It can be in anticipation of a favor or as gratitude, or you can mean it to be one but it'll end up being perceived as the other. I went up to him when he stepped away from the podium. "Wow, you guys are so hot. It must be fun to work here. I bet everyone does what I do and are always bothering you. I hope you understand we concierges are on the frontlines. Everybody looks at us like we're idiots because we can't get them in here. I'm sorry to bother you but it's my job." I shook his hand and palmed him $200.

He didn't make a show of protesting, as most maître d's in my experience tend to do before pocketing the cash. He pretended nothing had happened. But two seconds later, we were being seated at a table—and Hal Druiter was my new best friend, as nice as can be.

Hoping to be *seen*, I did a quick scan of the other diners. Were we even in New York City, let alone downtown? It didn't buzz like other places with that kind of hype. Where were all the alleged celebrities? The crowd was clearly a well-heeled bunch, but there were no air kisses. It felt a little bit like we were all guests at a wedding where we really didn't know the family.

The food itself was really, really good—just like at ten thousand other restaurants in New York. But the larger part of going to eat at a nice restaurant is the experience, and that's where it fell flat.

It's engaging to let people in service know that you're really enthusiastic about what you're about to experience. It makes them want to make the experience even better for you—if they're normal. But there didn't seem to be any sense of excitement from the staff at The Trough.

We got the menu and I looked it over. "It all seems so good. What's *your* favorite thing to try?" I asked the waiter.

He sighed with irritation. "Well, it depends on what you like. If you like fish, then this one is good."

After I left that night, I made sure to say good-bye to Hal. "Call me anytime," he told me. "You're the best. Let me give you our direct line."

Cool, I thought. *I got the number!*

A couple of weeks later, a guest wanted a reservation for a table. I called the number—but it was the same as the regular one, except it bypassed the hold music. Some secret! "Sorry," they told me on the phone. "We have nothing."

"Well, will you tell Hal that I called?

He actually called me back. "What do you want?" he said. He

wasn't very warm and he wasn't very cold; it was just very business-like.

"I'm so desperate," I said.

"What do you need?" he said.

"Can I get a four-top in at eight?"

"What's the name?" he said, impatiently. He didn't want to linger on the phone because he didn't need to linger on the phone. I had a short, specific request, and it was granted. The guest got their table and I did my job. Everyone was happy. *I'm so in now,* I thought.

Now I felt comfortable recommending The Trough to the guests of the hotel. The next time I called, I thought my old buddy Hal would be glad to speak to me. But it was my *old* buddy Hal—the one who didn't know me from Adam—who was on the other end of the line.

"Hi, is Hal there?"

"Hold on," the hostess said. "Who's calling?"

"It's Michael Fazio."

"Let me check." They put me on hold, and I was forced to listen to opera music for a few minutes. "Yeah, he's going to have to get back to you."

Crap. Crap, crap, crap!

I went back there after work one night, about eleven o'clock. I sat at the bar and ordered a drink. Hal was there at his station but, even though it was late, he was still busy. He didn't act like he really remembered me, which I didn't take offense to. "Hey, Hal," I said, when he had a minute. "Can I buy you a drink?" Obviously he doesn't need to pay for drinks at his own place, but it's a gesture of respect—just like when you buy strippers a drink.

"No, no, no," he told me. He didn't really say anything else or even engage me in conversation, which I also didn't take offense at.

As I was leaving, I stopped by him one more time. "Thanks again for everything," I said, palming him fifty dollars more.

I was a little taken aback that he didn't do what other people in his position usually do, which is to feign humility. "Thanks for coming in," he said, pocketing the money without any protest.

The next time I called them, I got the reservations that I needed—and then Hal stopped taking my calls again. *Damn,* I thought. *Here we go again.* But he had a bit of an excuse; the person on the other end of the line told me that he was in Italy on vacation. Since I knew "the number" I had a *little* bit of creditability with them. "Where is he in Italy?" I asked. "I want to send something to him."

"He's in Capri," she told me. Then she gave me the name of the hotel where he was staying.

Abbie speaks Italian, so she called his hotel. We sent him a beautiful bottle of wine, a bottle of Limoncello, and some pasticiotti. All this was not cheap. Abbie spoke to the concierge at the hotel and they attached a note, in Italian, to the gift. We thought we were being really classy, and we thought we were being kind of clever. We had found him all the way out in Italy and sent him a gift that was thoughtful.

Now we sat back and waited for the phone to ring. But there was no acknowledgment, not even a terse note. There was *nothing*. Nothing, nothing, nothing. Maybe we were being too upfront and honest for Hal's taste. We were establishing the boundaries of our relationship, but in doing so we were robbing him a little bit of his power. Maître d's—like concierges—cultivate an air of mystery about their position. They don't like their clients to feel totally comfortable. It's very much a situation where good service is given when *they* feel like it—not when *you* demand it.

But now I had to get a reservation that was very important. My friend Courtney worked at Bergdorf's, and she would always do really nice things for my clients and me. She would call and let me know that in ten days a certain collection was going to go on sale. I'd send people in. They'd pick out what they wanted, give it to Courtney, and she'd give it to them at sale price—and ring up the purchase ten days later.

Her corporate buyers were coming into New York, and she wanted to impress them. No surprise, but they wanted to go to The Trough for dinner. She called me right away, anxious that I make this happen.

"Of *course* I can do it," I told her. "Don't worry."

I managed to connect with Hal on the phone; maybe he was relaxed after having gone on his Italian vacation. "Incidentally," I asked him, "Abbie and I sent you something. Did you get our gift?"

"Oh, yeah!" he said. "That was great! How'd you know where I was?" He was more curious than grateful. I got the message: we weren't that kind of friend. I was *trying* to be that kind of friend, but failing.

"I really, really wouldn't bother you if I didn't need this one reservation," I told him. "This is a favor for a close friend."

"I'll see what I can do," he replied. It wasn't a yes, and it wasn't a no. He clearly didn't want to keep the door open for me to call anytime in the future. But I hoped that maybe he'd help this one time—and then I'd leave him the hell alone, like he wanted.

But Hal never called me back, and Courtney went ahead and told her guests that they'd be eating at The Trough.

I didn't want to be a pig and call him again. He had made it clear that we're not pals. None of my gestures was reciprocated. The Trough was literally—*literally*—the only place where those gestures didn't work. Maître d's know that concierges are kind of like matchmakers—we recommend their places to customers who would appreciate it, and we send them customers who would behave appropriately and add to their vibe. But no matter what you do, at The Trough you're still just an outsider.

It got to be the day of the reservation, and I started to get a bit of an attitude. I kept calling him, and calling him, and calling him, and calling him—and Courtney started calling me.

"This guy's being a dick," I told her.

"I already told them that we're going," she reminded me.

I imagined Courtney calling her buyers, who were totally psyched about eating at The Trough. She'd have to tell them that she was a loser and actually didn't get the reservation after all—and then she'd have try and do business with them in the future? It would be awful.

At around five o'clock, Hal finally got back to me. "I can't promise you anything," he said, "but just tell her to come and see me."

So I called Courtney. "Come by the hotel," I told her. "I want you to take something with you."

She didn't have that much money to throw around, and she didn't feel totally comfortable accepting money from me, but she had to do it so that she wouldn't have egg on her face. I didn't want Courtney to feel awkward, so I didn't tell her that it was money I was giving her—and certainly not how much. I put it in an envelope so she'd never know. "When you get there," I instructed her, "say hi to Hal. Give him this and tell him it's from Michael."

Courtney and her group went down to the restaurant—and I didn't hear anything the entire night. I was sure that it all backfired. But she called me first thing the next day. "You are amazing!" she said.

"What do you mean?"

"He took the envelope and sat us right away."

Abbie and I gave up on The Trough, and started playing by their rules. They take reservations thirty days in advance, and they open at 10:00 A.M. We would always start dialing at 9:56, a month before we needed a reservation. But even if we got through at 10:01, they never had 8 o'clock tables available. It would always be like 6:45, or 10:30. Maybe the 8 o'clocks are the ones that Hal uses for some sick I'll-decide-who's-worthy game.

I couldn't be more over The Trough if I tried—and I wasn't alone. I've yet to meet a concierge in the city who didn't roll their eyes at the name.

Whenever a hotel guest would request reservations for The Trough, I would always tell them, "You know, everybody wants to go there. I get it. But we get much better feedback from other places. The food *is* great, but they aren't going to make you feel very special."

Rarely, people would ask for other suggestions.

PLACES I WOULD REFER A CLIENT TO IN LIEU OF THE TROUGH

If You Are Looking for Great Italian Food:
  1. San Pietro—*Bellissimo! Beso, beso, beso.*
  2. Marea—Culinary talent and hospitality humility.
  3. Al Di La—Simply real. No reservations. (Please don't tell everyone!)

If You Are Looking for Foodie Cred:
  1. Little Owl—You need the cell phone of the maître d'.
  2. Bouley—Nothing trendy about a genius.
  3. Shaun Hargatt—Finally, a newcomer that is too expensive to be trendy.

If You Are Looking for Grossly Overpriced Cuisine:
  1. Masa—I "get" it . . . except that I don't.
  2. Gallagher's Steak House—This might have been cool, once.
  3. Valbella—Sorry you have to pass along the expensive rent, but *really.*

continued

If You Are Looking for a Totally Obnoxious Experience (Masochists Only):

1. Casa Tua in Miami—or most places in Miami, for that matter.
2. Any Graydon Carter restaurant—worth the punishment, if you want to be in an "it" place. They usually don't have a phone number. If you're lucky enough to get the private email address, you have a chance. But it's like hoping to get Fantasia Barrino to write you a letter.
3. The Park—It's still around, but so is Chevy Chase. At one time, they were the "first" not to publish their phone number. If you *were* lucky enough to get it, you were greeted with a computerized call-screening device that said, "Thank you for calling The Park, please announce your name at the tone." After you said your name, it replied, "Please wait while we check to see if your party is available." Rejected by a machine! (Gross, huh?) And today . . . *crickets.*

But the majority of guests didn't want to hear it. They knew about the reputation, but wanted to go there because, they say, they loved the way The Trough's famous chef/owner came off on TV.

"It's really difficult," I let them know. "This is the one place where we just don't get anywhere with them."

The thing is, I knew why the guests wouldn't take my advice. Everybody knows that The Trough is impossible to get into. That in itself is probably a good portion of the mystique. Saying you had dinner at The Trough is the kind of thing that would impress your friends.

A lot of people buy into the concept of who The Trough's chef/owner is. He's kind of a hippie, with this wife whose family used to own a goat farm, where they make their own cheese. He puts on this air like, "Look at me, I'm not a celebrity! Look at me, I wear

Crocs! I wear these all the time! I'd wear them to Steve Irwin's funeral, I'm so average!" I'm really not even exaggerating. The man wouldn't even put on a tie to meet the First Lady—at the White House. But he's about as rustic as Mr. Howell was on *Gilligan's Island*. Just because you're with the coconuts doesn't make you a native.

One snowy day, Abbie and I were walking around the Village. "I want some mortadella," she decided. "Where can we go?"

Abbie had lived in Italy for a number of years, and she loved anything that was authentically rustic and truly Italian. "Feedbag's a block away," I pointed out. It was another of the many restaurants in the Trough chain.

"They have the best carving board," Abbie grudgingly agreed. "We have to go."

We took our coats off, and took our gloves off, and took our snow boots off, and waited. We finally got seated into our little table, excited to have a good meal. The waiter came out, but Abbie interjected before he could say anything. "We don't need a menu," she told him. "We're going to get everything from the carving board. I want some mortadella."

"I'll have some bresaola," I added.

Minutes later, the waiter came right back. "I'm sorry," he said, "but we're out of mortadella."

Abbie looked at him as if he had punched her in the stomach. It was like a Five Napkin Burger being out of ketchup. Mortadella is hardly the food of the gods, but *real* Italians know what a staple it is—and a place like Feedbag is supposedly all about being *real*.

It was a couple of months later when Abbie and I were invited to a documentary festival along with a few other concierges from top hotels. It was sponsored by some TriBeCa organization as a way to promote local businesses and establishments. We were upstairs at the

Tribeca Grill, drinking cocktails, eating hors d'oeuvres, and watching the silent auction.

There, in the faux-rustic flesh, was He Who Wears Crocs—intentionally scraggly ponytail and all. He was standing there talking with Danny Meyer from Union Square Cafe and Tom Colicchio, who wasn't yet such a superstar. I had never met Tom but did a lot of business with his restaurants. I had met Danny Meyer, and he had personally given me his assistant's number when I needed something at any of his great restaurants. In my drunken delusions of grandeur, I believed that Danny couldn't have *possibly* forgotten meeting me.

Abbie and I saw this as our opportunity to finally get in good with The Trough. Here were two people with whom we had decent business relationships with, so it would be our in to join the conversation and score a relationship with the third.

DON'T MAKE PLANS WHEN YOU'RE DRUNK

Trust me.

"You start," I told Abbie.

"No, *you* start!"

"Well, what should I say?"

"I don't know." We stood there discussing the plan, downing more and more wine until we were kind of giddy. I remembered Dolores's advice: Be clever, and be quick. "I got it. Let's tell him about the mortadella. Don't be mean. Let's make it really nice."

We walked over, and I was so drunk that I was seeing six of each person. It was like 1,800 pounds of Mr. Trough, man of the people. Because they were the celebrities of the room, they were able to block out of their periphery that Abbie and I were standing right next to them and staring at their heads. It was that awkward twenty seconds where I thought that they weren't going to open up their group and acknowledge us. Finally, Danny Meyer turned his head enough that we sort of made eye contact. "Hi, Danny Meyer!" I said. "I'm sorry to jump in, but I just have to thank you for always keeping the door open for us—even when we knock ten thousand times a day. Your people really get it and they are so great at making things work."

"Okay . . . ," he said.

"I'm Michael Fazio and this is Abbie Newman. We're the concierges at the InterContinental Hotel."

"Oh, right!" he said, almost a little embarrassed. "Of course I remember you. How are you? Do you know Tom?"

"I don't know you personally, but we love your restaurant. Victor"—his maître d'—"is so wonderful. It's so nice to deal with professionals. You've got such a great team."

"I saw you speak at a concierge event a couple of months ago," added Abbie. "Everybody was so impressed. We really love your brand."

"Thank you," he said.

Now we were in conversations with two of the three, so Abbie went in for the kill. "I have a bone to pick with you," she told the Man of The Trough, playing up her Jersey accent with a joking wink in her eye. "We trudged through the snow to go to Feedbag, and all I wanted was some mortadella. Everyone knows you've got the best carving board in the city, but you were sold out of it! C'mon, man! A girl's entitled to a little mortadella after dragging herself through the snow, isn't she?"

It fell flat. *Totally* flat. "What are you talking about?" he said, as if she had been rambling for hours in a foreign language.

Now it was time for *my* drunken bad judgment to kick in. "You know, I just want to ask you something," I said. "Are we doing something wrong at The Trough? Every other restaurant shows us a little love, except for yours."

He looked at me like I wasn't worthy of being told to shut up. Danny and Tom turned away, staring into space, while Abbie and I tucked our tails in between our legs and slowly walked away.

RESERVATIONS: AN INFORMAL HISTORY OF CULINARY OBNOXIOUSNESS

1996: It's "who you know," and if you wanted to eat at Daniel, you'd better know Bruno. Everyone was friends with Bruno, however, which is how he has his own private club now.

1997: The birth of the charming "we're fully committed" euphemism. Asia de Cuba was the first to be so "professional."

1998: "We take reservations thirty days in advance."

1999: "Leave your request at the tone and we will call you back." Moomba seated Madonna and Leonardo DiCaprio but not enough other people to stay in business.

2000: A secret number no one else had. Becomes a problem when it kept people from calling. Commune became Rocco's, the first restaurant reality show—which became cancelled, closed, and sued.

2001: Call screening technology asks you to "please announce your name at the tone." "We're sorry," they continue, "we are not able to receive your call at this time. Please try back." People got sick of trying back at The Park, though they are still technically in business.

2001: Simply no number listed. Thanks, Man Ray!

2002: Allegedly, "we don't take reservations." Yet, somehow, there is a reservations book when you arrive and some people don't wait. Brasserie's dubious contribution to the food scene.

2003–2005: The dining industry wracks their collective brains on how to keep customers away while staying in business.

continued

2006: "We'll need a credit card to guarantee your table" at BLT.

2007: TableXchange.com sells reservations for cash at places like The Trough. Now it's "404 File Not Found."

2009: An email-only policy. I've been to the Waverly Inn many times, but have yet to meet this "Fritz."

7.
Mrs. Kinezevich, in the Hotel Room, with the Antique Russian Sword

When working in an establishment like the InterContinental Hotel, you just get a sense for people. She was probably fifty or fifty-five, but I had the sense that the woman was *traveled*. She was wearing a schleppy-looking fur coat, but the fact that it was so worn indicated that she had probably been carting it around *the world*. Her hair was pulled back really, really tight, and she accessorized it with ornate barrettes that matched the ornate jewelry and the brooches she wore on both sides. The jewelry seemed like there was some history to them; they clearly weren't just off the shelf from Van Cleef & Arpels. The pieces were very baroque, bigger than big. The entire effect made her seem like an old wall full of bad frames. She had a much younger guy with her, who had an odd air about him. Was he shy? Was he depressed? Was he planning a murder? She obviously had presence; he probably had skeletons.

She announced herself very elegantly: "Sofiya Kinezevich, Six Continent Club Member." The Six Continent Club was the platinum elite for the InterContinental hotel chain. Meeting them was like meeting hotel royalty. You knew you had to go a little extra for them, because they could complain and make trouble—and their complaints *would* be listened to.

"How can I help you?" I asked her.

"You know what I'd really love?" she said. "I'm looking for an antique Russian sword."

"No problem," I replied, as if there were several Russian swords in my desk; all I had to do was reach down and show them to her. *Russian swords, coming right up!* That was kind of the fun of the concierge experience. The customers didn't always just give us the task and let us do research; Sofiya stood there while I wracked my brain trying to figure out where to procure Russian swords—*antique* Russian swords.

She smiled. I smiled. Even the shy companion smiled. I picked up the phone and began calling every crazy rococo antiques dealer I could think of on 61st and 62nd Streets. Nothing. I hung up the phone and started to dial up Christie's; they could often point me in the right direction for things like this. If not them, I could call the Metropolitan Museum.

"One second," she said. "I'm also looking for some vintage Russian books, from the tsarist period."

"Have you tried Argosy Books, on East 59th Street?" I asked her. "That would be a great place to start. I'll be happy to do more research if you'd like to tell me any specific titles that you're looking for."

"In a moment. I think we'd like to get some food first. Can you recommend a Russian establishment? But *Slavic*. Not anything Ukrainian."

Oh my God, I thought, *this is crazy.* At first I loved this lady, with her kitschy jewelry. I thought she was fabulous, like Auntie Mame was staying at the hotel. But now we weren't accomplishing anything. It was like she was asking me questions just to impress me.

A lot of guests like to play the concierge equivalent of *Stump the Band.* They're the kind of people who go to the wedding band and say, "Do you know Mozart concerto number three, second movement? Allegro? And . . . go!" *All right,* I thought. *Enough of this, lady. What's really going on here?*

"I just need a car service," she said. "I'll find it."

"Sure," I told her. "When would you like the car?"

"Well, right now."

"No problem. There are usually cars right around the hotel. We can go see if there are any town cars out front." I walked her out to the car, glad to be able to move on to other things.

"I just remembered," she said, snapping her fingers. "The Russian embassy. I need the address."

"Of course." I sprinted back into the hotel and found our diplomatic directory. I wrote the address for her on a card, and ran back out to the car and gave it to her.

"Oh, you're wonderful," she told me. "Thank you so much."

She didn't tip me, which was fine. She was off and out of my mind now. The concierge desk was short-staffed, with three people covering a seven-day-a-week shift between us. There was no shortage of requests at the desk for me to handle.

Eight hours later, the car service dispatcher called me. "Uh, Mrs. Kinezevich has had our car since nine o'clock," they told me.

"Yeah, I know." I was surprised that they were calling me; she was hardly the first guest to use a car all day.

"But what do you want me to do?" the dispatcher asked.

"It's as directed," I told him. "You stay with her until she's done."

"Well, we dropped her off at the Russian embassy this morning and she told us to wait. But she still hasn't come out."

Aw, crap. A lot of times at the hotel, people would forget that they told the driver to wait—and drivers do as they are told. That's why booking a driver on an hourly basis is called an A/D ("as directed"). Car service in cities like New York is big business, and people rack up big bills—*especially* with A/Ds. The clock is ticking from the moment the car leaves with you until the moment you dismiss the driver. When people forget that the driver is waiting for them, the bill becomes hundreds of dollars. Even though it's the guest's own fault, they would almost always raise hell and contest the charges.

The hotel knew that we were getting a commission (read: kickback) for the cars we hired, so *anything* that came up became *our* issue. But we wanted to try to preserve the peace as much as we could. We had to try to placate the car company and the customers, and not let matters reach the hotel at all. We used to negotiate with the customers. If they were nasty, I would hardball them. They had signed a binding document, after all. Sometimes we would have to cough up the money ourselves, and tell the car company to hold it out of our commission. But Sofiya wasn't simply a regular guest. She was a Six Continent Club Member.

It was always better, for all parties involved, to disappear a problem now instead of contesting it later. *What do I do, what do I do?* I thought. *The car bill was already very high, but it's not like there was a back entrance to the embassy that she could have exited out of.* For now, the car would have to stay. As I finished up for the day, I called the dispatcher again. "Did she come out yet?" I asked him.

"Nope."

It had been like twelve hours already. "All right. Can you send the driver inside, to go ask if anybody had seen her?"

"Sure."

A few minutes passed while I weighed my options. I wished she had rented a cell phone from us; that would have solved the whole problem. I wished *all* the guests rented cell phones from us. It was new technology at the time, and people wouldn't know that they needed to turn it off. By the time they'd return it the minute counter would be in the hundreds, at a cost of two dollars a minute—and with no driver or concierge to blame.

"No one's seen her," the dispatcher told me.

"You know what? Leave. There's nothing you can do."

"Well, she left a couple of things in the car."

In a hotel our size, things got lost all the time. I felt responsible. "Just bring them to me. I'll take care of it."

Not too long after, the driver came and brought Mrs. Kinezevich's pashmina and a bulging manila envelope. It was clasped shut, but it wasn't glued. *This is really weird,* I thought to myself. *What is this?*

I took the envelope to the back, where none of the guests could see what I was doing. Inside the envelope was a stack of papers, on top of which was a very official-looking cover letter with a seal on it, like some fancy family crest. It was addressed to Chase Bank. Not to, say, John Farnsworth, Chase Bank Vice President of Client Relations. It literally began with, "Dear Chase Bank." I started flipping through the pages, skipping past the financial statements to get to the good stuff. I pulled up a chair, knowing that this was going to be a while.

"Allow me to introduce myself," she had written. "I am Sofiya Kinezevich Lermontov Kyansky"—she had sixteen names, every one Russian—"Romanov. I am the seventh generation of His Majesty" et cetera, et cetera. The point was that she was heiress to the Tsar and his fortune. It was quite formal and I'm sure the honorifics were accurate. Though it was gibberish, it made some sort of sense. In other words, I was clearly looking at the work of a crazy person. Crazy, but learned.

I immediately went to make copies.

She had all these attachments that I tried to make sense of. There were some bad snapshots of herself that were poorly Xeroxed, so that you could barely make them out. In one she looked at the camera and then in another she was in profile, like mug shots. They were meant to prove her resemblance to the Russian dynasty. Then she had different photocopies of every passport she ever had, from childhood to the present day. I recognized the barrettes that she had been wearing that morning.

There were pictures of her pointing to barely visible marks on different parts of her body. It was hard to tell if they were bug bites, bruises, birthmarks, or absolutely nothing. *What is she pointing to?* I wondered. I referred back to the text.

"In 1984," she wrote, "when I became the bride of Osama bin Laden . . ." This was before 9/11, and he was hardly in the public consciousness. Mrs. Kinezevich claimed that she was going into the Vatican and there was some controversy. She was kidnapped by conspirators who were working with the Pope, who poisoned her with a scorpion. She was pointing to the marks where it had stung her.

After I finished with the copies, I put the papers back in the envelope. I got a key to her room and I brought her belongings upstairs. I made it a point to fold up her wrap nicely, and put it next to the envelope on her bed. "I'm sorry if there was confusion," I wrote on a notepad, "but your limo driver brought this back and I wanted to make sure it was with you." Then I left a message for her on her voicemail to let her know that her things were in her room, and that we had tried to find her. "I'm sure it was a misunderstanding," I said, sounding very apologetic.

Now I was curious. The next day I looked into her guest folio, checking to see if other hotel employees who dealt with her had had weird experiences. But there wasn't anything remotely strange written in there. Quite the contrary. They were all quite positive and glowing: "Six Continent Club Member" "VVVIP" It wasn't *that* much of a surprise. The basic mentality of hospitality is to never be suspicious. I don't know why I was always the one wondering if things weren't what they seemed. "Wife of Dr. Kinezevich," I read on, "esteemed practitioner of Beverly Hills." I rolled my eyes. I could almost hear her dictating to somebody to write that in her file. (Any mentions of bin Laden, the Pope, or Tsar Nicholas were curiously absent from her guest folio, probably on orders from the CIA, the Care Bears, or the Trilateral Commission.)

I couldn't feel completely comfortable until I touched base with her again. I wanted to be sure that she got back to her room and that she had received her papers. But the next day there was neither hide nor hair of Mrs. Sofiya Kinezevich. Instead, the limo company sent over the reconciliation with the charge for her daylong adventure. The bill came to over $1,500, and I didn't know what to do. I worried about losing hundreds of dollars for the commission, and I worried about having to haggle with the car company about settling the bill, and I worried about having to deal with Russian royalty, exiled or otherwise.

The next morning she called down to the concierge desk while I was working, and I was relieved when I saw her name on the caller ID. "Good morning, Mrs. Kinezevich. This is Michael, how may I be of service?"

"You *peasant,*" she snarled.

I was too confused to even respond. *Did she just call me a peasant?* "Excuse me?" I said, wondering if I had misheard her.

"I need you to send housekeeping up here *immediately.*"

There were always problems in the old hotel, like toilets backing up or pipes leaking. "Of course," I said. "Is there any problem?"

"I think you know," she said, scolding me and sounding very alarmed.

Now I had no doubt that she was taking me to task because of something shoddy with the plumbing, that I should have known what kind of hotel I was working in. "I'm so sorry," I told her. "Is there anything that I can do?"

"I just want you to know that I'm fully aware of your attempt to poison me last night. I took your recommendation to dine at Planet Hollywood. The bathroom is full of towels that have cleaned my vomit and bile up from the floor. I haven't decided how I'm going to handle this."

PLACES I WOULD ADVISE A GUEST TO DINE BEFORE ADVISING THEM TO "DINE" AT PLANET HOLLYWOOD

Sonic Drive-In—save room for the cheesecake bites

50% off Sushi—go on a Monday

Pluck U—they deliver!

Taco Bell—we all mourn the retired bacon cheeseburger burrito

No. 1 Chinese Restaurant (the one in Bensonhurst)—chicken with garlic sauce

Домашняя кухня—конечно!

The Bucknell Bison—get the grilled ham hero

"I'm aware of your connection to them," she concluded.

It was like I had called ahead and said, "I'm sending you Sofiya Kinezevich. You *must* poison her. Just give her bigger portions of your regular menu."

Now I was starting to get it. The guy with her wasn't her shy, awkward son. He must have been her dealer, and she was totally on drugs. *The lady is whacked,* I thought, as she hung up the phone. I immediately sent up housekeeping to take care of the towels that had cleaned her "vomit and bile."

Then I started to get scared. I had the limo bill to deal with. I hadn't followed up that much on her Russian swords and books. If she wanted to make trouble, it would have been very easy for her. These were things that really could escalate. I started to do my homework to try to mitigate any havoc that she might wreak.

The first thing I saw in the system was that she had about 190 room nights that year; half the calendar year she had spent at an InterContinental Hotel somewhere in the world. It wasn't like she was just some loony off the street. I wanted to know if anybody else had any crazy stories so that I could start to build my case.

I started calling other properties around the world where she had stayed. It was still morning, so there was plenty of time to call London.

"InterContinental Hotel, this is Cyril speaking. How can I help you?"

"Hi, Cyril. It's Michael Fazio from New York. Listen, I need you to do me a favor. Can you look up Sofiya Kinezevich's file in your local database and tell me if you found anything unusual in there?"

"Sure." I could hear the clacking of the keyboard as he entered her name into the computer. "Oh! She's a Six Continent Club member!"

"*I know.* But isn't there anything?"

"What are you looking for?"

"I don't know. She's quite an interesting person." *Did she walk through the lobby naked? Something like that?*

"No, I'm sorry. She stayed here, but I don't have any record of anything like that."

"Thanks anyway," I said, hanging up the phone. *Where else do I know the staff?* I wondered, scanning the list of cities she stayed in. *Bingo! Chicago. It must have really hit the fan in Chicago. Please please please let it have hit the fan in Chicago.*

"InterContinental Hotel, this is Stephen speaking. How can I help you?"

"Stephen, it's Michael. Can you look up Sofiya Kinezevich—K-i-n-e-z-e-v-i-c-h—and tell me what you have in her file on her?"

"Huh."

I held my breath. " 'Huh'? What do you mean? What, what is it?"

"Well, she's a Six Continent Club member."

"Yes, yes. I know that!"

"There is nothing here about her. I mean, I can tell you how long her stays were but you should be able to access that yourself."

"I can. Thank you very much." I hung up the phone and looked into the empty lobby. Nobody could corroborate anything that I was learning. Nobody could help me in any way. Hell, nobody even knew who she was other than in her files. It's not like the Russian embassy would be filling out an affidavit against her.

Then it hit me. I dialed 310-555-1212 to get her husband's number. I wondered if he knew what she was up to. Frankly, I was most concerned about the car service charge. Money drama would bring scowls from management, instead of muffled laughter if I told them about any alleged poisoning attempts.

I called up Dr. Kinezevich's office. "Hello," I said. "My name is Michael Fazio. I'm the concierge from the InterContinental Hotel and I've been dealing with Mrs. Kinezevich."

"Yeah," he said, very lackluster.

"I'm afraid I have a little bit of a problem."

"Yeah?" he repeated, wanting me to just get to the point.

"It seems that she was using the car service and she didn't come back. It amounted to a pretty significant bill."

"Is that it?"

"Well, uh, she mentioned that she wasn't exactly feeling well today."

"Oh God," he sighed. "Yeah, you know what? Just ignore her. I'll pay the bill."

I felt so relieved. "Do you think I should call a doctor?"

"No, no. No, it's fine." He hung up the phone.

That's when I felt a little bad for her. Her husband knew that she's a total loony, and didn't even want to be bothered. Maybe I wouldn't have been as sympathetic if she caused me headaches with my job, but the husband paid the bill and I never had to deal with her again.

She wasn't a bad woman but a crazy woman, and the man with her was probably a handler to make sure she kept out of trouble as she spiraled out of control all over the world. There was fun-crazy and then there was *crazy*-crazy, and she was definitely the latter.

Julian, on the other hand, was definitely the former. He was fun-crazy. A frequent guest at the hotel, Julian was "out there" in the best possible sense of the term. He always challenged me to see what I could come up with next. There was some hot club in Vegas that he wanted to be absolutely sure he could get into.

"Well, you could do the paparazzi trick," I told him.

"What's that?"

"I had a client who wanted to get into Marquee, so I hired a paparazzo to follow him. He cut through the line like it was nothing."

I could see the gears turning in Julian's mind. "I *love* that! I could use it to get in *everywhere* in Vegas. Can you arrange it?"

"Sure," I said. Paparazzi weren't always guaranteed a paycheck for their photos anyway. I was sure there would be plenty who would be amenable to a flat fee for easy work, taking pictures and not having to worry about trying to sell them.

"How many can I get?" Julian said. "Do I get them all night?"

The answers were: eight and yes. He got in at every single club and it went off without a hitch—and now he had a hilariously absurd anecdote to tell people. So when Julian came to the concierge desk one day and wanted to do something special for his wedding anniversary, I knew I had to get creative. His wife loved white roses, and dinner at a nice place was fine, but those things weren't going to cut it by themselves. It was a few weeks away, so I knew I could really go over the top if I planned it right.

"How did you meet?" I asked him. "Maybe we can revisit it and do something with that."

"It was actually on the train, of all places, from Washington, D.C., to New York. We were on the same car and struck up a conversation. Now that I remember it, it was two cars down from the dining car. Wow, I haven't thought about that in years! Anyway, we ended up talking the whole way. It was almost like a movie. But a train ride isn't very romantic."

"Well, we can *make* it romantic," I insisted. "You can take the train again, and I'll have musicians waiting for you."

"Where, in Penn Station?"

"No, like on the platform. She obviously would never expect that. Talk about a movie! It'd be this big huge gesture and make a spectacle like when the credits begin to roll and our hero and our heroine finally get together."

"I *love* it," he said. "Then we can go to dinner at someplace fancy."

"Oh, that's easy. I'll have the white roses waiting on the platform and the musicians can hand them to her. So what do you think?"

He smiled. Now I could see that the gears had stopped turning. "Just go for it. This is it, this is *totally* it."

"I'll take care of everything."

"Thanks." He passed me a tip and left. I watched the smile on his face grow larger and larger.

That afternoon, I went to Penn Station to get permission for the performers. There's a police precinct right there, adjacent to the escalators that go down to the tracks. *They probably control the whole thing,* I reasoned. *I'll go and ask them first.* I opened the door and three cops looked up at me. I didn't seem particularly aggrieved, so right away they seemed to be on guard—they could tell that I was probably some sort of nuisance and not a crime victim. "I've got a *crazy* request," I told them, in an icebreaker that I regretted immediately. "I'm a concierge at the InterContinental Hotel, and one of my clients would like a string quartet to meet him when he gets off the train."

I totally fell flat. The energy in the room turned to total poison. "What are you talking about?" one of the officers finally said.

"It would be really romantic. He's recreating the route where he met his wife. Do you think there's some way?"

The cop rolled his eyes, not interested in parsing what I was telling him. "Go talk to the guy at the head of the escalator."

"Which guy?"

"The Amtrak guy who's in charge of tickets. You'll see him," the officer said, wanting me to be out of there as quickly as possible.

I took the hint. I found the guy the cop was talking about. He had on his Amtrak hat and was watching over the entrance to the platform. I meandered up to him as he watched me approach out of the corner of his eye. "Hey there," I said.

"Can I help you?" he replied immediately, in a tone that didn't sound like someone who actually *did* want to help me.

"Okay. I bet you've never heard this before." I explained the whole scenario to him, while he stared at me with no change in affect whatsoever. "This would be so great. Isn't it such a *crazy* idea?"

"I'll give you that," he said, chuckling to himself.

One of the tricks that often works in cases like this is to act nice and beg for mercy. It definitely helps to present yourself as a peer, who is in danger of getting in trouble at work. "If I can't say yes to this person, it's going to make my life miserable. You know how that is."

"I guess."

"Come on. It's good PR for Amtrak."

He shrugged and looked away. "Maybe so."

It was that awkward moment where I should have walked away and bought tickets for the musicians to get them access to the platform. But even if I did that, I wasn't assured that they would be able to bring their instruments—let alone play them by the trains. "Look at how cool this would be," I insisted. "This is bringing the romance back into train travel!"

He looked me right in the face, and now he started to crack a little bit. Clearly bringing the romance into train travel was not one of his priorities, and we both knew it. He started to laugh at me, but in a friendly way. "You're nuts."

I knew that I was winning him over. "When do you work? What's your schedule? This would be on a Thursday at six P.M."

"I don't work at that time," he told me.

"Do you know who does?"

He gave it the least possible amount of thought. "Nope."

"Can I give you a call and maybe you can find out for me?"

"I'll try to find out," he said.

"Can you give me your number?"

"Just come back and I'll see what I can do," he said. He wouldn't give me his phone number but I knew I had made the slightest bit of an ally.

"Okay," I said, "I'll find you another time." I didn't really feel like he was good for it—and he wasn't.

I went back three or four times, chatting him up and checking to see if he had done any research for me. "How's it going?" I asked him. "Did you have any luck? I'm sorry, I know I'm bothering you."

I thought that I should call human resources and simply just go over his head. But at that point I was too afraid that if I did that and went outside of his circle, I would be screwed. All he would have to say is, "There's some crazy person that wants to get on the platform," and it would be all over for me. He *had* to be my guy.

Instead it was me asking, "Do you want a coffee? How are you doing today? *Do you like candy?*"

Eventually, I was in the right place at the right time. "That's Elipto," he told me. "Go talk to him. He's got that shift."

I went up to Elipto and introduced myself.

"So *you're* the guy that keeps coming here," he said, laughing.

I gave Elipto my whole spiel. I didn't take credit for the plan; it was the "wacky client" who wanted to do this. It was amusing for him that there was a person out there who was willing to enlist this much effort to pull something off. Now it was like we were on the same team. I could tell that he felt invested in seeing this through.

"I don't really know what to tell you," he finally said.

"I just want to make sure that there aren't any issues."

It wasn't like he could give me some certificate in writing. "Just tell them to come and see me. It'll be fine."

"Thank you *so much!*"

Now all I had to do was find a string quartet that would be willing to do this.

HIRING PERFORMERS FOR CHEAP

There are obviously far more "artists" of every kind than there are paying jobs for them. The supply far outweighs the demand—which makes it a buyer's market of sorts. The problem is that many self-described "artists" are not very good, and many of the good ones charge a premium as coaches, consultants, and the like. Just as with any other service, the ideal scenario is to the get the best possible person at the lowest possible price.

continued

I once had a client that needed violin lessons. I reasoned that recent music graduates had no money, and they would be *overquali-fied* to teach someone how to play the violin—especially at the beginner level. They might not have had the roster or the résumé, but they definitely had the ability and passion. Not only that, but they'd be willing to work cheaper than someone who was an established tutor. Instead of sitting around looking for temp jobs, they could work in their own field, earn some cash, and spread their knowledge. It was win-win-win.

I had called the Juilliard alumni association in the past, and they happened to have a list of recent grads available for work. That's how I met Vicki. Vicki was a cellist who mostly did chamber music, moonlighting in little orchestras. I had a vision of these beautiful angelic women with long wavy hair and chiffon evening gowns, playing "My Funny Valentine" as the train pulled into the station. Vicki herself was attractive in a very classical music sort of way, with her black hair slicked back in a tight ponytail. She looked *sophisticated*.

"So can you help me out?" I asked her.

"Well, I don't really know a string quartet per se. But I can put one together myself. That won't be too hard. Where should we be standing?"

It was two cars down from the dining car. But I had no idea where on the platform that was, and if I estimated incorrectly then the effect would be lost. It would seem like the band was playing there at random, instead of putting on a show specifically for Julian and his wife.

I didn't want to go back to Elipto at Penn Station and figure out where it was. It would be like when a salesman keeps pushing after you've agreed to buy something, and ends up talking you out of the sale. Elipto and everyone else must have been joking about me and my attempts to bring romance back to train travel, and I was walking a tightrope between endearing and irritating.

I looked through the phone book and I called the number for Amtrak, working my way through the phone directory until I got to someone who oversaw Penn Station. I didn't want to risk having to explain the whole story for the twentieth time, so I just lied. "I'm meeting my cousin coming from Washington, D.C.," I said. "He's handicapped and I want to make sure I am precisely on the platform where he will be getting off. He's going to be two cars down from the dining car. Can you tell me how far back that would be?"

"Uh . . . I'm not sure."

"Well, can you tell me how long each train car?"

A very, very, very long pause. "I don't know."

"Is there someone else there who can help me?" I said.

"I'm not certain who would have that information," he said.

You know what? I figured. *I'm just going to go back. I've come this far.* I went back to Penn Station and dropped Elipto's name to get myself down to the platform. There was a train docked there already so I could see exactly where the people would be getting off. I found the nearest landmark—a garbage can with a big sticker on it—and counted the paces until I reached the door of the train. With flashbacks to Rosie Perez, I knew I couldn't leave anything to chance when it came to the directions.

The day of the event, I faxed Vicki an itinerary. I told her to ask for Elipto, and to mention his name if he wasn't there himself. I told her how many paces down from the garbage can, and which garbage can, and which track, and what Julian looked like. It was an entire flowchart to anticipate every possible problem.

Every possible problem except for my having forgotten about the white roses.

Oh, crap. There was a place right by Penn Station that dealt with roses and *only* with roses. I called them in a mad panic.

"We're already closing for the day," the guy told me. "Sorry."

"No, no, no, no, no!" I said. "You *have* to. You have to, you have to, you have to! This is a very big deal."

"I'm locking up."

"I'll send money right now. *Right now.* In a taxi. Please!"

"Fine. But if he's not here in fifteen minutes, we're leaving."

"He'll be there." I hung up the phone and went out into the street to hail a cab. I gave the driver a twenty-dollar tip, took down his medallion number just in case, and sent him down to the flower shop with an envelope full of cash.

The flowers made it to the platform. Vicki and her string quartet made it to the platform. Everything went off without a hitch, and it became a big deal. Julian was delighted, and his wife had the biggest surprise of her life. It even got some press attention—I really did bring the romance back to train travel.

Now part of me began to feel like I was some sort of concierge cupid. Instead of saving these great ideas for the guests who really appreciated it, like Julian, I started being more proactive in my advice. I obviously had never refused to offer service in the past, but now I brought up what I felt were better alternatives. Almost every single time, people took my suggestions—and they came out seeming wonderful in the process.

It wasn't that hard to make the hotel guests seem impressive, because most of them were so generic to begin with. Very quickly, the businessmen that stayed at the hotel all began to look the same to me. They were all so *polished* in how they acted and how they thought and how they dressed. Their hair was always smoothed back, like airline pilots. They wore Brioni shirts—with monogrammed cuffs—under Canali suits. The hive mentality even went a step further with some of them.

As a service to our guests—and a commission for us—we had tailors come to the hotel and set up shop for three or four days. The businessmen would go in and get measured and the tailor would make custom suits for them at a cost of upward of $3,000. Custom suits—that all looked the same. We even had a shoemaker. He would make custom shoes made to fit, for exorbitant prices. The plain, shiny oxfords would really stand out in a crowd, in the same way that Where's Waldo stands out in a crowd.

Their thought processes were often the same as well. Though it's the most obvious choice that anyone could possibly think of, each and every one of them believed that they invented the idea of strewing rose petals about the room to create an air of romance. I used to keep rose petals on hand just for that very purpose. It got to the point where, after an event, I'd go scour the flower arrangements. I'd even pull roses out of the garbage and just take the petals off. The chances were very high that, at some point, a guest was going to ask me—a complete stranger, mind you—to throw rose petals in a path from their hotel room door to their lover's bed. I had a couple of days before the petals smelled not so fresh. I'd go in the back room and find a cold corner to keep them chilled. If I got *really* desperate, I could pull out the moldy ones and use the rest. There would be no magic if I revealed that I kept a garbage bag full of second-hand petals, so I would charge twenty-five dollars to the guest as if they had come from a florist, and everyone was happy. It was like recycling!

One night I was approached by one of the generic InterContinental hotel guests. "I want to do something that's really special and really romantic," he said.

"Of course," I said, mirroring his energy.

"First I want to go to a great dinner with my wife, but I want a surprise when I come back."

"Do you have anything particular in mind?" I asked, bracing myself.

"I was thinking maybe if you just put, like, rose petals on the floor. Can you do that?"

He was a nice enough guy and he caught me in the right way, so I felt comfortable being honest with him. "Well, you know that's *okay*. People do that."

"Oh, really?" he said, deflated at the realization that he wasn't first to patent it.

Now the mercenary side of me kicked in, and I started seeing dollar signs. I started brainstorming with him like I did with Julian. "You know what could be really fun? Why don't you just fill the whole bed with flowers? Like the whole thing. Just buy two hundred roses—not the petals, the entire flowers—and cover the bed in them."

"Wow, that's pretty interesting," he nodded. "That's a good idea. What else?"

"What else?"

"Yeah, what else should I do?"

The thing with a brainstorming session is that you throw out many, many ludicrous ideas in the hopes of stumbling upon one or two fairly good ones. At least, that's how it's supposed to function. I started thinking of all the varied Valentine's Day clichés. "Well, does she like chocolate?"

"Absolutely."

"What about if you let me know before you come back from your dinner? I can fill the tub with chocolate and the two of you can take a chocolate bath." I don't know where the hell I came up with that one. Even as I said it, it sounded absurd.

He stood there quietly for a second, speechless. "You're *brilliant*. That's it! That's what we're going do. I love that. I absolutely love that. So it's tomorrow night that I want go to dinner at eight. Will you be working then?"

"Yes," I said. "I'll be here until midnight or so."

"Here's the plan. I'll call you when we're forty-five minutes away, to let you know that we're coming. And it's got to be Godiva. That's my wife's favorite."

"No problem," I told him. "I'll take care of everything for to-morrow."

"Thank you very much," he said, handing me a a hundred-dollar tip.

This can't be so difficult, I thought. Godiva had these little hot choc-olate kits. I could buy twenty of them and it would only cost around a hundred dollars. *I wonder if that'll be enough. How many gallons should I buy?* There was no point in me trying to figure it out on my own. I'd never had an aquarium, so water volume was lost on me. I picked up the phone and called Kraft Hardware.

"Hello," I said. "Can you tell me what the capacity of a standard-sized bathtub is, in volume?"

"Sure," the hardware guy said. "You're looking at just over eighty gallons of water before it reaches the overflow."

"Eighty gallons? Okay, thank you very much." I hung up the phone. Eighty gallons was a lot of chocolate. The Godiva came in eight-ounce packets. I'd need boxes and boxes and boxes of the stuff; if I got twenty, it would have just looked like frosting. We were already talking thousands of dollars.

When the guest came through the lobby not too long after, I called him over. "Is everything okay?" he wanted to know.

"There's an issue. The Godiva would be exorbitant."

"How exorbitant?"

"Thousands of dollars," I told him.

He didn't blink. "Well, what's the alternative?"

"We're going to need gallons of chocolate. I was going to start calling restaurant suppliers," I told him. The service bug had bitten me, and I was going to make this happen for him no matter what.

"Well, whatever works. That's fine with me." He handed me another hundred-dollar bill.

Now I realized that it couldn't even be chocolate at all—chocolate would harden. I needed to get chocolate *fudge.* There was nothing for me to do that night, since everything was closed. But the first thing I did when I came in the next day was to call around until I found a restaurant supply company.

"Yeah, we have Hershey's fudge," they told me. "It comes in big plastic jugs, and there are six jugs per box."

"I'm going to need about eighty gallons' worth."

"Eighty gallons? Well, each jug is a gallon so you're going to need at least a dozen boxes in total."

"Perfect!" I gave him the shipping information and took care of payment.

Later that evening, they delivered all the boxes to the hotel. *Oh my God,* I thought to myself. *This is actually happening now. I'm really going to be filling up a bathtub with fudge.* As the delivery guys unloaded box after box, I realized that it wasn't like somebody was delivering flowers. I couldn't just put all the chocolate in some corner and not draw attention to it.

I ran to the security office in the bowels of the hotel. "I've got a ton of chocolate because some guest wants to fill his bathtub with the stuff. I need you to cover for me while I get it upstairs."

"I'll help you," one of the guys said.

"Terrific." We went back to the lobby. I started opening up the boxes and pulling out all the jugs. I called to make sure the guest's room was empty, and then we started to bring the chocolate up-stairs. Thankfully the staff ignored what I was doing. They figured I was up to something marvelous—not, say, turning a human being into a living sundae.

Finally, I got it all up there and stood for a second looking at this room full of bottles of fudge. *Well, it's too late now!* I thought. *It's got to happen.* I went back downstairs and waited for my signal.

As planned, the guest eventually called me from the restaurant. "We're going to be there in about an hour. Will everything be ready?"

"Absolutely!" I told him.

"Thanks again. You're the best."

I went back upstairs. *Oh, crap,* I thought. *What a goddamn hassle this is going to be.* I stood there opening bottle after bottle and—*glug, glug, glug*—pouring it in. Forty-five minutes later, I was finished. It turned out that I didn't buy nearly enough; it must have settled, or maybe the tub was bigger than standard sized. But it *did* make a big impact. It was a *lot* of fudge—and it was a *big* mess.

I was a little disappointed because my fantasy was that it was going to be grander than it was. *This isn't that great,* I realized. *It's actually pretty gross. And it's not hot, either. It's tepid. I should have done a bubble bath and been done with it.*

Now I had dozens of empty, unwieldy jugs to dispose of. I got some commercial-sized garbage bags and schlepped the bottles out of the room. I took them through the back hallways where the housekeepers were so that no one would ask any questions. I didn't want to leave them in the hotel at all, so I just went out the back and took them out to the street on my way home.

I knew that I had to follow up the next morning. I wasn't working, so I called the guy in his room. "So?" I said. "How did it go?"

"Brilliant, fantastic," he told me, tickled out of his mind. "Thank you so much. You're absolutely great. I left a tip for you at the desk."

"I'm glad I could help."

"I've just got one question."

"Yes?"

"What am I supposed to do with all the chocolate?" he asked me.

"Don't worry about it. I'll take care of it."

"Okay, perfect."

We weren't really supposed to be at the hotel when we weren't working, but I couldn't have him call up housekeeping and explain that the concierge desk had filled his bathtub with gallons of chocolate fudge. I snuck into the room, and there I saw the tub again. It was just this smooth placid pool of velvety, dark liquid. In fact, it looked pretty much like I had left it.

Then I remembered that still waters run deep. And deep under these still waters was the drain, and I had to put my hand in through the muck and who-knows-what-else to pull the stopper. *Did they even step foot into it?* I wondered. *Did they fool around in the chocolate?* Out of the corner of my eye I saw a towel bunched up on the floor. If I didn't know that the stain was fudge, I would have been very much disturbed. As it was, I was indifferent. I just wanted to get it cleaned up and get the hell out of there.

I rolled up my sleeve and dove my hand into the fudge, feeling around for the drain. I pulled out the stopper and waited for the chocolate to pour down the pipes. I could see it start to drain—*barely*. There was a vague ripple on the surface. I waited, and I waited, and I waited.

It was very, very slow going. Now I started to get a little scared. It was possible that it would clog a pipe or something. Maybe it would take forever to drain and I'd get busted. I knew I needed some help, but I wasn't sure who to call. It wasn't like I could've dialed up Willy Wonka and asked for his advice on what to do.

Rupert, I thought. *Rupert will help me.* Rupert was the engineer in the hotel, which effectively meant that he was like the handyman for the entire building. He was an old guy I got along very well with. He also—like everyone else—loved to be in on anything scandalous. I tracked him down in the smoking lounge. There was only one thing for me to do: fess up and ask for his mercy. "Rupert," I told him. "I think I did something wrong."

"What? What did you do?"

"Can you come upstairs?" I whispered. "I need to show you something."

Now he knew something good was happening. I took him up to the room and showed him the pool. From the sides of the tub I could tell that it had barely drained at all while I had gone to get Rupert.

"What *is* this?" he said.

"A couple wanted to do something romantic, and I decided it would be a good idea to fill the bathtub with chocolate."

Rupert got a twinkle in his eye. Even though he was an old man, he still liked being witness to a room where naughtiness probably happened. "So now what?" he said.

"Now it's not draining."

"Did you open it?"

"Yes," I said.

Just to make sure, he stuck his hand in and felt around. I couldn't blame him, as I would have done the same. He thought for a second about what to do. "I'll get a plunger and some Drano," he shrugged.

It was an obvious solution, but I'd tried to think of something else and had come up short myself. "Thanks," I said, passing him a fifty. "And let's just keep this between us."

Later, I watched as he ran the water forever, and plunged the mess, and poured in the Drano—over and over and over. At the end of the day, I kind of thought, *Well, that was stupid*. I worked hard for that moment, and it totally wasn't worth it. Why did I have to do that? Flowers would have been fine.

And from then on out, I decided that flowers *were* fine.

Whenever one of the generic businessmen came up with that look on their face, I was standing there like a loaded gun. "Hi," they said. "I wanna do something romant—"

"Flowers," I interrupted.

"Really?"

"Oh yeah. Flowers. Works every time. They're fantastic and the women love it. We'll get tulip petals shipped from the Netherlands. We'll fly them in overnight." *Or pull them out of the trash in the Biltmore Room. There's a wedding there this afternoon.*

8.
Loose Lips

The concierge desk always had a dubious relationship to the rest of the hotel, and room service was no exception. If a guest called down and asked for, say, a bottle of scotch, technically the concierge should call room service and have them send it up. But what kind of service is that? The guest could have called them himself (and dropped ninety dollars for a bottle).

But why pay *outrageous* hotel minibar prices? What I would often do was give the bellman a ten-dollar tip and send him over to the liquor store to buy a nice bottle of scotch for thirty dollars—and since the liquor store guy knew the drill, "nice" meant different things for different kinds of guests. Then I'd add thirty dollars for myself and charge the room seventy. The guest saved twenty dollars, I got thirty dollars, and the bellman made ten. As long as the guest was happy, then the hotel was happy. No one bothered anyone.

Now I had to get reimbursed. We had a booklet of forms, like withdrawal slips, called "paid-outs." On each paid-out we wrote the date, the room number, the guest's name, and a description of the transaction. We were smart enough to know that if we wrote "bottle of scotch" in the description, it would be like rubbing the hotel's face in our business. The solution was to be vague. "Miscellaneous sundries" was never questioned or challenged—even though it describes nothing whatsoever. It could have been seventy dollars' worth of condoms for all they knew. The beauty of being a concierge was that nobody would ever ask us to give deeper details; that would be breaching the guest's confidence.

The only important thing was that the guest not contest anything. If I were a room service waiter and didn't get the guest to sign their check, then I'd be in trouble. But the concierge is slightly above the law. We rarely bothered to get signatures or give explanations; it was like "don't ask, don't tell." If the guest ever complained that we charged him seventy dollars for a thirty-dollar bottle of scotch, we'd just apologize and refund the difference.

It was very known that the concierge really was a confidant to the guests. One day I was approached at the desk by a Latin man. He was about forty-five years old, dark, and *really* handsome. "My friend," he said, pulling me over to the side, "I think I have a little bit of a problem."

Oh my God, I thought. *He can't get it up!* The foreign guests were notorious for asking the concierge to get them Viagra without a prescription.

WHO ASKS FOR WHAT

Los Angelinos: They love underground and edgy, thinking that something is "undiscovered." It probably comes from living in an environment that's so clean and "safe" behind tinted windows or inside gated homes.

Western Europeans: They love production values. Think big rooms, clean and shiny, and women dripping in diamonds. If they ask where the shopping district is, they're seeking the fantasy of a

continued

---

woman in a Chanel suit and gloves walking a white standard poodle on Fifth Avenue. She's going from Bendel's to Bergdorf's while negotiating a big business deal on her cell phone.

Scandinavians: They want Weber barbecues and lawn mowers. I'm not kidding and I still don't know why, but I made damn sure to point them to Home Depot.

American Tourists: P. T. Barnum, eat your heart out. They want the "World's Biggest," "New York's Finest," or "The World's Best" Anything. What they didn't know couldn't hurt them, so I occasionally steered them to "New York's Best T.G.I. Friday's." With the chain's world-class standards, every one of their dining establishments is the "best."

Gay Men: Even when talking to a gay concierge, my people are always too shy to ask for the gay area—and resort to euphemisms like "the fashion district." No one is judging you for wanting to go on a cruise (try 8th Avenue, the Townhouse, or the Gramercy Park Hotel roof).

He never really came out and said what the issue was, though I could totally feel his shame. "I . . . um . . . I was in Bangkok and I was with a woman. And my wife is coming tomorrow for the weekend."

I wanted to drop my professionalism and interrogate the man. "You certainly went to town, didn't you? Could you have been any more *stupid*? It's not like you met a girl in a bar, and then today you've got dickburn. You were in Bangkok. What were you *thinking*? Of *course* you got sick, moron!" But I keep it formal and instead started asking questions as if I were a doctor. "Do you have a sore? Do you have discharge? Does your penis itch?" *Do you want to show it to me?*

"So can you help me?" he asked.

"There's a house doctor," I told him. "I can get them to come and take a look at it, and see what's wrong."

"No, no, no! I just need to get medication. I can't have a doctor come see me. Absolutely not." He acted as if a doctor would have to register his illness with the government. "There must be *something* that can be done."

"No problem, sir. I don't know what can be done, exactly. Let me think about this. I want to help you. Just relax. We'll figure something out."

He tipped me like crazy, and then he gave me his room number. "Please, do not leave me a voicemail," he whispered. "This is confidential."

"Oh, yeah. Absolutely." I waited until he was out of earshot. "Hey, Abbie! Do you see that really cute guy?"

"Yeah, what about him?" she said.

"He's got VD!"

He came back to the concierge desk three times within the next twenty minutes, checking to see if I had made any progress. He was sure that we were going to call the embassy and get his passport stamped, as if he was the first Latin guy to get a venereal disease. It would have been easy for me to shrug my shoulders and send him on his way. But I could tell that he was a good guy who had done something naughty, and he was owning it—and terrified. "Let me see what I can do," I told him.

I had a connection at a pharmacy nearby. Dashiell would always help me out when I needed something discreet. I called the pharmacy and relayed to him the whole story.

"He needs spectinomycin," Dash told me. "But that won't work overnight."

"Well, isn't there *something*? Can he take an overdose of however much you normally would take in the pill form?"

"He needs an injection," Dash said. "If you want it to zap, you can't take pills. You have to get a megadose. I can give you the drugs, that's fine. I can do you this favor, but he really needs a shot if that's what you want."

"Okay," I said.

Now I needed the doctor to inject him without there being any sort of paper trail. This was a bit trickier, but I thought of a way.

I called the house doctor and told him what was up. "I got the guest five hundred milligrams of spectinomycin and I'm going to give it to him. But he doesn't want to see a doctor. Can we do this with no trace?"

"Sure," the doctor said. "I can see him off premises. You don't even have to tell me his name."

Minutes later, the guest circled back to my desk. I told him what the situation was. "A shot is the only answer if you want it taken care of before your wife arrives."

He looked down at his pants. "It's going to hurt, but if that's my only choice, then that's my only choice."

I snickered at his naïveté. "You don't get an injection *there*. It's in your *arm*."

"Oh! Thank you. Thank you, thank you, thank you!" He handed me a couple more hundred-dollar bills. It was so much money that I genuinely didn't want to take it.

"It's okay," I said. "Don't worry about it."

"No, you take this."

I sent him to the pharmacist to get the medicine and I arranged the meeting with the doctor. He wouldn't get the shot in the hotel and he couldn't be seen going into a doctor's office. He was so guilt-ridden that on some level he honestly felt "they" were watching him, and karma was going to come around and expose him—as if the burning in his groin wasn't karma enough.

The doctor's bill was a few hundred dollars, so I started doing algebra with the paid-outs until the combination of charges to his room bill added up to the exact amount I'd spent. An imaginary breakfast delivery: thirty-five dollars. Nonexistent flowers sent to the room: seventy dollars. Making sure your wife doesn't find out that you got gonorrhea from a Thai hooker: maybe not *priceless,* but damn near close to it.

The doctor called me after it was all done, so that I'd be sure everything was taken care of. "It's fine," he told me. "And he's a really nice guy. He was petrified, but he's going to be all right."

"Thank you," I said. "Thanks for doing that, really. I felt so bad for him because his wife was coming tomorrow."

Then there was a pause, and it was the kind of pause that never leads to good news. "Oh. Well, you didn't tell me that."

"Sorry," I said, a little bit confused.

"You're still a carrier for up to seven days after the injection. It clears up the symptoms, but you're still carrying the virus."

". . . *Oh.*" I got off the phone with the doctor, and now I had no idea what to do. Should I tell him and risk him getting upset with me, as if I should have known and told him earlier? Even barring that, somebody else was at stake here, too. My hands weren't clean in this whole mess. I could have walked away from the situation at the very start—and I hadn't.

I agonized over what to do until the next time he passed the desk. I decided that the moral thing to do in this immoral situation was, at the very least, to inform him. It was his karma what he did with the information; it's not like the disease was somehow life threatening anyway. When I told him what the doctor had told me, he was absolutely horrified. I could see the blood drain from his face. The really sad thing is that, in my gut, I knew that he wasn't going to tell her.

The guilt bothered me for a very long time. But on some level, a large part of my job is to help stupid and/or awful people with too much money continue to be stupid and/or awful. As bad as he was, at least he had a conscience about the whole thing. That, in and of itself, put him ahead of many of my other clients.

To be fair, using the paid-outs to cover an STD treatment was an isolated case. What we mostly used them for was the constant demands for theater tickets that all concierges live and die by. At the end of my shift, I would take all my paid-outs to the hotel cashier. They'd go through them and make sure that the rooms matched the names. Five hundred dollars was the absolute bare minimum amount that I would be cashing in. But four tickets to see *La bohème* at $400 a pop meant $1,600 for just one transaction—and the hotel *never* had big bills to reimburse me. It was crazy. On a typical night, I got $4,000 to $5,000 in twenties. I had to go to the back where, down to the Plexiglas, it was like a safety deposit box area, and separate out this wad of money for me, for Abbie, and for the house. Every night I'd be there for about an hour, divvying up the profits. It was like playing a poker game—and always winning. Sometimes it would get really bad and the cashier would only have fives and singles. There were times when I literally had hundreds of one-dollar bills. Hey, I didn't care. It all spent the same, and it made for a little fun at the grocery store. If anyone commented on my giant wad of one-dollar bills, I'd tell them I was a dancer.

The usual way we got theater tickets was to make a run to the box office. But we often received requests for really crazy, hard-to-get things like the Met Opera Gala or opening night at some hot show. Sometimes we'd have to just bite the bullet and deal with a broker. They'd then send somebody from their company to pick up payment—which was always cash and almost never in large bills.

The runners would sort of whisper where they were from so as not to attract attention. I would always have cash ready to give them in these big, overstuffed and worn-out envelopes covered with rubber bands. The fancy hotel guests with their fur coats and custom suits got to watch this not-so-refined guy in a trench coat and sunglasses count out the stacks of money that he pulled from my beat-up, rubber band–laden envelopes.

Yes, it often got a bit awkward.

One of the brokers had a runner named Alphonse, who was very, very old. He was into the semi-illicit nature of his job, and had a twinkle in his eye whenever he told me he was there to "pick up the money." He always made a show of looking around before tucking the money into his jacket.

One day, a police detective came up to the desk about an hour after Alphonse left. "Do you do business with Starbright brokers?" he asked me.

"Yeah . . ."

"And do you know Alphonse?"

"Yeah . . ." My heart started pounding. If it was bad for a *guest* to complain, a police complaint would be infinitely worse.

"Did you hand him money?"

"Yes," I said. "Is there a problem?"

"We're investigating something," he told me.

Oh my God, I thought. *The jig is up! There's counterfeit money in there.* If you deal with thousands of dollars in cash every day, it was probably only a matter of time. "Is everything all right?"

"I need your contact info. If we need to question you, do we have to go through your boss?"

I gave him my information. "No, I'll be glad to assist in any way."

"Alphonse got mugged."

Hearing that made me so *sad*. He had such bravado. "Is he okay?"

"They tackled him and knocked him to the ground. But he's fine."

The next day the detective came back and went to the manager's office. The next thing I knew, they brought the bellman into the manager's office. I was relieved. *He must have seen Alphonse leave and witnessed the whole thing.* The bellman had worked at the hotel for fifteen years, and had emigrated from the Caribbean to make a better life for his family. A little while later, he and the detective left together—no doubt to identify the assailant.

Except, it turned out, that he was the assailant himself. I hadn't even put two and two together. They had identified him from the surveillance tape at the Fitzpatrick Hotel, three or four blocks away. In hindsight it was obvious. There was no Plexiglas screen. There was no lock on my desk. I would open my drawer and there would be $10,000 sitting there. I'd go to the bathroom and leave my station completely unlocked. Who would ever think that there was a drawer full of cash? Clearly, over time, the bellman saw the pattern. He wasn't working that day, and he knew how much cash was floating around. He was probably just waiting for anybody to come to the desk to pick up money. He couldn't do something at the hotel itself, because we had cameras over the desk. But that didn't help Alphonse.

Despite the incident, I still always used cash to buy theater tickets—which induced some paranoia. (During the winter I was constantly convinced that bills were dropping through my cold-numbed fingers.) Every day, I would write down what tickets we needed for the next couple of days, and I would try and fish for them. The ticket brokers hung out at McHale's, and often they'd off-load inventory because they were getting scared that they had too many. As showtime approached, they'd start to get desperate. Those tickets were like bombs in their pocket.

SCALPERS

There's a myth that the people that stand in front of theaters offering tickets to passersby are scammers. They almost never are. Illegitimate tickets are quite rare. For some reason, they're more common at sporting events. But if they're selling tickets for a show, it's usually legit. What happens is that the brokers, who have a license to resell (though not on the street) might have one hundred seats to *Billy Elliot* that nobody bought. Even though they're not allowed to sell on the street, they still hire barkers to move as much inventory as possible.

One whirlwind day, I ran out of cash and had to use my credit card with the broker. The *Phantom* seats cost me $75, and the guests were willing to pay $200—each. But what I didn't realize was that when you buy a ticket with a credit card, they print your name on them. Abbie and I stood there staring at the tickets, wondering what we should do.

In our paranoid wisdom, we decided we were going to strike through my name with black marker. Somehow we thought they wouldn't notice a thick black line on the face of the ticket. Since the printing was glossy, we had to take the marker and dab it over and over until it took. It was so glaring that it had practically the same effect as using highlighter.

Tickets were pretty much the only time we had guests sign the paid-outs. We usually gave a little speech about how the face value was, say, seventy-five dollars, but it was hard to find seats so we used other sources. Most affluent people could not care less and were bored by what we were telling them. But then there were some people who really did listen to the whole spiel. *Them,* we got to sign off.

When the people came to get their *Phantom* tickets that night, I was so worried that I oversold the whole exchange. It practically became a show in and of itself, on the house. "Wow! Row *D*! You're going to have *such* a great time! That's just *wonderful*! Have a *wonderful* night!"

Not even an hour later, the phone rang at the desk. "Yeah, this is John from the Majestic Theatre box office. Is Michael Fazio there?"

I heard him talking to somebody and the sounds of a crowd in the background. "I'm Michael Fazio."

"I have people who I assume are guests of yours. Where did you get these tickets?"

"I gave my credit card to someone who bought them for me."

"Okay," he said. "I just wanted to make sure these were good."

I was horrified. I wanted to crawl under the desk and disappear under a trapdoor. I knew there would be drama when the guests returned. Sure enough, they came waltzing back from the theater—and they weren't happy.

One of the guests put the ticket stubs on my desk. "Can you explain this to me?" he said.

"I don't understand."

"Why did you put a line through your name?"

I tried to play dumb. "Huh? Oh, that? Yeah, sometimes we have to order on a credit card. I guess they printed my name on the card."

"Well, John at the box office said that a lot of times concierges will come the day of the show and they know that there is probably some last-minute availability. I want to know how you want to settle this, because you paid eighty dollars for these and you overcharged me. I would tip you, but you know this is not how it's done."

Technically, that *was* how it was done. "I absolutely did *not* get these tickets today. We work with brokers, and it's a gray market. We don't really know how they get the tickets, but they do."

"Well, you know what? Whoever you need to sort this out with, please do. Let me know what you intend to do. I'll speak with you tomorrow."

I called Abbie and we figured out a plan to put out the fire. The next day, I called the guest in his room. "I spoke to the broker who we got these from," I said. "Apparently there was a glitch. I apologize, and want to make you feel good about this." The paid-out was already on his room bill, so I went upstairs and counted out the money to him face-to-face. In a very classy move, he slid a hundred dollars back to me as a tip.

Going forward, I actually did sometimes get desperate again and have to use my credit card. But I never tried to blur out my name, and I made sure to have a speech prepared if the guests noticed anyway. "I don't know how brokers work exactly, but sometimes I think they have to just take my name. I'm not sure, since it's a gray market. But were your seats good?"

THE OVERCHARGE

No one thinks that tipping a waiter is really optional, even though that is what it looks like at face value. Things get trickier when you're dealing with other service professionals. People often believe there is a big distinction between paying for service and paying for a product. Somehow, because you're not physically making something, it's not valid to seek a profit. And if you're occasionally willing to do your job without getting a tip—as concierges are—to some, there's no *real* need to tip at all.

That's what the overcharge compensates for. When the Citigroup meeting planner wanted to find something that cost $500, there's nothing wrong with me doing all the work for him and saying that I found it for $300 and charged him $400 (at a profit of $100 to myself). If he wanted to go find it for $300, let him go spin his

continued

---

wheels. But in the end he saved $100, and no one got hurt. It's not like this was a group of old ladies on a volunteer vacation to help inner city kids. For the Citigroup-type people, the thing that they wanted meant much more to them than a few hundred bucks—and a few hundred bucks meant much more to me than a ticket.

Part of it is also a sort of Robin Hood syndrome. If someone is brazen enough to say that they need front row center, tonight—and the seats "had better be good," then they'd better be prepared to step up with the cash. (As if the show was going to be horrible and insufferable from the second row, right?) Nickel-and-diming many of these affluent guests was almost insulting to them. They told you what they wanted; why were you *haggling*?

But if people were looking for "decent" seats, it would always soften my approach. There were plenty of guests that used to come up and ask where the discount ticket booth was. I'd offer them the coupons and let them know that you could still see perfectly fine if you sat in the second mezzanine. I played to the crowd. All they had to do was ask me where the subway station was, and I knew what they needed. But if they came up and demanded "Service!", then I put on a different show. I checked out their coat and checked out their watch. Then I set the price and charged them for service; there isn't a concierge alive that doesn't do that. If you have the nerve to snap your fingers, there's a responsibility that goes with it.

9.
The Keymaster

The unions are very powerful in the hotel industry. It's a closed shop, so certain positions have to be staffed with union employees only. The union then dictates their shift and other parameters of their job. The bellmen's union is a good example of this. The hotel is only encouraged to hire so many bellmen, according to a formula based on the number of rooms. The union doesn't like the hotel to "overstaff," because it impedes on the bellmen's revenue. What actually happens is that the bellmen are chronically *under*staffed. I don't know if that's the goal or if it's just them being uninformed. What I do know is that we had four bellmen to cover over six hundred rooms—and there was never anybody standing at the bellman counter. The door right behind the counter would be locked, with all the luggage in there. People would just have to stand and wait their turn.

The guests would often start to pile up, and it was embarrassing. Even though I wasn't technically supposed to have one, I'd scammed a key to the bellman closet. Once, I decided to be the hero and save the day. The guests were lining up and I could feel their consternation. I walked around and opened the door. "What's your ticket number?" I asked the first guest. It wasn't rocket science. I gave the person their bags. When they tried to tip me, I refused. I still had the door open when the bellman finally came down. He and I had been friendly, but now I was standing between him and his meal ticket.

It was the closest I ever came to being fired.

His union representative contacted the hotel, and management let me know just what a big deal it was. Complaint cards and letters from annoyed guests were often met with a shrug. This was met with much wringing of hands.

I never tried to "save the day" for the bellmen after that, believe you me.

The U.S. Open was one of the groups that would always stay in the hotel. One day Anna Kournikova came down to leave for the day, and she needed things that she had in the bellman's closet. She was gorgeous, and you couldn't miss her long blond hair. Within a couple of minutes there were fans around her. In another couple of minutes, there were more people. She just stood there, looking around. "Where's the bellman?" her handler asked me.

I stood there, explaining the whole absurd situation. Skip, the ninety-three-year-old bellman, came pulling a cart. He was renowned for having the ability to fall asleep while standing up. As the place turned into an autograph session, he slowly shuffled his way across the gigantic lobby with no sense of urgency at all.

When I explained the bellman situation to most people, they were irritated but understood that it wasn't my fault. Sometimes people would argue with me about my inability to get in there. "There *must* be a way. *Somebody* has a key, right? What happens if there's a fire in there? You're telling me no one can get in? What happens if a woman's giving birth?" If it got really bad I'd pick up the phone and pretend to be making a reservation, having long drawn-out conversations with the dial tone just to avoid the inevitable venting.

Things reached a boiling point one day with a particular businessman. He kept hovering in my periphery, even though I was busy helping other people as a concierge. "This is crazy!" he huffed. "This is outrageous! I can't believe you can't just come out from there and get my bags!"

I paused with the people I was helping. "I really wish I *could* help you. Is there somebody that I could call? Do you want me to get the manager to come and explain it to you? We don't have the keys."

He kept shaking his head, getting more and more annoyed. "This is totally unacceptable and ridiculous."

I tried offering things to mitigate the situation. "Do you want to go sit at the bar? I'll have someone bring you your things. Just leave your ticket with me." To be fair, the man did have a point. It *was* ridiculous to pay $600 a night and not be able to get a bellman. But he was acting like I was part of the big amorphous "hotel problem," rather than the person who was trying to make things better for him. He really thought I was trying to spite him. Much like most people's approach to service, his perception became a self-fulfilling prophecy.

I made a decision to disengage from the people I was helping. I gave them a few restaurant review clippings to flip through for a minute, so they could decide where they wanted to eat. Very calmly, I spoke to the man. "It's *not* fair," I told him. "I agree with you. But honest to God, if I *could* go in there, I would."

"So where are they?"

"I don't know," I admitted.

"You mean to tell me that you have *no idea* where the bellmen are right now?"

"No, I'm sorry. There's no way for me to tell where they are."

He kept right on challenging me. "I can't believe you don't know where they are. What kind of system is this?"

"Well, there are four of them, and there are six hundred rooms, and I imagine that—"

"Don't you have a record of who checked out last?" he interrupted. "Maybe they're up in that room. Can't somebody go up to that room?"

I had to end it. He was forcing me to ignore the guests who were waiting in front of me at my desk. "We have not implanted the doormen with locating devices yet but when we do, I think we will have a much better handle on this." I didn't sound sarcastic, just totally businesslike. "Thank you for your input."

A few days later, I got called up to the manager's office. "We've received a complaint from a Mr. Nader."

"That name doesn't sound familiar," I said. I hadn't gotten the guy's information—he was just standing there and complaining.

"He's a very important executive at AIG."

I hadn't realized who I was talking to. A bigwig at a major corporate account was the worst-case scenario; losing a corporate account could have cost the hotel something like ten thousand rooms a year. We wouldn't be losing one guest, but dozens or even hundreds. "What happened?" I said.

"He sent in a comment card," the manager told me.

I relaxed, but only a little bit. A comment card was less poisonous than a letter to the hotel's corporate hierarchy. "Oh?"

"This is what he wrote." The manager read, verbatim, my conversation with Mr. Nader. "I think it was a little outlandish what you said. You said we were going to put *tracking devices* on people?"

"No, I can't say I remember this. *Tracking devices?*"

"He thought that you were being very sarcastic."

"Hm, I don't know." I didn't want to pretend he had made the whole thing up, but I still wanted to cover my ass. "The only thing I could think is there was a man, maybe a week ago, who was very,

very impatient and disruptive of my other guests. I explained to him that I wasn't able to go into the luggage closet."

"Ah, of course. It just sounded too outlandish."

"Yeah, who would ever say a thing like that?"

HOW TO HANDLE BAD SERVICE

In a perfect world, we'd all get good service all the time. But in real life, bad service is something that happens fairly often. There are people who are effective in getting a change in service—and people who aren't. My friend Annette was at the Peninsula in Chicago, and asked the concierge what he thought of a certain restaurant that she'd been recommended. "Eh," he said, "it's okay." That was the extent of their exchange. It rubbed Annette the wrong way because he was being dismissive of her suggestion. She gave the concierge a glaring look and walked off—and he let her walk off. The whole thing was unproductive, because Annette walked off without service and the concierge learned nothing.

In situations like this, I find that the passive-aggressive approach works best. Asking them something like, "Do you really hate it?" gives them a cue to either snap to it—or dig themselves deeper in the hole. You can follow that question up with, "Because here's how *I* feel." In service, you don't have to act contemptuous of the person's suggestion. You can see what they're going for, and try to steer them in the right direction without being a snot about it.

It certainly works both ways. Some customers know *everything* and don't let you do your job. If they wanted to sing the praises of T.G.I. Friday's, I'd tell them it was a *great* choice and make reservations. It was pointless to try to educate them, and they robbed themselves of learning about Five Napkin Burger. They weren't seeking advice; they were seeking validation.

If you want to be vindictive and punish the service person you're dealing with, it's very difficult. The appearance of service is that you're the boss. But you're really not. The only time people get

continued

fired on the spot is in movies where the character needs a change in occupation. For a business to fire someone on the spot in front of a customer is to admit that they're staffed with incompetents—not a very healthy image.

If you want to just be a jerk, the best thing to do is to write a letter. But here's the thing: Unless the bad service is grossly repetitive—and sometimes it is, and those people are clearly not in the right field—those letters do nothing except make you feel good. Letters do get to somebody's eyes, and then there's a whole chain of people that need to explain the issue. But there's no way you know an employee better than their managers do, unless their manager is completely out of it—in which case they're too stupid to take effective action anyway. Further, if someone has been consistently giving bad service for a long time, they're probably entrenched in that position. You're not going to be the tipping point to get them fired.

Another alternative approach is the classic "Let me talk to your manager!" You will get your instant and ephemeral gratification, because human nature means that the manager will try to come in and save the day. You'll get some modicum of submission, but the idea that you've somehow "fixed" this person is absurd. You and your power play will be quickly forgotten by all parties involved. The only way you will be remembered is in a *bad* way, if your attitude gets you a scarlet letter. Restaurants and hotels do it all the time, marking rude customers' profiles with comments. Our special code for this was abbreviated to "PITA"—as in, Pain In The Ass—in case they saw the computer screen's reflection in our glasses or something. Positive comments also got registered. A "BFT" was a Ben Franklin Tipper who dropped hundred-dollar bills.

My personal approach is to try to educate the person. At first glance, it seems like a waste of time. But educating someone is actually a very good investment, because you instantly become memorable. Instead of being angry, act surprised. "All I did was come up here and ask you for a restaurant. Correct me if I'm wrong, but that's kind of what you're here to do." It's kind of like the Dog

continued

Whisperer. You snap them out of their bad-service mode and bring them back to earth. You're no longer some amorphous guest, but a real person with real needs.

Now that they're listening, it's important to frame the issue correctly. Service professionals are prepared to defend their company, but they're not prepared to defend injustice. "This is unacceptable! This is not what your website looks like!" cries out for an explanation, not a remedy. You'll get the excuses as to why it has to be acceptable. "I'm sorry we're oversold this weekend," they'll tell you. "There's nothing we can do." But what *does* work is, "I booked this reservation two months ago. I know that the hotel is oversold but my room is horrible. *This isn't really fair.* I was looking forward to a great weekend and I'm not going to be happy in there." *That* cries out for a remedy. No one wants to be unfair.

People who are very confrontational expect that they're paving the way for their future. The idea is that if you try to assert your importance every time you walk in the door, then everyone will salute you. Machiavelli's "it's better to be feared than to be loved" is an adage that might work when you have real power—not the illusion of power that the service relationship actually is. With service, it's just the opposite. It turns everyone off and creates stress. You're not going to get good service from somebody who's afraid of you. It's the same reason people don't keep porcupines as pets: Yes, there might be some upside. But the big downside is glaringly obvious, so it's safest to simply minimize any interaction.

10.
On the Case

There is absolutely nothing wrong with coming to a big city and not being that good at finding your way around. That's one of the main functions of a concierge: to help guests navigate the area. There *is* something wrong, however, with being a know-it-all when you're actually a know-it-not.

Many people that repeatedly visit New York feel like they've earned some imaginary, invisible badge. It's usually awarded around the sixth visit, but I've encountered it with people who had been to the city only once before—or even on their first visit, but they'd "read a book." They'd ask me a question, but they'd never *ever* let me finish a sentence. "We want to go downtown to Harlem," was one that I heard.

Harlem *is* downtown—if you're on 175th Street. But since the hotel was on 48th Street, that would make it uptown. I never really knew how to respond. It was more them showing off than actually asking for information. But knowing the simple fact that Harlem exists is not exactly an impressive bit of trivia.

Tourists loved to say that something was by "the river." "Well, there's the East River and the Hudson River," I explained. "Which river are you talking about?"

"You know. The *river*."

Thanks to *Sleepless in Seattle,* every concierge in New York has had to argue until he's blue in the face that, no, there *isn't* a restaurant at the top of the Empire State Building. It *hasn't* closed recently and you *didn't* eat there last time you were visiting New York. It doesn't matter how certain you are and how much you swear up and down. *It did not happen.* That was a *movie,* not real life.

The Muppets never really "took" Manhattan, either.

It's not a question of "asking the right way." I'm a concierge, not some freemason who could only grant access if presented with a certain keyword and a rare feather. To be sure, there *are* hidden gems in major cities of the world. At the D'Orsay in Paris, there's a wonderful little restaurant up on the top that many people would overlook. But I guarantee the French concierges *do* know about it, and they *will* tell you about it without any secret handshakes.

The one request that happened constantly—*daily*—was to have breakfast at Tiffany's. Even the people that know it's a very upscale jewelry store believe that there must be some VIP café where they serve tea and croissants. There isn't. Technically speaking, there must be some room in the back where you can bring in some food and eat in a windowless office. But that's as close as you're going to get.

Late one evening a man came to the desk with his coat on, ready to go out on the town. "How far is Atlantic City?" he asked me, with a thick Eastern European accent.

"It's about a hundred and twenty miles," I told him.

"So how long will it take me to get there?"

"Three hours, roughly."

He was *distraught.* In his mind, Atlantic City was another bor-ough of New York. "That's impossible," he said, kindly but firmly.

Now I knew I was in for an argument. "It's not impossible," I said.

"Isn't there a subway I can take? Maybe something at Grand Central?"

Oh, of course! *The Grand Central Atlantic City Express!* "No," I insisted. "There really isn't."

"Isn't there *some* way to go faster?"

"You'd have to charter a helicopter!" I said, trying to show him how impossible it was.

"Okay," he said.

He was one of those. After you got past the arguing, they'd pretend to be interested in some extravagant adventure. Then, after I did all the research to find out what it entailed, they'd change their mind (but never admit how ridiculous they were being in the first place). Just from the way he was postured I could see that he thought he was a big shot. "I mean, it's probably going to be about three or four thousand dollars," I said, trying to nip this in the bud as fast as possible.

"Each way or round trip?"

"Probably round trip."

"How fast can you arrange it?"

Crap. It wasn't like I could call my friendly neighborhood helicopter pilot. The only helicopter companies I was aware of were the tourist ones, and I knew that they were closed. I wasn't sure what to do. I had to start brainstorming about aviation. Teterboro was a private airport; maybe there were helicopters there. Now that I had a minute to think, I realized that the price I quoted him was quite high. I was looking to pocket a clean $1,000, easy—*if* I could pull this off.

I called Teterboro but got a recording. ". . . If this is an emergency," it concluded, "press zero."

Oh yeah, I decided, *it's an emergency.* I got connected directly to somebody who was in the air traffic control tower. "Look, I'm sorry," I said, embarrassed. "I know I did this wrong. It's not like life or death, but I have a dilemma and I'm just desperate."

"Did you call Liberty Helicopter?" he said, after I explained the situation.

"They're closed."

"Hold on a second." I heard him rifling through some papers. "Call this number. It's the cell phone of the guy who owns Liberty."

"Thanks!" I called the guy—and got his voicemail. I told him what I needed as succinctly as I could. "If you get this within the next ten minutes, *please* call me back." I hung up the phone and started to think of where else to call. I got the idea to contact charter companies in Los Angeles, where it was three hours earlier.

It was a bit of a challenge and kind of fun, but what made it even more of a challenge is that other guests started to come up to the desk. Nine o'clock was always a very busy hour for us, and now I had the annoying people coming up and asking for a table for six, at Babbo, in fifteen minutes. I was juggling the phones and the wheels were clicking, but nobody else mattered except for the Russian helicopter man.

The guy from Liberty soon called me back. "What's the matter?" he said. "What do you need?"

I had a good relationship with his company, because helicopter tours were a very premium attraction. "I need someone to fly a guest to Atlantic City. Like, now."

"Let me see if I can get one of my pilots. They might still be around." He called me back in seconds. "All right. I have someone. Is this guy for real?"

"Yeah."

"Well, it would be his own helicopter. Your guy has got to pay for the whole thing himself. It'll be twenty-seven hundred."

My rule of thumb for pricing things was to take the expectation, then take the reality, and meet in the middle. "All right," I told the guest. "I've gotten a private helicopter ride to Atlantic City, round-trip for $3,500 if you're still interested." It was less than he had been expecting to pay, so I'd procured him an apparent bargain.

"Fine," he told me. "No problem. Do it."

Now I had to process the paid-out. Thirty-five hundred dollars was exorbitant, even by our usual high-ticket standard. I'd require manager approval, and there would be some questions. "How do you want to pay?" I asked the guest. "Do you want to put this to your room? Do you want to put just part of it now, and then part of it tomorrow?"

"Can I pay cash?" he asked.

"Sure." I knew that the pilot would have no issue with that, but I called anyway to make sure they knew what was coming. The owner was also more than fine with that.

"How do I get to the heliport?" the guest asked me.

"I'll get you a car," I said. I was terrified he was going to change his mind, and I'd be out a huge commission. It would be worth palming twenty dollars to one of the drivers out front to do me a little favor.

While I got on the phone with the car company, the guest took his valise and put it on my desk. It was like I was watching a James Bond movie through the corner of my eye. He popped open the valise— *click, click*—and I saw that the entire briefcase was *full* of stacks of bills. The stacks even had the little bank wrappers around them.

He started counting it out while I grew instantly aware of the cameras that hung over my desk. *Oh my God,* I thought, *don't let anybody see this. This is so great . . . but I'm so scared!* He handed me the cash for the full amount, and then he handed me a couple of hundred dollars extra. "Thank you so much for your time," he said.

A few minutes later, the driver came in from outside. "Is this the gentleman going to the heliport?"

"Yes!" I told him, sending them off on their way.

Now Murphy's Law kicked in, and I got extremely busy. It was even harder to focus on minutiae than usual, because my brain was still processing everything that just happened. In a few minutes, he'd be in Atlantic City after all.

Then, all of a sudden, I could feel the blood drain out of me. *What is he going to do when he gets to the heliport on the other side?* I realized. *I didn't make any arrangements for him!* Urgently I called Caesars. "I need to talk to the pit boss," I told them.

It was kind of like calling the White House and saying that you have to talk to the president. Maybe not the president, but at least like the secretary of state. "*Sure* you do," they said. "What is this call regarding?"

"A man with a suitcase full of cash," I blurted out, "from Russia, is on a helicopter that I just charted for him for thousands of dollars. If you don't want him to come to Caesars, just tell me that you're not interested."

They paused. ". . . Hold on."

The pit boss got on the line, more than a little skeptical. "What's this regarding? Some man from Russia . . . ?"

"Here's the deal," I told him. "I'm the concierge at the Inter-Continental Hotel. The man's on his way. He's got—I saw it with my own eyes—a ton of cash, and he's a really good guy. You're going to love him. Somebody needs to take him by the hand from the heliport and treat him like a star, because this is a very good thing."

I kept following up the entire night with Caesars, and I found that they really did treat him like a star. They dispatched a car for him, and the pit boss himself came with the car to welcome him to the casino. Everything was going off without a hitch. Now I got nervous again. *What if the guy is just going there to hire a hooker?* I wondered. *I've got this pit boss joined to him at the hip. It's like some really tacky buddy comedy.* I didn't *know* the guy; I was simply trusting my instincts. He had seemed no-nonsense; he wanted to go to Atlantic City, and he got what he wanted. He wasn't mean or demanding or insulting. But maybe he *was* horny—and not just horny, but tactfully horny.

The next day I followed up. God only knows how much he spent at the casino, but the helicopter waited and he came back in the wee hours of the morning. It was all done and it was all good, and everyone was happy. "*Any* time you want to come to Atlantic City," the pit boss said to me, "just call. Your rooms are taken care of."

When I needed concert tickets for somebody performing in Atlantic City, the pit boss was my contact—and he always came through. And I like to think that the next time someone asked me what seemed like a stupid question, I hedged a bit before giving them a sarcastic answer. I always wondered if they had a valise full of cash, sitting there just outside of view.

HOW TO WORK CASINOS

Every casino has a host. Sometimes they're called guest services, but they're never referred to as "VIP" or anything. The host is provided a list of the high rollers at the hotel. What most people don't realize is that you can establish yourself as a high roller proactively. You can literally go to a casino host and ask what their policy and parameters are for being a high roller—and they'll very candidly tell you. It's usually a minimum commitment to gamble a certain amount of money. No, you can't commit to that amount, then cash out immediately and cheat the system. They're watching, and you'd be off that list in no time.

continued

The casino host has the power to comp dinners, to comp shows, to comp anything that's within the confines of that casino. Even if you don't want something comped, they have an allotment of tickets to distribute. When Cirque du Soleil first came out, it was the hottest thing in town. Theoretically, the host was supposed to give his tickets to the high rollers. But the high rollers are notorious for no-showing. They get taken up at a table while the show comes and goes. They know they've been invited, but they never pick up the tickets. It's a crap shoot (ha ha) but it's a good last-minute place to check for tickets to a popular event. You don't have to pretend to be a guest; you just need to offer to buy the unspoken-for tickets.

11.

The Best Seat in the House

Like many other fancy customers, the man on the phone was very businessy and matter-of-fact. "I am staying at the hotel next week," he told me. "I need to get a car service. I would like to go to the theater at some point. I have meetings in Connecticut and New Jersey, but the location I'll be at most is 1180 6th Avenue."

"That's five blocks away," I told him. "You don't really need a car."

"Well, I'm in a wheelchair."

"Okay, that shouldn't be a problem. I'll figure this out and I'll get back to you." He was so gruff and logistical-minded, that he sounded like he was a world champion skier who fell and now had his leg up. He was going to go to scores of fancy dinners, fold up his chair, and throw it in the trunk.

I'd never had to make accommodations for someone who was disabled. But I just went and hit the phones to call the car services. How hard could it be?

Well, it's pretty hard when you don't have any information.

"Is the wheelchair electric, or is it foldable?" the dispatcher asked me.

"Huh. I'm not sure."

"How much does it weigh? Is he absolutely wheelchair-bound, or does he have some mobility?"

I sat there with the receiver in my hand, trying to see if there was any way to guess—or if there was any way for me to find out without calling the man back and making things awkward.

There wasn't.

I got off the phone with the dispatcher and thought about how best to approach the situation. I knew the worst thing that I could do: use the overly fake tone that guests always used with me. "Hello, little crippled man! My grandmother's in a wheelchair; we have *so* much in common."

Instead I just took his cue. It was a nonissue to him, and therefore it would be a nonissue to me. "Everything's going to be fine," I said to him in my most businesslike voice, when I called back. "I just have a couple of questions to ask you. First of all, can you move your legs?"

"No, I'm a paraplegic. I have no use of the lower half of my body. I would need to be lifted out of the chair, but I prefer a car that could take me in the wheelchair."

For me, to hear "prefer" meant that I *had to* find it.

I got it. I wasn't thinking any longer of requesting a very strong driver to lift him. Now I started thinking of dignity, of Donald Trump as a paraplegic. I had this fantasy of hiring a totally shiny black van with blacked-out windows. It had a wheelchair lift and everything, and was exactly what he wanted. I really wanted to make this happen for the guy.

My fantasy was perfect except for one thing: It doesn't exist.

My research expanded to a day's worth of work. I called whomever could conceivably have a connection that could help me. I called the Disabled American Vets. I called hospitals. I called every possible provider—and I couldn't find a van that would accommodate a wheelchair.

After I exhausted every number in New York City, I started expanding my calling circle. Lo and behold, there was *one* company in New Jersey. They had a black wedding limo van—and it had a wheelchair lift. Bingo!

"We're one hundred miles outside of the city," they told me. "We charge a dollar a mile just to get it there, as well as the hiring fee."

The guest's handicap wasn't interfering with his financial success. I doubted it would be a problem, so I just called him.

He was fine with the expense, and wanted to plan out his restaurant- and his theater-going. "Let me put together some choices for you," I said. "I'll do some research and call you back as soon as possible." I got the limo secured for him all day, and was already spending a fortune. Then something clicked inside my head. I realized that if the fancy limo companies weren't as accommodating to his needs as they could have been, it was possible that the restaurants wouldn't be, either. There was no way I was going to have this man compromise his dignity.

Restaurants are to code; technically, they need to be wheelchair-accessible. But my job meant never assuming anything and always confirming everything. I called Chanterelle. "Hi," I said. "It's Michael from the InterContinental Hotel. I have a guest staying at the hotel who is in a wheelchair. I just wanted to confirm if you have a ramp?"

"Of course we have a handicapped ramp. But we do have stairs up to the dining level."

"You do?"

"It's only two stairs," the hostess said.

"Only" two stairs? Having him be lifted up two stairs was about as plausible to me as having him walk up them. "So he has to eat at the *bar*?" I sputtered.

"Gee, I'm afraid so. But we *do* serve the full dining menu in the bar area."

That crossed them off my list. It's not like I began to pity the guest. But I realized that to be wealthy, fancy, and handicapped was kind of a contradiction. It was just obstacle after obstacle after obstacle, and in counterintuitive ways. I hit the phone for hours to be sure to secure a first-class experience for him.

At eleven o'clock one night, I was finishing my shift. The doors opened, and in came a man in a wheelchair. It was obvious who it was, but I had brainwashed myself into thinking of him as just any other guest. *I don't know if it's him!* I chided myself. *He's like anyone else! He's just sitting down, is all!*

He wheeled up to my desk while I was on the phone. I motioned that I'd be right with him—he's like anyone else!—and he nodded in acknowledgment.

That's when Glen happened to walk past.

Glen was the general manager of the hotel. Glen was also a frat boy who grew up and happened to get a job. He was the kind of person who incessantly hung out at the hotel bar, making sure that everyone knew that he was the general manager.

Glen came in between us and squatted down in front of the guest. "Well, hi there!" he said. "Is Michael taking good care of you?" In a tiny way, I understood where Glen was coming from. His intentions were somewhat good, but he was completely not clued in to the guy's stature. It wasn't as if this were a pitiful-looking person. The man had a fancy wheelchair and was dressed impeccably. He was probably the owner of a Fortune 500 company. But Glen was talking to him like he was a kid, or someone's elderly mom.

The guest was totally dismissive of him, barely turning his head. "Yes, he is. He's fine."

Glen did not take the cue. Glen wouldn't normally take a cue anyway, but Glen also happened to be drunk. "Are you having a good stay? We want to make sure that you're comfortable!"

I wanted to die, but even if I died that wouldn't have stopped Glen. I could only pray that he wouldn't start asking about the wheelchair. After a bit more stilted dialogue, Glen must have spotted a skirt to chase. He got up and walked away.

Over the next few days, the guest took the opportunity of being in New York by the horns. He did everything that everybody else did, and was able to afford to do it in the way that made him feel comfortable. "Loved the restaurant," he said simply. "Great call." He didn't gush when he left, even though he must have known how much work I put in to accommodate him. The hundred-dollar bills he tipped me said it all.

THE EXCHANGE

When you use the right tone, you're on your way to receiving good service.

The guest himself wasn't too nice to me from the beginning—but he wasn't unfriendly, either. It was very much a business-to-business kind of relationship, which is what all service effectively comes down to. Some people are often uncomfortable being served, so their impulse is to be sickeningly sweet. "Hi, how *are* you? Listen, me and my friends are using my talking-to-a-dog voice. You've got to accommodate me, right?" That might work at Applebee's. Those people are just happy to have somebody who's not yelling. But once you leave the mall, service is different. Speaking that way to someone who is serving you is the same way Glen spoke to the guest in the wheelchair. Just because you're standing and they're sitting doesn't mean they should be talked down to—or will be oblivious to it.

There's nothing wrong with being "nice." The niceness that works is creating some sort of cool and detached acknowledgment—but not

continued

aloofness. It can be going up to a bartender and asking "So, what time does this place get busy? Around six thirty, seven?" You're making a statement and creating a conversation. If you want to pick up a girl, you don't just walk up to her and ask her out. There needs to be some sort of icebreaker.

What always worked with me and what works when I do it to other people is to go to their world. If you know a little bit about their world, you're subliminally getting the point across that you know a little bit about what they're doing. Now, it's "us" versus *them*. It's implicitly saying, "Look at all of these people waiting for a table. Aren't they ridiculous? What time am I getting in?"

If you don't know anything about their world, there's another technique you can use. People in service often have name tags, and people with name tags always hate the fact that they have to wear them. Everywhere I see that, from the bank to the airport, I immediately ask them what their last name is. It kind of breaks the wall and identifies them as a human being, not some faceless name-tag drone. I don't do it in mid-dialogue; then it sounds like I'm going to report them. And I don't bother *using* the last name, because it's needlessly formal. But asking for that last name shows that you get the situation and are on their side—and people in service bend over backward for customers who get the situation and are on their side.

At my desk there was a big concierge sign. It was one of those fancy glass rectangles, like a transparent brick with a marble stand. That's what told people that I was a concierge. What told people that I was a *good* concierge was how quickly I processed requests from guests who needed help.

The thing that I admired were the people who got it. Conversely, the thing that I loathed were the people who didn't. Some were too chatty and fake-friendly, which I didn't have time for. But the worst were the people who did not feel that they had to wait in line. All they had to do was use their logic and open their eyes. They could see how fast I was going. They should realize that my attention was seconds away.

The dinner hour was always a busy time. That's when people had a tendency to say things like, "I just have a question . . . !"

"That's what the other people in line here are for," I'd say with a super-positive tone, gesturing at all the people queued up. "They *all* have questions. I've got to help them first." I looked upon myself as kind of a service counselor, and I was too codependent for their approval to be nasty about it. (And I really *was* genuine about trying to enlighten them.)

Sometimes it got more out of hand. Instead of forming a line, people would form a cluster in front of the desk. There was no regard for allowing the person I was with to get the help they needed. "I just have a question . . . Where do you suggest I go for dinner?"

That was not "just" a question. The only questions where you can cut a line are ones you can ask in one word—and be answered in zero. "Bathroom?" "Phone?" "Elevator?" I would point and continue helping whoever was there first, without breaking out of the conversation.

Unless, of course, it wasn't phrased in the form of a question. Alex Trebek, eat your heart out. "Bathroom."

"Would you like to know where the bathroom is?" I always said, correcting them as subtly as possible. "It's just around the corner to the left."

One dinner hour, this woman in a mink stole who looked like Diahann Carroll tried to cut the line. I was already helping somebody and there were three or four people waiting ahead of her. She moved to the side of the line and kept trying to interject.

It didn't work.

She started strumming her fingers on my desk, and it made a

very distinctive sound because of the big ring she had on. But that didn't work, either. She may have thought she invented strumming the desk with the big ring, but people did that a lot. In that environment, spoiled people snapping their fingers at me was not unusual at all. They'd even ring the bell, even when I was assisting somebody else.

I was always nice at first, no matter how rude the guest was being. "I'll be right with you," I told the strumming woman. "I just need to finish with *these* people since they came first."

She just kept sighing and trying to chime in. The people I was helping started to get distracted by her. I made direct eye contact with the lady, painfully aware that the ring she was clacking against the desk was probably giving it a good scratching. "Do you have a quick question?" I said.

"Well, I'd like to get some help!" she snapped.

"Of course. If you could just give me a moment to take care of these nice people in line ahead of you, I will be very happy to help you. If you wish, perhaps someone at the front desk can help you. I can see there's no line there."

"This is crazy," she yelled. "I can't believe it!"

I knew very well how to keep the flow moving quickly. But the bitch in me couldn't resist adding a tiny drop of fuel to her fire. The others in line had cameras, tour brochures, and copies of *Where* magazine. It was obvious that they didn't exactly know how to process the tension she was creating. To them, it was a great New York moment like out of the movies—and they had front row seats.

Out popped my tour map and a Sharpie. The others in line gathered as I slowly detailed practically every sight to see in the city. "If you're a chocolate lover, you must go to the third floor of Henri Bendel to Chocolate Bar. When you enter the store, you'll want to take the elevator to three. When you get off, just look to the left past the evening gowns."

Mere inches away from me, she just kept grunting and sighing in disgust. "These stupid tourists," she muttered to herself.

My patience was extinguished and I snapped. I slammed my hands on the desk at her. "This is a *line*. These people were here *first*. This is how it works: I'm going to help them, and if you'd like to stand behind them, then your turn is coming next, that's when you get all of my attention."

"You bastard!" she yelled. She lifted up my heavy glass concierge sign and threw it at me. It clanked across my marble counter and bounced onto the floor. The glass broke, and the pieces scattered *everywhere*. Everyone in the lobby heard it. Shattering glass is not a quiet sound.

Then: silence. It seemed like a year passed before anyone reacted, including her and me. I was startled, and the adrenaline started kicking in.

Very sternly, I looked at her and said, "Look at what you just did. Is that how you behave? Are you *proud* of yourself? Everyone else had the decency to follow the rules. The rules are easy. You wait for two seconds and I'm going to help you."

The people in line started to chime in with agreement. "Yeah, lady. We were here first." From the lobby came a little spattering of applause and laughter. It wasn't like where they started cheering in *Norma Rae,* but it was apparently enough to make her feel humiliated.

She started to cry, mink stole and all.

It wasn't long after that I got called to speak to the manager. "She threw the sign at me!" I said. "I didn't *scold* her. I simply told her that she'd have to wait for the next person."

Nothing came of it in the hotel, but something came of it inside me. No matter what happens, some people are just not going get it. That woman must leave a trail of blood everywhere she goes. She must constantly have very bad experiences. She just needed to realize that it's the service person who is in the driver's seat. They can help you get to the destination that you want, or they can roadblock you.

But good service often means allowing for bad behavior. She might have broken my concierge sign, but it was the concierge desk that was beginning to break me.

THINGS RICH PEOPLE CAN'T DO FOR THEMSELVES

Remember if they like it: "Did I like Turks and Caicos?"

Take ownership of their demands: "We really need to make sure *we* get seats in the first five rows."

Say "I don't care what it costs"—and mean it: "I don't care," *as long as it matches my unrealistic expectation of what I think a private jet charter should cost.*

Book a dinner reservation: I have a job because of this.
  1. Call the restaurant.
  2. Say "yes" when the reservationist answers and immediately asks you to hold.
  3. Don't hang up and call right back.
  4. Don't watch your clock to see how long you are holding.
  5. Don't tell the reservationist how long you were holding.
  6. Say hello to the reservationist when they pick up again.
  7. Ask if they can accommodate your request for a table.
  8. Allow them to respond with the perfunctory "we can take your party at five thirty or ten forty-five" even though you asked for eight thirty.
  9. Remain cordial and sell yourself with all your heart, just like you would if you were interviewing for a job.

Interview for a job: What is this, a deposition? I'm not on trial!

continued

Deal with a coach seat: Is first class sold out? Just book three coach seats all for yourself.

Enjoy a concert without meeting the star: Maybe we're all just thirteen-year-old girls at heart, but I stay very busy scoring backstage passes for my clients, at thousands a pop.

Write love letters: If I had a nickel for every person who asked me to "just write something" to go with the flowers . . . Wait, I do. I have many, many nickels because of this.

Wait: I have people in my resource database who will stand in line for a fee. Time is money.

12.
New York Loves You Back

I was home watching the *Today* show when Jeffrey called me from Union Square. "A plane just crashed into the World Trade Center," he told me.

"What?" A lot of other people thought the same thing that I did when they first heard the news: a little Cessna had hit one of the towers, and nothing would come of it. After all, one had flown into the White House not that long before, and it had done no real damage.

But then the *Today* show flashed on with the news. It was so weird that it took me a while to register. I got up and looked out of the window. On the street below there were all these people standing outside of their cars. I went downstairs to see what was going on; by this time the second plane had already hit.

I have to get to the hotel, I thought. I felt like there was a call to action. People were going to need transportation and people were going to need help. Not lifesaving help, obviously, but these were people who would be trapped in a foreign city. The alternative was for me to sit at home and freak out, and I wanted to be doing *something*.

I went back upstairs to get my work suit, and slung it over my shoulder. I wasn't sure how long I'd be gone for. I walked the thirty blocks to work because the subways were shut down and traffic was insanity. When I stepped into the hotel, the lobby was a mob scene of frenetic energy. I'd never seen it like that before. There was a line around the concierge's desk, and in front of the front desk was a crowd four people deep. The staff had brought down all of the televisions from the conference rooms on those high rolling carts. Everywhere you turned in the lobby, you saw the news right as it was happening. They had electrical tape holding down all the wires for the televisions and, between that and the noise, this fancy lobby looked like a construction zone.

I was living in Los Angeles when the earthquake hit in January of 1994. It was a scary period, and it had the effect of making everyone instantly nice. When I walked into the hotel, that was my fantasy. I expected to come into a place where it was group-think. I was going to arrive, help everyone who needed help, and be the hero. But that fantasy was crushed very quickly. There wasn't a lot of softness. For many of the people, this day was all about *them* and *their* problems. The only real difference between September 11 and September 10 was that now they were somehow inconvenienced. They found this hassle to be inexplicable and outrageous—while images were flashing in every direction they turned, while the news was blasting at full volume, and while the smell of death was literally in the air. Every New Yorker remembers what it smelled like that day; at least, those of us who paid any attention to begin with.

"What do you mean, I can't get to the airport?" one man asked me. "How am I going to get out of here? You must know *somebody* that you can get on the phone with."

People would sometimes get that way when the airport was shut during snowstorms, and I could understand where they were coming from. They felt like there must be *one* flight leaving, and the concierge *had* to find it for them. But this wasn't exactly a snowstorm. I made a show of calling American Airlines on their behalf. All I got was a recording that said, "You've reached American Airlines. I'm sorry, but our lines are blocked and we can't accept any more calls. Thank you, and good-bye."

"I apologize," I told the guest, "but they're not taking calls."

"Well, how am I going to get to Stamford for my presentation?" he asked me.

Buddy, nobody's going to Stamford for your fucking presentation.

A young woman came in and sidled up to the desk. She was about thirty and really attractive. She looked expensive, like a Madison Avenue debutante. "Where are your banquet rooms?" she asked me, irritated that she'd had to wait for my attention.

I assumed she was there to attend some conference in the hotel. "There's nothing going on," I told her. "Everything's canceled."

"You're not understanding me. I just need to look at the space. Just call someone who can show me the rooms," she sighed.

"Can I just ask—did you have an appointment or something? What is it that you are interested in doing?"

"I'm looking for a wedding space."

"I don't think it's probably going to happen today."

"That's ridiculous!" she said. She literally said it was *ridiculous.* "Why not?"

"I have a *feeling* that they are probably putting rollaway beds in the conference rooms right now, because all of the people that didn't check out today are still here, and all of the people that got in today are here, and we need room."

"Don't you want my business?"

I just stared at her. "You know what? No, we *don't* want your business." That day, of all days, I had the ability to simply say no. Part of me even expected her to write a note, complaining. *I came into your hotel to inquire about space for my wedding. It was September 11, about an hour after the second tower fell. I have never been treated so rudely in my life as I was by your concierge Michael!*

The frenetic energy stayed like that for the next two days. Everybody was stuck, and not many people could get home. Our hotel was always packed, with practically every one of the almost seven hundred rooms occupied all the time. If there were three hundred checkouts, then there were three hundred check-ins—but now that meant that we were overbooked by three hundred. Every hotel in the city was like that; there were *no* rooms to be had. We moved cots into conference rooms, and people just had to make do—though they didn't like it. Guests could have given up their rooms, and slept on couches in their coworkers' suites. But instead they chose to call down to the desk to complain about how long room service was taking.

It started to soften when the airports opened up, and there was a bit of an exodus. We suddenly had to struggle to make space and get rooms ready: the people from Cantor Fitzgerald were coming to stay with us. They had been headquartered at the top floors of One World Trade Center, and two-thirds of their workforce had been killed.

CEO Howard Lutnick came in with a whole crew from his company. They stood at the front desk, and from everywhere in the lobby you could hear them crying. They weren't trying to hide it, sniffling into a handkerchief or something. These very successful people were just absolutely devastated. It's not like they lost one friend or one family member; they lost their staff, everyone who they used to spend hours at the office with, day in and day out. Their emotions were so raw that I started to panic.

Suddenly things became real. All of the greediness and brattiness was gone. It was replaced by a somber, humble, and depressing energy. In a selfish way, that's when I got scared. I realized our whole city is built on those people who snap their fingers and make demands. "Get it now! Get it *now*! I don't care what it costs and I want more! *More!* Bigger! Closer to the stage! Louder!" That attitude that I sometimes resented was gone—but without people like that, who was I going to provide service for?

Over the following days, the hotel started to empty out and things became weird. We were only booked at around 50 percent capacity when it came to rooms. Every single person was calling to let us know they couldn't get in, and wondering what to do about their theater tickets. I obviously wasn't going to tell them that they had legally committed to the purchases, so every cancellation was money out of my pocket. It was just *spiraling.* Our concierge desk was very formal and old-fashioned. Instead of doing things in the computer, we had a big logbook with the ribbon down the middle to mark the page. Every sheet was filled with line after line as we crossed out the various reservations, one after another. *I'm not going to have a job,* I thought. Everything that had made me crazy about my job instantly faded away. I was into my work. I was a great concierge and things had been going well, and I mostly did love this business. I loved the air of power, I loved the mystique, and frankly I loved the money for doing it all.

One quiet evening, the lobby was deserted. Literally every phone call I took was for people canceling their dinner and/or theater ticket reservations. *Oh my God,* I thought. *People can't stop coming. Now is the time to come!* There was tremendous damage that had been done to the city—but it was just getting worse and worse. *This* damage could be mitigated, in some small way. *How do we convince people to come to New York without sounding greedy?*

It was the same thought process I went through when a show was sold out. I always knew that there *must* be *some* way. Like my most demanding guest, I absolutely would not and could not accept the notion that there wasn't at least *something* that could be done. Maybe I could get someone from the theater industry to call all the incoming guests to leave a message or send a letter out to people that would encourage them to come. I knew who was listed as scheduled to check in and I had all their contact information. Maybe there was a way to reach out to everybody due to come in the next month. I obviously didn't want to make it something like, "On behalf of the hotel: We need your money!"

There seemed to be a lot of help and support for those who lost loved ones in the towers, but as dirty as it made me feel, I couldn't help but think about the next wave of residual damage. More bad things were happening. Shows close when seats are empty. Waiters don't make a living from empty tables. Concierges are useless without a hotel full of people snapping their fingers. I was terrified of trivializing, in any way, the anguish New York was going through. Yet I couldn't help but think that this, of all times, was a good time to bury some sorrow in great food, music, theater, and art.

Then I thought bigger and I began to feel that there really wasn't anything wrong with my message. What the message needed to make it legit was star power. I was fixated on all those public service announcements that celebrities do for various causes. *Was this a "cause"? Could I pull something like this together? Would it seem odd for me to reach back to my Hollywood contacts, as someone now on the outside?* Thoughts of Dolores gave me a sense of fearlessness.

I needed to get a star who was really famous and really recogniz-able. *Who do I have contact with,* I wondered, *that knows someone with a famous, distinctive voice? Charlie Sheen would be good, and I certainly know how to get to him. Salma Hayek? Now there's a distinctive voice—but I just couldn't. I do have an in with Rosie O'Donnell. She's all about New York. But would her voice be instantly recognizable?*

Whoopi Goldberg was *blaring* in my inner monologue. She was on Broadway, she had won a Tony award, and her voice was totally distinguishable. She just seemed like someone who I could be real with about my mission—and someone everyone loved.

Whoopi was on my periphery because one of my acquaintances from Los Angeles was Tom Leonardis, who I knew as her assistant. He was one of the people I had tried to network with by sending little notes and articles about themselves to. I had a little bit of pull with him but not a lot; I hadn't talked to him at all since I moved to New York. I found his number and gave him a call.

"Tom Leonardis's office," *his* assistant said.

I did a quick double take. I knew that he was still with Whoopi and I knew that he had risen in the organization, but I didn't know the extent. I had eventually stopped reading *Variety*. He had actually become the president of Whoop, Inc., her production company. "Hi, this is Michael Fazio."

"Can I ask what this is regarding?"

"Oh. I'm an old acquaintance of Tom's, and I just wanted to say hello and to run something by him." I didn't want to get into detail about what exactly I wanted, and I *definitely* didn't want to mention Whoopi. I felt like that wouldn't warrant a response, or would pro-bably even put up a wall.

I got the typical tepid assistant's answer. "Okay, I'll take your num-ber and let him know you called."

Oh, crap, I realized. *There's no way she's going to do this. What the hell was I thinking? Tom is going to blow me off.*

I got more down-to-earth about the kind of person I was looking for. I brainstormed people who would be known to guests of the hotel—but who would also have a direct vested interest in what was happening. Daniel Boulud was a famous restaurateur with a great French voice and Abbie knew him very well. Danny Meyer was an icon in the restaurant industry, and I knew his assistant. Both of them agreed to do it on the spot.

I started calling my contacts in the theater industry, since they would have access to actors. They were all cautiously polite, but they didn't really want to promise me someone who they couldn't deliver.

I looked through my old L.A. book to see what contact info I had. I put calls out to everyone that I could, but Whoopi was far and away my best choice. I decided to call her office again; the worst thing that they could tell me was no. By this time I knew that Tom wasn't likely to return my call anyway. I came up with my thirty-second elevator pitch of what I wanted; the first time I'd called, I just hadn't been prepared. I rang him up again, and again I got the assistant.

I thought about what worked and what didn't work with me, as a service industry person. I wasn't going to get through by being dismissive, or fakely nice, or needlessly aggressive. I couldn't take his caution personally. The assistant was just trying to do his job, which was to be a gatekeeper for his boss. So I was truthful and to the point about what I wanted. "I hate to be impatient and I know Tom hasn't called me back but I would just like to get his ear for twenty seconds. This is something that's kind of time sensitive and it would mean a lot to me. I don't work in the business anymore; I work in a hotel. I have this idea that I think would be really positive, and help bring some attention to the tourism industry in New York, which is in really bad shape."

It worked. "Okay," the assistant said. "Hold on one second."

Tom got on the phone. "Yep?"

"Tom," I said, "I hate to be calling you for this because we haven't spoken in so long. I work in a hotel now and I'm scared out of my mind, because the hotel is emptied out. I'd like to know if Whoopi might consider doing some sort of public service announcement. This wouldn't be broadcast nationally or anywhere in the media if she doesn't want it to be. It's just to play to our hotel guests because everyone's calling and canceling, and we are all flipping about our jobs."

His tone changed, and he warmed up. "Oh . . . Wow, when did you move to the hotel?"

I gave him the condensed version about becoming a concierge, and explained what the situation was like in the New York tourism industry. "Look, it's a crazy idea to think that somebody of her stature would even be interested."

"You know what?" he said. "Fax me over what you're asking, and put it exactly how you told me. If we can keep this to around five minutes, I can find a slot. She's going to be in a recording studio, and I can just put it in front of her."

I couldn't believe it. "Of course!" I wrote up exactly what I was envisioning, and sent it over to him.

He called me back the next day. "I still can't guarantee it," he said, "but just looking at it quickly she said okay. But I think we need to have a script."

I sat down immediately. *What do I write?* I remembered my friend Brendan's answering machine. He paused after saying hello, and I always thought that it was him picking up the phone. I would start talking as the message continued with, "I'm not here to take your call right now."

I envisioned the guests calling the hotel. When you're on hold, you're kind of brain dead and not paying attention. It would be a great way to jolt people, to have Whoopi Goldberg say "Hello?" Then, when they started talking to the recording about how they needed to cancel, she could continue with, "Are you still there? Oh, there you are. I just didn't want you to get cranky while you're on hold. Hey, it's me, Whoopi Goldberg. Your visit can really help lift us up, and I know that once you experience some of what this city has to offer, you'll be lifted up, too." I kept it cute and I kept it quick.

"Oh, this is perfect," Tom said. "This is all she needs to do?"

"Yep!"

Just like that, I had the brass ring. I had underestimated how accommodating she would be—just like I underestimated how accommodating so many other people would be. Rather than getting doors shut in my face all over town, celebrities willing to chip in started calling me back.

I told everyone's people the same thing: "I work in a hotel; our business is a catastrophe; the city needs all of this tourism. This is how so many people make their living—not just me. Here's my idea, to broadcast this to people to stop them from canceling." It wasn't like I was sponsored by some big corporation. It was just little ol' me. People took the cause on as their own. My friend Nancy Richards, head of a theater marketing company, brought in tons of Broadway celebrities. The roster grew bigger every day:

HALL OF FAME

Charlie Sheen	Michael Feinstein
Dominic Chianese	Bernadette Peters
Fran Drescher	Billy Crystal
Vanessa Williams	Ray Romano

continued

Helen Mirren	Paul Shaffer
Ossie Davis and Ruby Dee	Cindy Adams
David Hasselhoff	Wynton Marsalis
Anne Meara and Jerry Stiller	Bea Arthur
Christine Baranski	Mayor Bloomberg
Marc Anthony	Joan Rivers
Tony Bennett	

I was shocked by the people who were saying yes, but I was even more shocked by the people who were saying *no*. When I had Valerie Harper and Joel Grey calling me personally, it was hard to believe that a Bebe Neuwirth would be turning me down. There were so many people signing up that if Brooke Shields didn't want to do it, it wasn't any problem. When you own that belief and when that really is your philosophy, things have a way of snowballing in a very positive way.

HALL OF SHAME

Sarah Jessica Parker

Mathew Broderick

Billy Joel (but what about "New York State of Mind"?)

Brooke Shields (not-so-pretty, baby)

Rosie O'Donnell (the "Queen of Nice")

Barry Manilow (it would have been such a personal triumph)

I am absolutely certain that of those famous people who refused, none of their representatives ever even took it to them to begin with. It was very much like being back in Los Angeles. Instantaneously,

I could tell if the contact was going to be a yea or a nay. The refusals probably came from those who wanted to hear that this was the next "We Are the World," with people flown to New York in private jets for a huge press extravaganza.

The campaign soon took on a life of its own. Steve Karmen had written the "I Love New York" jingle and donated its use. It occurred to me that this should be a love letter *from* New York to its visitors. With "I Love New York" playing behind each message, I decided the perfect tagline would be "New York Loves You Back." I called a studio in L.A.; they donated time. Sony in New York donated studio time as well. Tapes were constantly coming in the mail, from celebrities all over America.

Then one of my contacts pulled me aside. "Why don't you share this with other hotels?" she said.

"I didn't tell anyone here that I was doing this," I replied. "I didn't know it was going to get this far."

"It's not right to get all this free stuff, and just have *your* hotel benefit."

I thought about what she said for a second. "You know what? You're right. But I didn't ask any of the people if that was okay."

"Are you joking? It's all good. Don't worry about that, and just push this whole thing out there."

She was right. I took it to the Hotel Association of New York, and they had twenty-five hotels playing it on their hold button. She knew Gerry Schoenfeld, the head of the Shubert Organization, and they got on board; whenever you called Telecharge to buy a Broadway ticket, you heard the campaign while waiting for an operator. Then Ticketmaster picked it up, and a slew of restaurants followed suit.

It kept my mind off all the crappy stuff that was going on in the rest of the city. Because all this happened within a month, I could keep myself distracted from the horror. Then I got a call from one of my publicist friends. "You know what?" he said. "This is really cool. I think you should call *New York* magazine and just get something in there. You might as well bring more attention to the fact that people should be going out to dinner and to see shows."

I saw what he was saying but I felt very conflicted. I had made a difference, but on some level it felt like the most opportunistic thing imaginable. It was like I had the ethics of an ambulance chaser, using 9/11 to guilt people into coming back to New York—and somehow this was turning into something about *me*. I felt like I had medicated myself with the whole campaign and been an opportunist. Maybe what I should have done was to go to some kid's house who had lost a parent and, say, mentored him at the hotel and taught him a vocation.

After *New York* ran a piece on it, *Crain's* and Channel 5 news came calling. That was when it got too much for me to be the face of this whole, huge expression of love for the city. I roped Abbie into being my partner for the larger rollout as the project continued to take shape. Instead of it being the Michael Fazio show, it became the story of this creative duo who did this crazy, zany thing for the city that they loved.

Between all the press and all the attention, I had addressed the problem as best I could. Things definitely improved—somewhat. Now, instead of being at 40 percent capacity, the hotel was at 42 percent capacity—and next week looked to be at 43 percent. *They're not coming back,* I realized. *And there's nothing I can do about it. Dozens of stars have joined this fight, but they only managed to stop the bleeding. It's going to be a long time before New York is a tourist spot again—and before this hotel needs me as a concierge like they did just weeks before.*

It seemed like it was time to pay the bill and get out—but despite all my contacts, I didn't feel like I had any place else to go.

DEALING WITH CELEBRITIES

Concierges constantly get requests for meetings with celebrities but it's not as simple as just calling the stars themselves. A typical celebrity has: (a), a personal assistant; (b), an agent; (c), (often) a manager; (d), (often) a business manager—which is a nice way of saying accountant; (e), a lawyer; and (f), a publicist.

People have this idea that if they only happened to run into a star in an elevator, they could pitch them their project and then be discovered. After all, this kind of thing happens all the time—*in movies*. In real life, you can't ignore the fact that these gatekeepers' very reason for existence is to guard the celebrity from people who would waste their time. You want to get *through* the gate—and not somehow sneak over it. No one, famous or not, is going to overrule their closest associates for the sake of someone they ran into in an elevator.

There is a certain system that you have to respect, just like when getting a discount for rooms or getting a table at a hot restaurant. You might get through by being creative or even tricky. If you were tasked with crossing a minefield, for example, getting a metal detector would help you navigate the situation. But getting through is not the most important part: you still have to have something *real* on the other side. The idea of being able to bullshit a star whose entire career is based in *Hollywood* is absurd. You can trick someone into taking your call, but you can't trick someone into doing something they otherwise wouldn't do.

Agents are all about how much a celebrity is going to get paid, so that is usually a bad person to contact first. Publicists are sometimes good way to go, especially if there's something they can spin in a positive direction. They are often a little bit more open, and they are always looking for something "interesting." My fellow concierge Daria got her name into Page Six because she had been tasked with finding a beard-braider for ZZ Top. Lawyers are also often good to contact. They have the famous person's ear, but they're not in entertainment themselves. If you can present your

continued

case (ha-ha), they can be helpful. Many times, I've gotten theater tickets from musicians' lawyers.

Put out what it is you would like, and don't take it personally or get offended when they tell you that they don't take offers or that they don't take unsolicited material. You have to constantly skin it. "What if I just send you a treatment, and I sent you a disclaimer?" "Can I send you literally one paragraph to read, for your feedback?"

You have to have a very legitimate thing that you want. Let's suppose you wanted Beyoncé to sing at your birthday party. That's not *not* legitimate—but you had better figure out what is going to make that compelling for her *and her gatekeepers.* Maybe you're going to charge everybody who comes fifty dollars that's being donated to an after-school program. You should also have a plan B and a plan C. "Can she call and wish me a happy birthday?" "Can I send her a sign saying 'have a great birthday,' and you just take a photo with her phone and send it to me?" Provide various levels, so it doesn't have to be all or nothing. If they're nice and they don't want to just say no, giving them choices will allow them to say yes to one of them—so you get something out of it after all.

One of my clients wanted to get backstage at a famous country singer's concert. I didn't approach his people with any expectations. "I would be excited," I said, "if they could just go to the stage door and somebody there would have their name." Not a big deal. What ended up happening is that the singer came out, brought them into his dressing room, and it became this whole big thing— which I would never have gotten if I made such a bold request to begin with. I kept it real, and things ended up happening. It works that way more often than you'd think.

Another trick is to read celebrity magazines like *In Touch* and *People,* as well as all the celebrity blogs. They constantly name-drop what restaurants a celebrity ate at and what hotels they were staying in. There's nothing wrong with calling the restaurant or calling the hotel, especially if you don't ask them to break their code of silence and confirm a certain person was there. Very often, you'll get

continued

someone on the phone who wants to show off. You could even get somebody who is actually friends with your targeted celeb. If you're compelling and real, getting them to do you a minor favor would be just that—a minor favor.

It's very important to validate whomever you're speaking to by knowing their name, and not just their title. In any bookstore there are agent directories. Thanks to the Internet, all of this information is readily available online as well. Because of the unfortunately named WhoRepresents.com (aka WhorePresents.com), IMDb.com, and IBDB.com, you can easily find everyone who a given star has ever worked with.

The Hollywood Creative Directory has not only agency listings, but also film production credits, production companies, and listings where you can see people's titles. If you look up Columbia Pictures, you can then drill into what actors have deals at Columbia Pictures, who's the director of development, who's the production coordinator—and you can kind of aim your contact request at the right level. If somebody's represented by the real-life equivalent of Ari Gold (i.e., the Ari Emanuels of this world), you're never going to get the agent on the line. But look to see if they have a production deal somewhere. Look at who their director of creative development is; that's probably somebody who's a little more eager to be nice. Having contact with celebrities seems more exciting than it really is. Being able to make that connection for you might be one of the few chances that contact will have to seem like a big shot.

Let's suppose you have a name but you can't get their exact phone number. In that case, my favorite thing to do is to use the prefix and dial randomly. Most companies have a bunch of phone numbers formatted something like "555-9xxx." Try dialing a random sequence, like 555-9865. "John Geiger speaking," they'll say.

"Oh, I'm sorry. I was trying to get Leslie."

"Leslie who?"

"Leslie Langford. What extension did I dial?"

continued

"She's at extension 3499." Then they'll transfer you, but even if they won't, they'll have given you the extension. But again: Make sure you have something specific and legitimate to ask Leslie. Respect the system and her role in it.

13.
The Great Escape

Eric Stepansky was a frequent guest at the hotel. He owned a commercial lighting company and was wealthier than God. He also happened to be a very nice guy who treated Abbie and me like we were his pet charity. "Is it supposed to rain tomorrow?" he asked me one day, walking by the desk on his way out.

"Let me look," I said, flipping open the paper. "No, it looks like it's going to be good tomorrow."

"Thanks," he said, passing me a hundred-dollar bill.

Whenever he made some dinner reservation with Abbie in the morning, he would give her a hundred-dollar tip. By the time I got there, she'd have a "confirmed" card for him—and when he came by to pick up that confirmation from me, he's give me a hundred dollars as well.

Eric's company eventually bought a corporate apartment, and he stopped staying as a guest at the hotel. But he would still pop in every so often. If he wanted a reservation at a place like Daniel or if he wanted to see a hot show on Broadway, he would simply ask us— and we always took care of it immediately.

"I don't want to come here every time to give you money," he finally told Abbie. "Can I just give you a check once a month, and then I know that you're going to take care of me?"

"What do you want to do?" she asked me when I came in to work. "Should we do it?"

One of the things I admired most about Abbie was how hard she worked to provide for her son Ali. She scrimped and saved to pay for his tuition to the ultra-elite Allen-Stevenson School. It was the kind of place where his classmates were the sons of Goldman Sachs chairmen—while she was making do in a one-bedroom apartment. I knew that every little bit of money helped.

"Well, *yeah*," I said to her. "Why shouldn't we take Eric's money? Who cares that he's not at the hotel? We're still providing him a service."

"How are we going to deal with him on tickets?" she asked. "We can't put it to the room. There isn't a room."

"Maybe we could get a credit card machine ourselves," I said. "Or PayPal. I'm sure we can figure something out."

"Fine. Let's just charge him two hundred dollars a month," she said. "We'll split it."

A couple of weeks later another of our favorite patrons was staying at the hotel. Kevin was a very frequent, very rich guest. He loved Abbie and me because we always covered for him when he brought his mistresses by the hotel. One week it would a girlfriend, and the next the wife; but we always acted as if we hadn't seen him in forever.

"You know I only stay at InterContinental hotels," Kevin told me, "but I don't have the same relationship with the concierge in London as I do with you and Abbie. You and Abbie are the best. The next time I'm there, can I just call you and have you take care of things for me?"

"Of course!" I told him.

"I'm not going to do it unless you let me give you something."

"All right," I said. "Whatever you think is fair."

"Do you share everything with Abbie?"

"Something like this, we definitely would. She's here at the desk sometimes and I'm here at the desk other times. To make sure that you're never disappointed, we can just split it. We'll make an arrangement so someone will always be around to take care of you."

"Terrific. How much should I pay you?"

I shrugged. I felt so awkward. I liked and respected Kevin; despite his libido, he otherwise was a class act who always treated us well. I didn't feel comfortable putting a price on myself with someone like that. "I don't know . . ."

"Just give me a number."

"Five hundred?"

"Perfect." He counted out five one-hundred-dollar bills, and threw me a hundred dollars extra as a tip.

After a few weeks of this, I got to talking with Abbie. "You know, we should think about just charging people. Why should we be embarrassed? We're really good at what we do. We should come up with an official fee, and maybe even start telling people proactively."

"Like who? What kind of people?"

"Like our big high rollers. There's a lot of people like Eric and Kevin. If they're not at the hotel and they live in Atlanta or whatever, we can still do stuff for them."

"Yeah, that sounds great. Why not?"

Abbie has a very broad perspective on things; she likes to see the big picture. But I have to analyze things. That night I went home and wrote up a spreadsheet of fifty of the high rollers that she and I had a relationship with. These were people who I thought we could approach and would actually be receptive to what was, effectively, a novel concept. If each of them gave us $500 a month, that would mean $25,000—cash. That wasn't even counting what they'd be booking, and the tips and commissions that would generate.

I knew right away who our first target would be. Zinovy Dimitriov was basically an attaché to hugely wealthy people, and could be a bit imposing. He handled people like Saudi princes and Russian oil czars. He would travel five-star, while his clients stayed in places like the penthouse at the Waldorf Towers. It was clear that he had a high-stakes job and there was zero tolerance for anything less than perfection.

Facing away from the guests, Abbie made the call while I intercepted anyone approaching the desk. We had such different styles; whereas I was all business, she was queen of schmoozing the client. It sounded like she was talking to her long lost best friend rather than making a pitch. Finally, I heard her tell Zinovy about what we were looking to do.

When she got off the phone with him, her face said it all. "He's completely into it," she told me. "He needs a private boat for his client to go back and forth between Venice and Nice for ten days. He asked if we could gather the information for him by tomorrow."

Abbie was picturing herself on the boat with the clients. I started thinking about where in the world (literally!) we'd begin looking for this boat and how many cabins he wanted. *What size crew did we need? Did they want a chef? What about a dock? What if there were no docks available in Nice? How do we arrange payment for the boat? Who are the clients, anyway? Are they Russian mafia, doing a drug deal?* I called Zinovy back and gathered the info. Their idea of a "private boat" was more like a small cruise ship.

Abbie and I got to work, and the task was as difficult as I had anticipated. The Internet wasn't a worldwide source yet; it was still at the point where people would tell you to put "www" when they gave you the URL. We looked online for hours. Then we talked to yacht dealers, until we realized that they were all representing the same five or six boats. We knew we could do better (read: make more of a commission) if we could get directly to the owners' primary representatives. It got to the point where Abbie was calling fishing villages overseas, speaking to them in Italian and asking if they knew anyone who knew anyone that dealt with yacht owners directly. The best we could come up with were these miniature cruise ships that ran about $300,000 a week. If we hadn't gone directly to the owner's rep, it would have been *$330,000*! We knew Zinovy would never go for that; it was just ridiculous, even with the "reduced" price. But we couldn't find anything else, no matter how resourceful we tried to be.

Wanting to show him *something*, we printed up the pictures of the crazy mini–cruise ships and left them for Zinovy to look at. "Maybe I didn't understand exactly what you wanted," I said, sliding the pics across the desk to him, "I'm sure there are less extravagant options if we go with something smaller."

He looked them over briefly. "Perfect," he told me. "See if this one is available."

"Oh yeah," I said. "Of course. I was going to say that one. That was my favorite."

"How are we going to work the commission?" he asked me.

It dawned on me that Zinovy's position was similar to that of a concierge on some level. My commissions usually came from theater tickets. His commissions came from $300,000 private yacht charters.

Dare I go there? It seemed safe enough. "Should we just split everything down the middle?" I asked him.

"That's fine," he agreed.

Now I was empowered. "It sleeps twelve," I explained, "and there's additional room for the crew of ten. The chef will send sample menus. The three hundred thousand includes fuel and slip fees. We got it directly from the owner's rep so it's about thirty thousand less than what the others were asking. Are we going with *that* price?" I said, wondering if he himself was going to upcharge his clients.

"That works," Zinovy agreed.

That $15,000 wasn't just a huge bonus: it was the gasoline on a fire. Now I really thought that we had an actual business going. The two of us needed a name for ourselves, instead of just being Abbie and Michael from the InterContinental Hotel.

We both agreed that we needed to aim for something that sounded very distinguished, like "Golden Keys International," "International VIP Services," or "Concierge International VIP." But names like that were also very affected, and didn't really sit well with me. They were cheesy and sounded like an escort service.

I started playing around with our respective initials. "ABMF Enterprises"? Too generic. "F-BAM!" was just absurd. Then I thought of things like "Michaelcierge"—and then I realized these were all awful as well.

"Well, you know people like *us,*" I reminded Abbie. "Why are we trying to mask ourselves? This isn't going to be some big corporation. This is more like our own lemonade stand. Why don't we just say 'Abbie and Michael, at your service'?" Then I played with our middle names, but Helene Patrick made no sense. But "Abigail Michaels" . . . ?

It was a little bit of a cheat—"Abbie" wasn't technically short for "Abigail"; Abbie was actually her full name. But Abigail Michaels sounds like a very well-heeled society matron. She's somebody that might have gone to school in the U.K. or at the Sorbonne, speaks nine languages, and lives on Park Avenue. Abbie liked it because her name was first. I liked it because it sounded anonymous enough to get away with it at the hotel; we weren't exactly prepared to quit our jobs yet.

When I'd worked in Dolores's office, I really liked that she brought a seriousness to the entertainment industry. She didn't have some trendy or crazy font for her letterhead; it looked like it came out of a legal office. I just ripped off her idea, and wrote out our new name across the page, manually spacing it out for effect in Garamond:

A B I G A I L   M I C H A E L S

We next got a new phone number and forwarded all our business calls to the hotel. Since the last of our four phone lines *never* lit up at the concierge desk, that was the number we forwarded to. When it rang we knew that it must be an Abigail Michaels client calling.

The thing was, Abbie had been at the hotel for seventeen years. The hotel was her career. I was a different story. After seven years, I was addicted to the cash but still wondering what the hell I was do-ing with a goddamn name tag on. I started to impress upon Abbie that we needed to get the hell out—and that this was our own golden key, so to speak. I was so taken with the light at the end of the tunnel that a few days later I almost snapped.

Abbie hung up the phone, glowing. "Do you know who I just made a reservation for?" she said. "The head of White & Case. Their kid goes to school with Ale."

All these fancy parents would call Abbie at work and ask her to get them into restaurants. It drove me crazy. They had entire *staffs* at their disposal. If these people were so important, they should have been able to get their own reservations. It seemed disrespectful to treat her like she was their assistant when their children were peers at school. "Why are you doing it for free for him, and for all these other parents?" I asked her. "He's a major lawyer. Do you think you can go to him for free legal advice? If you slipped and fell in the lobby of the hotel, would he pro bono your representation? All those people who call here from the school, you should just stop. No more professional courtesy. That's a goldmine of potential clients. Do you think any of them wouldn't be able to afford us, anyway? Five hundred dollars a month? That's nothing to them."

She nodded, but I could tell that she wasn't totally convinced so I didn't mention it again for a while. To my surprise, it was Abbie who brought it up a few weeks later. "Okay," she said. "I got the nerve up and spoke to someone last night at a parent-teacher event. I think this is the perfect family. They own a national housewares chain, and the guy I spoke with manages Chloë Sevigny. His name is Alan Chiles."

It was all actually starting to happen. We made an appointment with the family's personal financial advisers, a firm by the name of Ferro Capital. My ambition wasn't simply to get $500 per month for taking care of Alan. I wanted to go to Ferro and ask for $5,000 a month—for *all* their clients. If they had five hundred clients, that boiled down to only ten dollars per client. That was nothing.

Abbie and I decided on the services we would be offering and I put together a PowerPoint presentation for our big meeting. I was expecting to come into a huge, luxe office building. Instead, when Abbie and I arrived at Ferro, it looked like we were paying a visit to a State Farm. The place was completely vanilla, down to the generic industrial carpet.

The head of Ferro, Ken Nolan, took us into his office and proceeded to tell us a little about the company and who they represented. "We represent the Chiles family," he told us.

That was it. He couldn't tell us a lot about the company because there wasn't a lot *to* tell. Obviously Ferro represented a huge amount of wealth, enough that they could call themselves Ferro Capital. But it was basically four sets of in-laws with four bank accounts. My fantasy of servicing five hundred clients went out the window.

A couple of days after the presentation, Ken phoned to let us know that they were interested. "But we can only pay nine hundred and fifty dollars a month," he told us, "and we would like to pay it quarterly."

"That's fine," Abbie and I said in unison.

"Terrific. Bill us in three months. I'm assuming you have some sort of standard agreement form?"

"Absolutely," I said. "I'll get that right over to you."

The fact that they wouldn't even be paying us in advance should have been my first clue. The wind might have been let out of my sails, but at least we got an account. I wrote up a contract in my best legalese—"heretofore"; "the party of the first part"; "we agree whereby"—and sent it over to them.

The ink wasn't dry before Alan Chiles started to call us. "So *you're* the new assistant!" he told me.

It was exactly the kind of thing that I despised about working at the hotel, and what I was attempting to get away from. I wanted to be a wheeler-dealer, not the guy who has to come to attention when fancy people snap their fingers. But from that point on, that's who I was for Alan. As soon as *Bon Appétit* and/or *New York* hit the newsstand, Alan was on the phone wanting the latest hot restaurant. "I heard Fiamma was good," he'd say, as if he had been in a conversation—and not reading about it in a periodical like all the other amateur foodies in the city. "I want to go there *tonight*."

"I'll see what I can do."

"Your letter says that you provide dinner reservations," he reminded me. "So where are they?"

Every request that he had—and it was almost always restaurants, restaurants, and restaurants—was the most impossible reservation to get. Riding high on Abbie's depiction of him, I often threw out that he was Chloë Sevigny's manager. I had to beg, borrow, and bribe to make sure that he got what he wanted. I was learning the difference between charging for a service and hoping to get a tip for it. I couldn't really tell him I had failed.

With Alan, no news was good news—a concept I hate. There were never any sign of gratitude; not even a five-dollar gift card for his housewares store or some rank scented candle that they couldn't sell. But then Alan did start calling me with the wonderful icebreaker of "I have some feedback for you." He took it upon himself to start giving me feedback so that I'd be better trained.

"Is everything all right?" I said.

"When I got to the restaurant, you told me that it was at eight thirty and they had eight fifteen—but I'm not gonna bother you about that. They sat me at a table, and it wasn't the best table—*just so you know.*" He was trying to be my buddy in some quasi-bromantic way, but it felt like he was scratching a chalkboard. Always, the underlying message was that I would never be allowed to step foot in these places, so he was scoping out the place for me. It was very noblesse oblige of him.

After about a month, Alan appeared at the hotel and introduced himself to me. He had the exact vibe of Jason Alexander—or to be more exact, Jason Alexander as George on *Seinfeld*. He was just this little man, physically and spiritually, and a total nebbish. Even though we were about the same height, I could tell that *his* size was an issue for him—and he was compensating for it in the worst way. It was the obese, homely girl who constantly mentions that she's "done some modeling."

Now my brain began to play a montage. I did a mental recap of all the great restaurants that I had gotten him into, telling them how impressive he was and singing his praises. I felt like I needed to go back and apologize—and I worried how I was going to continue with this.

"*You're* Chloë Sevigny's manager?" I eventually asked him.

"Her business manager," he told me. "Well, technically, I'm her accountant."

He was wielding his way through the New York social hierarchy like a killer, and I was the one who'd been sharpening his knives. He lived for being seated next to Heidi Klum at the Zac Posen show at Fashion Week—but fashion wasn't his craft. It was just a matter of place-dropping being the new name-dropping.

One of the places Alan asked me to get him a table at was Fred's, a really hot lunch spot. Fred's is on the top floor of Barneys, where it's sort of camouflaged. It's the kind of place where you see the corporate who's who of New York—and where they don't normally take reservations from anyone.

Unless, of course, you're a concierge who has the hostess's number.

Alan wanted to eat lunch there at 1:15, so I called her to 12:15 to let her know that he "was on his way." By the time he got there, his name would be at the top of the list. I specifically told him to approach her away from the hostess stand, because he was effectively cutting the line and needed to be subtle. He didn't *need* to be happy that it all worked out and that he had a table waiting while the other shmoes were standing around—but it *would* have been nice.

At 1:20, the phone rang. "Hi, Michael," he said. "It's Alan. I'm here at Fred's, and I'm really not happy."

"What's the matter?"

"They have me at the crappiest table. I can't sit here. You've got to move me."

"Okay . . . Where do you want to be moved to? Where are you sitting now?"

I tried to visualize Fred's layout in my mind. He must not have been at what he considered a "power table." I tried to figure out where this elusive location was supposed to be. For normal people, *there's no such thing.* But people like Alan *imagine* that there's a table, so I had to start thinking the way he did. *What would Alan Chiles do?* I asked myself.

Annoyed that I was oblivious to table-politicking, he explained the situation himself. "If you walk into the restaurant, the bar is to the left and there are a couple of tables up against it. One of those tables is empty. I want to be at *that* table."

What could I say? *Just ask the manager, Alan?* I called Fred's back on my little secret number; from all the background noise I could tell that they were as busy as usual. "I'm so sorry," I told them. "Alan Chiles is really not comfortable where he's sitting, and he would feel much better at the empty table by the bar. Would that be okay? Are you holding that for someone? Because if not, he really wants to be there." I couldn't denigrate Alan, because then Fred's would be wondering why I was sending them this pain-in-the-ass guest in the first place.

"Yeah," the hostess said, "let me see what I can do."

To make sure the best possible service was provided, I called Alan back. "She's going to come over to your table and she's going to move you," I let him know.

The consequence of this was so obvious that I am amazed I didn't see it coming: I created a monster that put Frankenstein to shame. "Where should I sit?" Alan always asked me when I got him a reservation.

Even if they sat him exactly at what I told him was the "correct" table, he would still call me and have them move him. It was a power thing, I guess. Finally, one of my contacts simply refused and I had to call Alan back and let him know that he would be staying put.

"Well," he huffed, "don't they know who I am?"

No, Alan, they don't—which is how I got you the reservation in the first place.

BEING SEEN

For restaurant seating, the generally accepted rule of thumb is this: In trendy places you want to sit in the back, and in old establishment places you want to sit in the front. The whole psychology boils down to the fact that with trendy places, it's all about hype. What makes them explode is word that Fergie was seen there making out with her boyfriend. But if they ever really were there, or if they really frequent it, or if it was just a one-time appearance (possibly compensated), is a whole other question.

What many of the trendy places have now is a sequestered dining room. It kind of replicates the VIP sections of nightclubs. But with restaurants, when you get seated in there it doesn't really make a difference. You might feel as though you're in the right place, but it's not as if there's some secret menu.

My personal take, as far as entertainment value goes, is that you don't want to sit back there. That back room is a place where you can cut the tension with a knife. If there *are* famous people in attendance, everyone else is just nervous. They feel like they've scored because they're sitting next to Jessica Simpson and you can feel that awkward energy. There's such an effort put into acting nonchalant that it's like a group of hunters terrified of spooking the deer.

If you're in the front, on the other hand, you see the whole parade. You see whatever controversies there are in the front, with all the customers complaining that their names are not on the list. You can legitimately ogle at people when they're coming in or when they're hanging out at the hostess station or at the bar. The only thing the back room does is allow you to tell people that you went in the back room. Is Jessica Simpson's conversation really going to be that entertaining? Are you even going to be able to hear her? I'd rather be in a room where it's a little bit louder, where the celebrities have to speak up.

With the brown-derby, established places, you want to sit in the front, as well. The vibe in those types of restaurants is very

continued

communal. If you walk into Nobu or BLT on any given night, you'll see a Barry Diller or a Ron Perelman. These places might deny you a table, but it's not because they're hoping Britney Spears is coming so they're holding them all until she calls. Instead, it's a virtual who's who. If you go to the Regency for breakfast, for example, every media mogul is in there. Everyone in publishing goes to Michael's for lunch; there's even a website dedicated to who was sitting at which table on any given day. Their average-at-best cuisine is a running joke in the industry, but it's still where they end up going. If you sit at a front table, you can see everyone go by and you can greet them—even if you don't know them personally. It's the same strategy politicians have when they stand outside stadiums or subway stations. Everybody has to walk past you, and that makes for infinite opportunities to break the ice.

There's also the matter of knowing where to go to begin with. When a client calls me for recommendations in a city I am unfamiliar with, I do my homework. I look through *Vanity Fair* and *Town & Country,* or any of the niche media publications like *Gotham, Capitol File,* or *Ocean Drive.* If there's a fancy charity event pictured, wherever it's being held is guaranteed to be a cool place to be seen in.

This approach is way better than scene blogs or sites like Yelp. Once the bloggers show up, you know the party's over. Despite its origins, blogging has become completely mainstream—to the point where big conglomerates can afford to pay people to blog all day about how great their places are. I'd rather look for an article that shows Nicole Kidman having Stumptown coffee after dining at the Breslin. That tells me that it's the place to go to be seen, if that's your thing. It might not be *good,* but it is getting the right traction.

Celebrities themselves don't need to know the right places because they *make* the right places. Nine times out of ten, a hotspot will have some sort of celebrity involvement. Dolores's son, for example, was a record executive. He also loves to DJ, so he DJs at the Rose Bar. Because he's who he is, all the cool people show up. Then,
continued

when those people show up, the paparazzi cover it. Then it's in *In-Style* magazine and it's on *Entertainment Tonight*. Suddenly, the place is on its way to being made.

The scene formula is much more predictable because there are certain people whose recipes are almost certain to be a success, like Rande Gerber, Keith McNally, or Graydon Carter. Any club launched by Noah Tepperberg or Ivan Kane is going to be A-list because of the people they know. It's only natural. They know many celebrities, so it's only fitting that the celebrities tend to fraternize their places.

14.
Feet of Clefs

Ferro Capital technically had one other employee, and Jerry Chu was *technically* the financial manager for Alan and his family. But Jerry came across as so browbeaten and humiliated that she was really reduced to the status of a receptionist. She had been the one taking care of Alan until now, and she had been the one reverently insisted that Alan "don't like to just sit anywhere." She had also been the one, I was sure, who Alan used to call with "feedback" about the places he had eaten the night before.

Because Abbie and I were the ones who dealt with Alan now, Jerry began to appreciate us more and more. "You guys should do this for my friend's new apartment building," she told us. "I'm going to introduce you."

I got the call and gave the man my spiel.

"Hold on," he quickly said. "How do you operate? You still work at the hotel?"

"We have a whole system in place," I explained. "It's not just the two of us, and if it ever got too busy we would pull in one of our friends from another hotel. That would never be a problem. We have resources. There's an entire concierge community that we can tap into."

"There is?"

"Of course. Let me explain."

THE CONCIERGE COMMUNITY

There's an array of concierge associations, especially in the big concierge cities like New York, San Francisco, and Chicago. It's a lot like in high school, where you have the cool kids and the not-so-cool kids. Except, in this case, none of them are the cool kids. They're the smart kids, and smart is *very* cool as a concierge.

But the smart kids have organized and inflated their coolness so they think that they run the world. Like so much else with concierges, a lot of it is smoke and mirrors—and it's often a blurry line between delusion and reality. It's just like with Christmas: No one claims that a present comes from a workshop run by elves. But no one says that they picked it up at JCPenney's warehouse sale, either. The mystique itself is part of the gift, and that air of mystery is what the concierge community thrives on.

Concierge events bolster this sense of a magical community. They're held at establishments like Cipriani, the Rainbow Room, and the Astor Ballroom the day after the place hosted visiting heads of state. There aren't many professions that those venues open their doors to for free. It goes with the whole idea that concierges have the keys and, therefore, no doors can be locked to us.

The funny thing is that most of the concierges act disinterested or even disdainful of how cool that is. They claim—or actually even believe—that they're going to send *hundreds* of people to book the room in return for the favor. Please!

The events are sponsored by distilleries or distributors; by Bloomingdale's and art galleries; by theater companies and Madison Square Garden. The mix of businesses runs the gamut, because everybody wants our referrals. It's like a trade show, and the swag bags are amazing. I've been to very fancy society events and the concierge giveaways are usually way better. They'll also try tricks to
continued

get us into their places. You won't just get a Loro Piana sweater at the event—but you will if you take the enclosed card, make an appointment, and go to the store. Bergdorf's or Bendel's will have a raffle for a $5,000 shopping spree—but in order to register you have to go there, and you have to be a concierge.

The sponsors think we're going to open the door and flood them with business. Sometimes we do—but it's rarely equivalent to the extent that they've solicited to us. Yet there's a whole group of concierges who get lost in the grandeur and don't keep it in check. They really do believe that they are an absolutely vital channel to which these places should market. Many concierges fancy themselves curators, critics, and arbiters of the finer things. Me, I feel a bit guilty about the whole thing. I try to reciprocate to the vendors as best I can. Exposure to the concierge community can't hurt, and it's probably a lot more cost-effective than other forms of advertising. The trick is to get the concierges to understand that their referrals are more valuable than their critiques. Even if something doesn't suit my taste, one of my clients will like it. I definitely keep that in mind every time I'm comped.

The biggest and most prestigious concierge organization is the Clefs d'Or (pronounced *clay door*), which started at the turn of the century in France. At the very upper echelon of society, people needed connections. One concierge would call another concierge to call another, and so a loose circle was created. It very much became a secret handshake kind of society. It reached its peak during the '80s and '90s, when concierge culture came into the forefront and it was hip to be grand and international.

You had to speak three languages to join—they *would* test your fluency—and they put you through a rigorous exam of knowing your city. It would be trivia like, "If you're in Geneva, when is the opera season in Vienna?" You would have to get all sorts of different letters of recommendations. You'd have to go before a board, write an essay, and plead your case. It attracted a pretty amazing bunch of people.

continued

These days, the members of the Clefs d'Or are mostly in their fifties. They almost look like they're from another time, which in a way they are. They wear their tiny little glasses at the tips of their noses. The women—the few of them that there are—are dripping in jewelry, with their hair all sprayed and done. Everything is formal and just so, which can be read as stuffy but is also really taking pride in one's work.

What's impressive about them is that being a concierge is truly their vocation, and something that they take pride in. In Europe especially, concierging is still very much a mark of elegance, and you *really* have to know your stuff.

One time at the hotel, Abbie was *ooh*ing and *aah*ing over a guest's gold ring. Me, I would use jewelry to size up how much I could overcharge someone for things. But Abbie was taken by the lady's semiprecious stone. "Here you go," the woman said, handing it to her. "It's yours!"

"I can't take that!" Abbie said.

"No, darling. Take it, take it. It's yours. Love it, and wear it in good health."

All the Clefs d'Or concierges have stories like that. It'll be cuff links from Winston Churchill's niece or a necktie from Brooke Astor. Once I brought Whoopi Goldberg to a Clefs d'Or congress, and a concierge came running up to her. He had gotten her a pack of Marlboro Reds many years prior, and she gave him a lighter to hold in case she needed a light. She left his hotel and never picked up the lighter—and he wanted her to know that he still had it, because it wasn't his to throw out.

Nowadays, all you need to join the Clefs d'Or is $250 and the ability to speak one language. The city quiz is something as simple as naming six restaurants in your town that have a Zagat's rating of 25 or higher. Little by little, the magic is fading away.

It doesn't help things at all when you have people with absolutely no reverence or even simple appreciation for the profession. They

continued

seek the prestige and they're at every event. Hell, they're at the opening of an envelope. Their greed is up-front and explicit; it's the same snapping of the fingers and "Get me . . . !" attitude that I abhorred at the hotel. Oftentimes restaurants will have concierge meals in which the chef prepares a special preset menu to show off the food at its best. These "newcies" (nouveau concierges) inevitably want to order off the standard menu. If the chef is offering a veal chop for us, they'll ask for the veal shank. *If* they vet you, and *if* they approve, they will supposedly unleash the door to their army of golden customers.

They also never, ever tip. When I get a free meal, I plan on spending at least half of what it would have otherwise cost me. The Four Seasons always invites us for dinner, which is around $150 per person. You don't go in there, have a $300 dinner, and leave without taking care of somebody. A tourist might not know any better— but it is a concierge's *job* to know the system, and to respect it.

On the flip side of that, there are businesses who aggressively market to the concierges and give everything away. They explicitly let us know that we can come in for free any time we want. It's like when you work at a radio station and you end up drowning in CDs. If I get one more spa gift certificate for a free manicure, my fingers might just fall off.

Some of these concierge events are held in nontraditional spaces as well. I once went to an event at Bloomingdale's, which they had for us one evening after regular store hours. Already it was kind of cool being in that huge landmark establishment when it was closed to everyone else. Even though I knew I was welcome, it still felt like we were trespassing. I was very careful of their stuff—but there was still the temptation to just run and knock the clothes off the racks.

They sent us on a scavenger hunt, which was a very clever way to get us to know all of the different components of Bloomingdale's: the personal shopping, which is called At Your Service; the fur salon; the wedding gowns. I didn't know about those things. I

continued

didn't know that they had a visitor center, where anybody with a foreign passport and a hotel key gets 15 percent off for the whole day.

After the scavenger hunt they brought in a little riser and had a private fashion show for us. They were treating us as though we knew all about fashion, even though concierges don't really deal with it. We're just service people. But, at the same time, waiters and personal assistants don't get private fashion shows at Bloomingdale's.

The woman from Bloomie's came out, and she addressed us as though we were a group of experts. She spoke to us as though we truly were tastemakers and influencers. I felt like an imposter, but all my colleagues seemed to own that cloak of importance. I was so afraid of being the type of concierge who's pretentious that maybe I undervalued the influence that we do have. I always do try my best to make my recommendations person-appropriate. I didn't want to be like my colleague who sent the German guests to see *The Producers*. If I wasn't making good recommendations, I would be out of work.

"I'm going to put you in touch with Solomon," the guy told me. "He owns the building and will probably be receptive."

Immediately, I called Solomon up and gave him the same pitch.

"Can you meet me in an hour?" he asked, in his really thick Middle Eastern accent.

"Sure!" I told him.

I called Abbie. We frantically got ready and went to meet Solomon. He had a beautiful cashmere trench coat, and out front he had a black Mercedes with a driver. It was totally that real-estate, Donald Trump vibe. He took us inside and gave us the tour, showing us all the amenities that the building had to offer. It was one of the first times I had been in a recently completed building like that, and it really did have that same smell as a new car. It was gorgeous, with every possible fancy convenience.

"Come!" he said. "I want to talk about business!" He took us next door to a little Turkish kabob place. I didn't really understand what we were doing, but I wasn't about to argue with the man.

"Let me tell you about what services we provide," I began.

"Can you help people with dry cleaning?" he interrupted.

"Of course," I told him.

"We can get dinner reservations and theater tickets," Abbie told him. "If they have guests coming into town, we can book the hotels and tours."

"The people want their dry cleaning," he reiterated.

We finished our food, and went back to the building. Solomon took us around by the elevator, where there was a Dutch door. He opened both halves and pointed to the room behind it, all eight-by-four feet of it. It was unfinished, and had a folding table in it. It was not really a room; it was a supply closet.

"This is your office," Solomon said. "Don't disappoint me." He was acting like he was giving us a break—but it sure wasn't *feeling* like a break. Even Hannibal Lecter eventually got a window.

"Let's explore this," I said. "We'll see what we can do."

"Today is Friday," he answered. "When can you start?"

"We'll have to get back to you," Abbie said. "And we're going to have to run some numbers and make sure."

"If you can start Monday, yes. If not, forget it."

Monday it is! Monday, just like we said!

As soon as we left, Abbie and I discussed the logistics. "We have to put our mark on that room," I said. "We just have to fluff it up with some paint and a few sleek accessories. We'll dress it up." We'd been given a beautiful building—and been thrown into the toilet. The least we could do was make the water sparkle.

We went to IKEA and worked all weekend putting everything together. I didn't get a chance to sleep before our debut. As Abbie and I prepared to open for business, we could hear the tenants gathering outside. It was our first day, and we were excited. I opened the top half of our Mr. Ed door, and saw that there were four people standing there already.

"Hi!" I said. "Can I help you with something?"

"Is this where I'm supposed to leave my clothes?" the woman grunted.

"Yes!" Our experience with dry cleaning was from the hotel. Guests would put their dirty clothes in a bag, and attach a slip with their room number. The dry cleaner would pick it up and bring it back, and everything was fine. As far as I was concerned, it might as well have been handled by elves.

I looked at the women with an armful of clothes, and saw that the other three tenants had clothes for us as well. I looked around the room for a second, knowing that we didn't think to have bags prepared for this. Abbie pulled out some garbage bags, and we put the clothes into them. "Can I get your apartment number?" she asked the woman.

"Twenty-four twelve."

I wrote down the apartment number and put it in the bag. "So," I asked her, "do you have dinner plans for the evening?"

She looked at me like I was asking her out or something. "Yes . . ."

"Well, we can provide that service for you in the future." By the time it was nine o'clock, over thirty people came around with their clothes—but we gave our sales pitch to every one of them. We even got a few nice comments about our fancy little space. Abbie and I realized that people very much loved the concept, but nobody had heard about something like this before.

The more people thought about it, the more they saw how useful it was. "So you can also book a car to the airport for me?" they asked. "Or do personal shopping?"

Because of how receptive everyone was being, we were feeling really great. Then, at five o'clock, the dry cleaning truck came back with two hundred pieces of clothing. To them, it was just one pickup location so they'd mixed everything together—and Abbie and I tried desperately to remember who "2412" was and what he or she had brought. Like a game of Memory, we tried to match the outfits with the faces. We were mortified, but we still laughed at how farcical it was. Fortunately we charmed our way out of any problems and spoke to the dry cleaner. Before the end of the week, we had a whole system down with duplicate tickets and everything.

Instantly, business started to pick up. Within a month we started to make around $1,000 per week, which quickly grew to $2,000 and to $3,000 and to $5,000. Rather than spend all this time trying to get corporate accounts, we realized that we should just go get twenty more buildings. But the only way we could manage that is if we hired staff, and I was there full time.

Leaving the hotel was not that difficult of a decision. They'd changed management a couple of weeks before, so I didn't feel embarrassed giving them short notice. There was kind of a whole new regime that I wasn't really invested in—and I wasn't going to invest. There were no stakes anymore. What should have been a ceremonial moment felt kind of melancholy. I was literally handing back the keys after years at the desk. The movie was ending with me walking off into the sunset and everything looking good.

But the people who formed my experience at the hotel weren't there anymore. Ian, who had first suggested that I become concierge, was long gone. Glen, the general manager/barfly, had left—as had Rupert the engineer. The institutions that had made the hotel quirky and crazy and interesting to me weren't there anymore. There was nobody to wave me off, wishing me good luck and letting me know that they were proud.

I fantasized that all of the bad guests would be staying at the hotel my last week, the people who were demanding in a mean way and those who were downright unruly. It was going to be my time to say, "You know what? I've given you such amazing service, and you're despicable. You don't even *know* what bad service is, but now you're going to. You're never going to have anybody jump through hoops like me. And, *plus,* you really are evil, and you make people unhappy, and I'm smart and strong. You don't bother *me,* but I want you to know that you're going to have the worst karma because you *do* bother people."

I was working the night shift, and I was working it alone. Everything went off without a hitch. Nobody needed to fill a bathtub with chocolate. Nobody needed confidential VD treatment. In a way it was anticlimactic because I was just waiting for one last bit of drama. Every reservation was attainable, and every ticket was the best. When I called hot restaurants, they told me to send the guests right over. I almost wanted to ask them if they were sure.

It happened to be a good money week, too. I did all my paid-outs with all the singles and five-dollar bills. I was struck one last time by the smell of money, how my hands smelled of it after counting so much cash. I locked our drawer, and I made the envelopes for everybody. I walked into the manager's office and put the key in their desk.

I went to the locker room and I took my work suit off. I wadded it up in a ball and I threw it in the laundry *without* my bag; it didn't need to come back to me anymore. I yanked my name tag off and threw it away. I walked through the lobby in my street clothes and right out the front door. The entrance in the back was for hotel employees.

There were no fireworks going on. "Pomp and Circumstance" didn't suddenly play from the speakers. I just went home and woke up bright and early the next day, ready to provide service for the people who lived in our new building.

HOW TO TELL A SERVICE NATURAL FROM A SERVICE NIGHTMARE

There are two major kinds of people who are not good at service. The first is blatantly obvious and doesn't require much insight to spot. They're disengaged and they don't seem to have any kind of connection to the fact that they're in a position to bring professionalism and spirit to their job. You can see it from a mile away; they will treat you as an intrusion when you approach. Just visit any post office.

But someone who is enthusiastic and engaged is easily mistaken for a service natural. I once stayed at a hotel and the person who checked me in was very outgoing and bubbly—but everything with the encounter was wrong because it became about her. "I'm going put you in *this* room," she told me, "because I just love this room." It became uncomfortable because I didn't really care. She didn't ask me if I loved the room or what I was looking for in a room. What people in service sometimes don't understand is that it's really all about the person getting served.

These service nightmares can be very engaging—for a minute. At first you think that it's great. But they're just trying to show off, rather than actually working to do things for you. They'll tell you all about the great restaurant and how you'll be treated and what the experience will be like. But they want validation from you more than they want to serve you. They're living for that moment when they can watch your face get all excited—and then, they're pretty much done. What happens is that they overpromise, underdeliver, and take up way too much time and attention. They don't understand that the preview isn't as important as the actual movie.

continued

Service naturals are easy to overlook because they might not be the most gregarious, smiley, bubbly people—but neither is a really great stockbroker. I generally try to look for people who are not engaging, but who look focused. They're not *un*friendly. I was never unfriendly at my job, but I was much more focused on what people really wanted than on chitchat about how they were doing this fine spring morning.

We're instinctively drawn to people who are cute, young, and bubbly. Yet those people are usually just passing through the service world. They often don't have real power or anything invested. I always look for the oldest, least glamorous person. They might not be nice, but they rule the roost—and they don't usually get any validation, so you'll get a lot more mileage.

Here's an easy way to tell the difference: Per Se is a quiet restaurant, and Applebee's is loud. When I ate at Per Se, they weren't really that receptive to when I tried to be chummy and fun—but they weren't cold, either. "That's very funny," they said, "but how's your meal?" Meanwhile, if you went to Applebee's, you'd have a very different experience. The service is boisterous. They tell you where they're from. Everything about it is *screaming* about what a fun place it is to be. Where would you like me to make your reservation?

15.
Bands of Gold

Everything Abbie and I did was operating under the hotel mentality. But when we reached out to our hotel connections for new hires, we weren't looked upon too kindly. We were wild cards. Whether it was jealousy or whether they were upholding the credo of conciergedom, people were expecting us to come crawling back to the hotel fold. They didn't want us in the associations; they didn't want us accredited by Clefs d'Or. Concierge meant hotel, period.

We managed to find a girl named Missy who had worked at a hotel spa. She was an itsy-bitsy girl with a little chipmunk voice who reminded me of an Olympic gymnast. Missy was somewhat nice, but somewhat uncooperative as well.

I was in the "office" with her one day when a tenant came down with some dry cleaning. "Here," Missy said, handing him a bag. "Can you put your clothes in there for me?"

The man looked at her sideways, but did as she asked and didn't say anything.

I waited until he left. "What was that?" I asked her. "That's not very customer service–focused. You can just take his clothes and bag them yourself."

"I can't touch his gross clothing," she said. "That's disgusting!"

"Missy, these are fancy people. It's not like he was handing you his dirty underwear. Those were dress shirts and a Canali suit."

"Well," she said, crossing her arms, "I'm not comfortable doing that. Would it be all right with you if we compromised?"

"Sure," I said. "What's the compromise?"

"I'll do it if you let me wear sanitary gloves."

"Fine. But you're paying for the gloves."

She left the company not too long after that. To be fair, it was an environment that demanded a very specific type of personality. If you didn't own our supply closet/office, it could have felt pretty repressive. There was no window, and the air got full of the Clean Crisp White Votivo candle scent. I loved my lilies, but I also changed the water every day. If I left for two or three days, the vase would stink rancidly. The whole ambience backfired because it took maintenance, and other people didn't maintain it.

We decided to try to expand our search from just the hotel world. "Let's just put it out in the *Village Voice*," I suggested, "and get some young, collegey kids." Our ad emphasized the hospitality aspect—and we got people who were really only tangentially from the hospitality field, like former employees of YMCAs in the Bronx. We booked four hours' worth of interviews at the W Union Square, and we had every conceivable type of person come through the door. It was like *American Idol*. The good ones we did get ran in the other direction when they saw our little closet workspace. We tried a couple of people, but they didn't work out because they weren't scrappy enough.

The next time around we just knew we had to keep it real. In a way, it had been just as difficult to explain what we did to a potential employee as it had been to explain it to a potential client. It was innovative and people were confused; a concierge without a hotel was like an astronaut without a spaceship. We just took all the sex appeal out of the job description in our next ad: *You take dry cleaning. You book housekeeping. You walk people's dogs.*

That's how we found Teddy. Teddy was super-effeminate, with a voice that was higher pitched than any soprano I had ever heard. He spoke faster than speed-readers go through books, to the point where you couldn't even follow him sometimes. If somebody told him that they wanted their apartment cleaned, his response was frantically long winded. "Oh, it's no problem. Is it a one-bedroom or a two-bedroom or a three-bedroom? Do you want coffee started or should we just do the bathroom and the kitchen? Would you like to go out for dinner? Because you know we also book car service for you." But he had such a spirit that I thought he was going to be *great*.

One day Teddy screwed something up with dry cleaning. But he was also smart and very industrious, so he discovered that another tenant had picked up the clothing by mistake. By tracing the receipts, he knew that Mrs. Yates had Mr. Fishbach's clothes. Unfortunately, Mrs. Yates was a miserable and confrontational person. Innocently, he called her up to get the matter straightened out. "I think I messed up," he told her, "and I think that we gave you Mr. Fishbach's cleaning."

Instead of taking the information and checking her closet, she put Teddy through the ringer. "Well, *why* do you think so? Is this how you deal with people's personal belongings? Don't you have a *system?*"

He got off the phone with her and told me the whole scenario. Shades of Lucinda Oskar flashed in my head. "Don't worry about Mrs. Yates. Let's just write a check to Mr. Fishbach and make this thing go away."

"But I feel so guilty!" he said.

I cut him off before he went on a monologue. "It's just a growing pain. These things are inevitable as we get busier and busier. Just find out exactly what Mr. Fishbach is missing and we'll pay him."

A couple of days later Teddy pulled me aside, ecstatic. "I got Mr. Fishbach's clothes back! I *knew* that Mrs. Yates had it."

"That's great! Did she finally bring it down?"

"No, I just went in and took it."

It was like time froze. "Hold on. Let me get this straight. So you went into her apartment *with* her?"

"No. You know that I've got really good relationships with a lot of people in the building, so I went to the doorman and asked for the key to Mrs. Yates's apartment because I was *convinced* that she had the cleaning. So I went into her place while she wasn't home. Sure enough, there were the clothes, still wrapped in plastic and everything."

It always took a second to process what Teddy was saying, but this took me more than a second. He had just admitted to me that he was guilty of breaking and entering in the name of Abigail Michaels. Or, at the very least, guilty of *entering*.

The sick part of me was glad that that miserable woman was busted. But the smart, business part of me realized that Teddy had just robbed her house. I wanted to go back and work at a hotel and never have to deal with people ever again. "You can't do that, Teddy," I told him calmly. "It's not worth it. This is going to be a huge problem. That was *not* the right thing to do."

Teddy had created this huge liability for us. If Mrs. Yates noticed that the clothes were gone, we'd be gone from the building as well. People like that *enjoy* causing trouble, as I had witnessed over and over at the hotel. I knew that I had to confront the situation and call her, because it wasn't going to go away.

"Hi," I told Mrs. Yates, acting calm but inwardly rattled. "You know, we have a bit of an issue. We've been looking for these misplaced items of clothing, and it seems that my employee got a little overly ambitious. He was so happy to have solved the mystery of where they ended up. His enthusiasm got the best of him, and he went to your apartment and took the clothes back. I just want to make sure you know that nothing happened. Nothing got broken and everything's okay."

She wasn't mean and she didn't yell at me. Instead, Mrs. Yates just treated me like the biggest idiotic piece of crap imaginable. "Okay, okay, okay. Let me just understand this. You're calling me to tell me that your employee broke into my apartment and went through my things?"

"No . . ."

"How is that incorrect?"

"He didn't 'go through your things.'" But the fact of the matter was, she wasn't incorrect. The fact was, we *had* robbed her that day—but since the clothing didn't belong to her in the first place, we didn't *really* rob her. We'd *un*robbed Mr. Fishbach.

Calmly—and evilly—she said, "I need to talk to somebody about this first, before I can even reply to you." That was terrifying, because I knew that her "somebody" meant that she was going to talk to a lawyer.

The next day I got a call from property management. I had told them what Teddy had done, but assured them I was going to take care of it. "Well, it's getting more complicated," they said. "She claims that she had something around $15,000 in cash and she can't find it now. She kept it stashed in her closet, like in a secret coat."

Now I needed my own "somebody," and that *definitely* meant a lawyer. It turned out that if you're in possession of property that isn't yours, you're still culpable in the eyes of the law—and she *had* signed for the clothes.

Emboldened, I called her back. "Yeah," I said, "you totally have me here. But let's just be realistic. Look at what you did. I don't know if you were doing it out of spite, or if it was oversight, or if you were feeling like you needed to teach us a lesson for making an honest mistake. Whatever the case was, you were holding on to things that didn't belong to you—and you *knew* they didn't belong to you. They had Mr. Fishbach's name on them!"

She paused, letting what I had said sink in. "Well, what are you offering?"

"If you sign an agreement that you understand that you took possession of these clothes, and that this is the remedy for the mistake, then I am prepared to compensate you."

"How much?"

"Two thousand dollars."

"Twenty-five hundred," she said.

"Done." I lost some money. But, sadly, I had to lose Teddy as well. I was starting to wonder if Abbie and I would find *anyone* who would be as much in sync with us as we were with one another.

That's when we reconnected with Daria.

Daria had been a concierge at the RIHGA since before it first opened. It was originally going to be launched by Scandinavian Airlines, but they lost money and so they sold it to the Japanese. It wasn't like me at the InterContinental, where it was a chain. They were basically the only hotel run by Royal International Hotel Group Associates.

It was a beautiful building—the only all-suite property and the tallest hotel in New York. But nobody knew who they were. They would literally accost people on the street and ask them to come take a tour of the amenities. Then they got the idea to approach the celebrity market and become a go-to place for movie junkets. They had a whole floor dedicated with the right lighting for celebrities to come and do interviews for places like *Entertainment Tonight*. Even if the celebs were living in New York at the time, they still came to the RIHGA to film their interviews.

They then branched out from junkets into the music industry. Daria jokingly called the RIHGA the Has-Been Hotel, because of all the old-time stars who stayed there when they were performing in New York. Take the Bee Gees, for example. They all had to have fully stocked bars with very specific drink requirements, which is not that uncommon or even remotely unreasonable. What I found hilarious was the fact that Barry Gibb had to have a whole huge process to make sure that his hair was perfect each and every time. The hotel staff got so sick of renting full-length mirrors for him that they just bought some and kept them in the back for when he returned. The dehumidifiers in the room were a must as well. He couldn't very well blow-dry his hair and then have it collapse before he even stepped out of the door.

Even though the RIHGA was a five-hundred-suite hotel, there were only thirteen rooms on each floor. It was a tall building, but it was still somewhat intimate. It wasn't like at the InterContinental, with our huge lavish lobby. Their lobby was *tiny*. They had four club chairs in the lobby: two on one side, two on the other—and that was *it*. It added to that semi-secluded vibe that they were going for.

HOTEL LOBBIES

If you're looking for a place to sit with your friend and chat, most people think of Starbucks, since they're so omnipresent. But in big cities, hotels are just as common. The locals don't even register that they're there, or ever think of stepping foot inside. Why would you go to a hotel if you aren't a tourist or there on business?

continued

Hotel lobbies are designed to represent the establishment at its best. The seats are much better than at a Starbucks, the ambience more appealing, and there won't be people hovering over you to finish your coffee so they can take your chair. You won't be the only one "squatting," either. Lobby lizards are a common issue with hotels, where not-so-fancy people come in off the street to read their paper and eat their Egg McMuffin. The hotels are loathe to shoo anyone out, for obvious reasons. Some hotels are even experimenting with having the lobby off the ground floor just to discourage walk-ins. But if you carry yourself with class and don't take up space, I guarantee that no one will bother you.

If you want a *really* quiet place, go to the floor where the conference rooms are. Oftentimes there's a mini-lobby there. If they're having corporate meetings at the time, they'll set up catering tables with coffee, fruit, croissants, and things like that. Go ahead and help yourself. It won't be missed.

Because they catered to a celebrity clientele, the RIHGA zealously protected their guests' privacy. Over the years Daria had to fire a few people for speaking to the press about who was staying there and what their proclivities were. She almost had a heart attack when her mom called her to let her know that she was in Page Six—for hiring a beard-braider for Billy Gibbons of ZZ Top. The hotel's PR director had planted it herself to show that the concierge at the RIHGA will "do anything" to keep their guests happy.

I always went above and beyond with my clientele, but celebrities have the nerve to request things that even the most notorious guests would never dream of. It's not so much that it's crazy or obnoxious, but that it's simply *weird.* When Prince came to stay at Daria's hotel, all the furniture had to be moved out of his suite. Everything was replaced with his own things by his people—down to the candles, the lighting, and the pillows. When they were done, it was stunning. They staged it like a movie set for him—for the one night that he stayed there. Yet even though it was an outlandish request, it's not like he was pitching a fit every five minutes over how long room service was taking him. He was particular, but he wasn't *mean*.

Kathy Griffin was another case in point. Many celebrities who tour have their luggage FedExed independently of them. There might not be enough turnaround if they're hopping from city to city on a daily basis. Daria would get Kathy's luggage, take it upstairs, unpack it, and spritz the clothes with water so all the wrinkles got out. Then she would open an attached envelope. Inside the envelope were Polaroid pictures of Kathy posing in her different outfits. Daria matched up the pieces to the picture, down to the shoes, so Kathy would know what to wear with what. When Kathy left, she always made a huge spectacle of thanking the staff for how great they were, putting on a big show of gratitude—before jokingly palming them a one-dollar bill as a tip. But she made sure that they would all get invited to her concerts, too.

Surprisingly few celebrities carried themselves as difficult individuals. There's rarely any need to, because their "people" are there to be difficult on their behalf. Despite claiming that she was still "Jenny from the block," Jennifer Lopez's people said the room could only have white flowers—okay, no big deal. But she once kept the massage therapist waiting for three hours while she got on the phone and had screaming arguments with her boyfriend at the time, P. Diddy. Every time he called, she'd chase her assistant and all the handlers out of the room. The poor masseuse had to stay there, hanging on, while J.Lo cried and screamed hysterically. This was somebody who worked hard, and who booked appointments one after the other because it was her livelihood. But everyone else had to subordinate their schedules because J.Lo was having personal drama.

But J.Lo was an exception. When Norman Schwarzkopf stayed at the hotel, for example, he found out that a dozen employees were in the Reserves. They worked as dishwashers and in maintenance, things like that. The general came down to the lobby and met with them all as a surprise, thanking them for their service to their country, and got the entire staff all emotional. U2 were similarly humble. When they stayed at the RIHGA, they told the paparazzi to wait for them across the street. That way, the other guests wouldn't be disturbed and the entranceway wouldn't be blocked. True to their word, they came down, crossed the street, and got their pictures taken and signed autographs. Wealth and fame don't always lead to class—but they don't necessarily have to lead away from it, either.

At one point the management changed at the RIHGA, and Daria decided to leave. She got hired by a company named Marquee Concierge, which was trying to do something similar to what Abigail Michaels was doing—but they were doing it all wrong.

They had three big investors and their business model was predicated on having clients pay $10,000 a year for 24/7 concierge service. They hired a big staff with exorbitant salaries, and took nice offices in the Empire State Building. The overhead was tremendous. Meanwhile, it took them four months and a fortune just to put together a brochure.

One of Daria's clients followed her from the hotel. The other thirty or so Marquee clients were all free memberships, or given a "promotional rate" of 75 percent off. There were only two concierges and, because the service was 24/7, they both had to be on call at all times. Unfortunately for them, this was the same time that Marquee the nightclub opened up. Daria would get woken up at two in the morning, because some drunken partier was calling 411 looking for Marquee.

They had a core group of financiers who did spend money and traveled a lot. But those people weren't enough to sustain the business—not when management was renting a house up in the Hamptons using the company's money. Not when management was dropping thousands of dollars at nightclubs, entertaining clients with models and bottles.

They fired everybody, and the business shut down—and I got Daria to join our team and oversee our expanding operation.

16.
Circle in the Sand

The more Abigail Michaels expanded operations, the more calls we got from people who wanted to work with us on their projects. Andrew Miller made his fortune through a very popular infomercial product. "I have this resort in the Hamptons," he told us, "and I want to have concierge service. Would you be interested?"

Abbie and I were always interested. We met with Andrew in a nice restaurant on Lexington and 46th Street. He was about forty years old, a short guy with a big mop of brown hair and a very intense demeanor. When he spoke, he leaned forward like he was whispering CIA secrets. His assistant was named Ilse and looked like a cliché of the hotel industry worker: She wore a little scarf and her hair was pulled back in a very tight ponytail. She had a leather book to take notes in, and she totally exuded a crush on Andrew. Even if there wasn't any romantic inclination between them, you could just tell she was fantasizing about beating the crap out of him in bed.

The only resort that Andrew had, unfortunately, was a conceptual one. "Here's the idea behind the resort," he told us. "I have friends who are bazillionaires, and we have these gigantic, elaborate homes all over the world. No one is ever there and it costs a fortune to maintain a home like that. St. Martin's, St. Bart's, Aspen, Telluride, Vail, Nantucket. Everywhere you would expect."

I knew exactly what he meant. There's a lot of wear and tear on homes like that, especially when it's an oceanfront property. The house gets eaten away, and yet the owners are only there once a year—if that. They have to hire a house manager (often with a six-figure salary) to live in the house for free to make sure that the salt doesn't erode the façade. The house managers have to paint—or rather, hire painters—when needed. They have to make sure that the gardener shows up, make sure that the mail gets in, and really run the house as though it were an ongoing operation. With places like that, it's not okay if the grass grows six feet tall until the owner gets there. The neighbors would flip. The owners wind up spending $40,000–$50,000 on a gardener for lawns that they don't even see.

"A lot of people are starting to take advantage of the big boom in the market," Andrew pointed out. "There are fifteen-, twenty-, thirty-million-dollar homes on the market, but they stay on the market for two or three years. These are marquee value homes. We're talking about things built by famous architects. I know of a Lapidus that's been on market for over two years. The house has a whole history and it's just sitting there."

"Eating away money," I added.

"Exactly. They're paying all of this upkeep, and nobody lives in it. So my idea is to go after the very high-end vacation market and find people that really don't want to go stay in a hotel. Let's basically duplicate their lifestyle, but in other locations. The Hamptons is an international destination for the rich and famous, and there are no hotels there."

Andrew was right. There must be some zoning regulations that keep it from happening, because otherwise Hyatt would have built a beautiful beachside hotel in the Hamptons. There *are* a couple of bed-

and-breakfasts and a few really disgusting motels—but that's it. It's part of the reason why the Hamptons is so cliquey. You're not going to get invited to a party if you live in Queens. You get invited to a party because you were at another cocktail party the day before, at someone else's house. The party circuit is this little incestuous buzzing around.

"I want to homogenize all of the houses," Andrew continued, "so they have a certain congruent aesthetic. They're all going to be outfitted in Frette linens and they're going to have certain bath products, just like a hotel—except instead of a hotel, it's going to be a twelve-bedroom home."

"We expect to be able to charge a hundred thousand dollars and up per week," Ilse chimed in.

It actually sounded like a good idea, or at least a feasible one. It would be just like when we rented the $300,000 yacht for Zinovy. It would also be a great way for Abigail Michaels to expand our operations, both in a new framework and in a new location. Abbie and I were downright giddy. To be fair, if a dog spa had approached us to have a concierge examine dog poop, we'd go get our gloves. But the Hamptons seemed a little more up our alley.

"Do you think you'll be able to service these big estates?" Andrew asked us.

"Oh, of course!" I told him. "We'll anticipate everything they need. There are vineyards in the Hamptons, and they're going to want private tours. They're going to want to go to all the hot nightclubs, like the Pink Elephant and Tsunami. And they *definitely* will want to eat at Nick & Toni's."

"We're just gonna crack the shell," Abbie chimed in. "We know how to do all this, and everyone is going to love it. It'll just be magnificent."

"The only hitch is that *we* don't have a place to stay out there," I pointed out.

"I'm going to rent a house just for the staff," Andrew told us.

Even though Hampton Estates was still just a concept in Andrew's head, he was an aggressive businessperson who picked a start date for things to get going. Abbie and I started designing how the service was going to work. While Ilse was off with her clipboard, busy picking out the official Hampton Estates–brand soaps, we were left to figure out the logistics. To be honest, I started to get scared. The hotel concept and procedure didn't necessarily translate to what Andrew was envisioning. Where did the people go to get the keys? Where did they check in?

Ilse spent a lot of the time trying to get pool companies to wear a Hampton Estates shirt whenever they cleaned the pool at one of the homes. We couldn't employ a pool cleaner full time, mind you, so he would have to do a few other jobs, then put our shirt on, and then change his clothes again. She was picturing this beautiful Aryan pool cleaner, with his blond hair greased back, disrobing in the sunlight and putting on his fancy Hampton Estates button-down oxford shirt. He would sparkle like gold as he went to clean pools in the one-hundred-degree weather. The more we discussed things, the more it seemed like a fantasy that wasn't going to come to life.

Abbie and I made our way to the Hamptons, and got hit with another solid dose of reality. The Hampton Estates offices were in a disgusting stucco building across the street from the Southampton Car Wash, and were totally industrial and generic. Down the block was the bus stop for the Jitney. If the wind was right, you could smell the Armor All and chemicals from across the way. There was nothing luxurious about any of it at all.

We made appointments to sit down with the doormen and the owners of all the nightclubs and the restaurants. The one place where everyone goes to in the Hamptons is Nick & Toni's. If we couldn't get our people into Nick & Toni's, we might as well have boarded up our imaginary twelve-bedroom houses and told our theoretical Aryan pool guys to go home.

Nick & Toni's is a little place that looks like a cozy bed-and-breakfast type cottage, tucked away among tons of foliage. It's supposed to be Italian, but it's more like a mix of everything—in other words, rich people food. It's not formal at all, and is very laid back. You can go there in jeans and no one will blink.

The restaurant doesn't hold a lot of people, but it's one of those places that is full of A-listers. But a Britney Spears isn't A-list to Bonnie Munshin, the manager. To her, an A-lister is more like real estate developer Harry Macklowe or the president of the New York Stock Exchange. It's high-culture cred, not pop-culture cred. The only glitterati that matter to Bonnie are the ones that are known in the Hamptons: Billy Joel, Steven Spielberg, Chevy Chase, Calvin Klein, and Liz Smith.

That's why Nick & Toni's is the kind of place where you have to practically send in your résumé to get in. It's not a rude sense of self-importance, like with Trough. It's actually not about pretense. Bonnie tries to create a home away from home. It's the opposite of a trendy nightclub: She *doesn't* want lookie-loos bothering people. If you want to gawk, go somewhere else.

Obviously, *everyone* in the Hamptons wants to be Bonnie's friend. She's the Texas Guinan of her scene. My friend Robert knew her—and he was my only in to get a connection. There's a Nick & Toni's in Manhattan, which is perfectly fine as a restaurant but nowhere near as exclusive as the Hamptons branch. Whenever I had run into her there with Robert, I'd really tried to get on her good side.

First I tried to call. "Hi, may I speak with Bonnie?"

"Who is this?" the reservationist asked.

"It's Michael Fazio."

"Does she know you?"

"Oh, absolutely!" I said.

"I'll tell her you called."

I waited a day and called again. "Hi, is Bonnie there? It's Michael Fazio."

"May I ask what this is regarding?"

"Oh, she knows me. I'm friends with Robert and I know her from Nick & Toni's in New York." It was kind of amateurish, but it was my only link to her. It wasn't really about me name-dropping. It was more like me showing to her that I was vetted, because her friend is my friend so she doesn't have to worry. I *get* it. I'm one of you!

I guess she didn't think I got it, or that I was one of you. She didn't call back.

I tried my next trick: sending her flowers.

This time she called, but she wasn't being all warm and fuzzy. "The flowers were very sweet—what do you need?"

"Are you there right now?" I said. "I'll be over. Just wait for me. I'll be right over." I tried to keep it light and breezy, as if my Hamptons concierge career didn't depend on it.

I ran over there and gave her my spiel of who I wanted to be sending her way. "There are fifteen-thousand-square-foot oceanfront homes that are empty. This guy's going to be renting them for a hundred thousand a week. These are really rich people. You have nothing to worry about. These are going to be high-profile people, too. They're not going to want to bother anybody. I get your vibe, completely."

The entire time I was talking, she sat there literally making faces. "Where are these houses? The owners are going to let you put some stranger in their *house*? *What?*"

"I know it might sound crazy but that's only because no one's ever done it before," I insisted.

"I can't promise you anything, but just call me. Ask for me if you need something."

One month in, and there were no bookings. Andrew wasn't really finding any houses, either. Apparently there weren't as many people interested in renting homes for $100,000 a week as he had thought—and apparently there weren't as many homes sitting around and getting salty and run-down, either. At least not owned by people who wanted to convert them into quasi-hotels.

Fortunately, Andrew himself had a very flagship kind of home himself. It looked like South Fork, with big gates, his Ferrari parked out in view, and horses roaming around this beautiful grassy knoll. While we stayed in the staff home—Abbie and I alternated between the Hamptons and New York—we found out that Andrew enjoyed pot. He would crash there with us, popping out joints and wine like it was a frat party. He was also hiring people to be house attendants, even though there weren't any houses yet. He was running things as if we actually had customers.

Eventually, Andrew managed to get some traction. "I've got the Honigs coming to stay," he told me. I'd heard of the Honigs; *everyone* had heard of the Honigs, which is why I'm not referring to them by their actual name. "I'm thinking they'll be influencers who'll then go back and spread the word to everybody that we're really the thing to do this summer. Can you get an itinerary ready for them?"

"Absolutely." I started planning an itinerary—but everything was difficult because the Hamptons was very closed. The golf club that everyone wants to play at, for example, is private. I was making my rounds, but what I was describing was totally a foreign concept to everyone. I was forced to try and sell the credibility of the whole thing. "Of course you haven't heard of this. It's very off the radar. Nobody knows about it. It's exclusive."

Sometimes that got me somewhere. When it didn't, I said, "It's the Honigs. I'm not supposed to tell you, but it's the Honigs who are going to be staying in one of our homes this weekend." That *always* worked. I even let Bonnie know, because I was positive she was friendly with them.

"They're coming?" she said. "He didn't call me."

I knew that since it was the Honigs, I could make the ultimate reservation with her: eight people for nine on a Saturday night—when they only had one table that held eight people. I pulled out all stops. They got the golf, they got the vineyards, they got first-class treatment every step of the way. Hampton Estates was firing on all cylinders.

The Sunday after the Honigs came and went, I got a phone call. "Hi, may I speak with Michael Fazio?"

"This is Michael Fazio," I said.

"Hi, Michael. It's Steph calling from Nick & Toni's. I have a message from Bonnie."

"Is something the matter?"

"She just wants you to know that you don't have to deceive her to get reservations. She really didn't appreciate being tricked. You should've just told her what you needed in the first place."

"Wait, *what*? What happened?"

"I don't know. That's what she told me to say."

"Is she there? Can I talk with her?"

"No, she definitely is *not* here to talk with you at the moment."

I was *horrified*. I couldn't think of what had gone wrong. I wracked my brain trying to think of every other time I had a reservation go awry. Did they show up with only four people? Did they not even bother to show up at all?

I practically started stalking Bonnie, doing everything I could to get her on the phone. Nick & Toni's was closed the following day, and all I could do was obsess about how I had "tricked" her. It was such a blunt message that I was completely confused.

Finally, I managed to get her on the line. "Bonnie, I understand there was some sort of problem. What happened?"

"What happened was, those weren't the Honigs!"

"What? They *were* the Honigs! I swear to God they were the Honigs!"

"No they weren't, honey. It was some guy who happened to be named Honig, and his buddies."

I hadn't even considered that. It was a house, a big price tag, and the Hamptons—of *course* it was going to be *the* Honigs. But it was only *a* Honig. "I'm dumbfounded. I am so sorry. But I wasn't *lying*!"

"No, I know. But you can't do that. You have to really know next time."

The fact of the matter was, she was absolutely right. If my job is to be a connector, I have to be damn sure that I knew who I was connecting to what—especially at a place like Nick & Toni's, where they were trying hard to cultivate a certain vibe.

By the end of the summer, we had no clients, no houses, and no realistic chance of returning to the project the following year. Abbie and I returned to New York, focusing on what it was that we did best.

GOING TO THE COUNTRY

The expression "The Hamptons" is a bit misleading, in the same way that being from "New York" can mean Manhattan, or it can mean one of the boroughs, or it can even mean upstate. Coming

continued

from New York City, Southampton is the closest. It tends to attract old money and newbies all at the same time. It's where the Paris Hilton bars are. It's where the share houses are. Because it's the first one, you think you've hit gold when you get there.

Next comes Bridgehampton, which is just a bunch of rich white people who golf. East Hampton isn't technically the farthest of the Hamptons, but it's far enough. You don't want to go past it. That's where you'll find Steven Spielberg, David Letterman, and Jerry Seinfeld.

The flashy nightlife is almost always in Southampton. Most of the "Hamptons" places that you read about are in Southampton. It's great—on the surface. Yet it's also where the *Jersey Shore* cast would be seen. On the other hand, you're going to see Gwyneth Paltrow when you get to East Hampton. You might not see her in a nightclub, but you will see her at a charity dinner at somebody's house.

There's this idea that Hamptons life is really glitzy, like going to some trendy hotel and dressing up for stylish restaurants. The media treats it as though it were Palm Beach, where everything is polished. In reality, it's the opposite. If you go to most places in Louboutins and a beaded cocktail dress you'll be completely out of place. It's not like Los Angeles, where people *try* to look sloppy. It's a weekend community and the hippest and most famous people treat it that way. All those things that people fantasize about *are* happening. They're just not happening with neon signs on them.

As with any community, there are subliminal ways to gauge someone's status. If someone has a phone number that starts with the 324 prefix, you know that they're the real deal and have been there forever. It's the equivalent of having a 212 area code in New York; 324 is almost always "south of the highway," which is where the most expensive homes are.

Another status symbol is the number of beach stickers you have on your car. You need to have a sticker that says you're a Hamptonite
continued

to park at the beach. The fancier the car, the more beach stickers it tends to have on it. They wind up accumulating like tree rings.

When people want to size you up directly, they won't ask if you rent or own like in most other places. Instead, they'll make comments like "I can't stand the summer here" or "Are you year-round?", which are based on the idea that the renters are tarnishing their quaint little town.

The Hamptons is like a gated community—without the gates. The only gate is a knowledge gate. If you're in the "right" place, everyone is approachable and even friendly. Anything that Guild Hall puts on will always attract the right crowd. ARF, the animal charity, always attracts the right crowd. There are two gay events that are very celebrity-studded. One is for the Center, which is the Gay and Lesbian Center in New York City. The other is the Empire State Pride Agenda, which is on the beach and always gets a big celebrity clientele. The East Hampton film festival is a pretty obvious place to go see people.

If you're cool enough to know that you should be at a Guild Hall event and you run into a Billy Joel, it's very easy to strike up a conversation. Provided you're not gushing over his music, the event itself will provide something to talk about. Everybody's approachable because of this sense of guilt-by-association. You're there, so you must be okay.

In the Hamptons, rich people give their homes to be used for these big charity fund-raisers. The funny thing is, no one says that they're going to the Amaryllis Farm Equine Rescue event. Instead, they're "going to Steven's tonight" because the party is at Steven Klein's house. But it's not like Steven invited them to some exclusive event. Anyone can get out a checkbook, write out a donation—tax-deductible—and be welcomed in. I feel like a trespasser many times because I'm walking through somebody's house. Granted, they often have undercover security or an area closed off. But it's still kind of weird to take a pee in Steven Spielberg's home.

continued

Unlike in a club, there are no bodyguards and no VIP sections at these events because everyone is ostensibly a VIP. Don't drop money to visit a club where no one will be, or where you can't approach the people who are there. Drop money to send those poor horses to the Amaryllis Farm, and your hand will be reaching over Madonna's to get a shrimp off the table.

17.
Good Housekeeping

The Abigail Michaels plan was that each time we got a new building, we were going to do the same thing that we did with our first one. We had that system figured out, and we knew both how many people we needed and what kind of people they needed to be. This ended up being a total mistake, because every building isn't the same—and not every group of tenants is the same.

Our first building was mostly populated by rich kids (read: up to age thirty-five), whose parents picked out their apartments for them. The parents asserted that they liked to come to the city, that it was nice for them to have a great place to stay, and that their children *needed* a three-bedroom so Mommy and Daddy could keep some things there and never have to unpack. Our services were used so frequently that the building became a total cash cow.

Because these kids moved straight from college to their fancy apartments, they never learned how to handle everyday chores—and thanks to Abigail Michaels, they never had to. We had a girl whose mother booked a car service for her every morning to get to work. One couldn't expect her to take the subway; there's a *reason* why it's underground.

Abbie and I thought we had discovered gold with our first building, so we took on a bunch of others as soon as we could. We didn't realize that new buildings are often *empty* buildings. We started our operations in places with five hundred apartments—but it takes a long time before five hundred apartments fill up, even in Manhattan. On the flip side, everybody and their brother was getting into the real estate business because of the housing boom—but the technical knowledge was not always there. In one of our new buildings, the giant glass doors didn't really meet correctly. In the winter, it was literally colder and *windier* inside because those doors created a vacuum of cold cyclonic air. The developer never thought of important things like that. He also didn't think that they should vent the heat all the way back to our space, which meant that there was condensation on our little aluminum countertop. We sat in our coats, trying to help the six residents through our chattering teeth. Abbie and I brought in so many space heaters that fuses would blow.

It was catastrophe after catastrophe. Another building had a major, disgusting rat problem. Rats are a very common sight on the New York City subway tracks. They know that people can't get to them down there, so they're utterly unafraid. We had the same situation in the building. The rats just walked around in our space, looking in the garbage cans for anything good. If we shooed them they'd simply back away a few feet. It was more like they were politely getting out of our way rather than being actually intimidated.

Abigail Michaels became so spread out that we were losing money hand over fist. It felt like we just weren't going to make it, like everything was upside down. The last straw was when the main water line for the heating and air-conditioning unit burst in one of these brand-new buildings. I came in that morning to find people's deliveries and their dry cleaning submerged in inches of water—and then we had to try and explain to some wealthy lady why her entire wardrobe got ruined. I felt like I couldn't do it anymore and I simply wanted to leave.

In essence, that's kind of what we did. Abbie and I bailed on our whole in-house concierge concept, and instead set up a centralized virtual presence. We still offered services, but now people would call us from their building and would never really get to see us. That's how it worked in a hotel, after all. Half the time the concierge there is just a voice on the phone.

Because we didn't have an on-site office in most places, Abbie and I threw meet-and-greets in building lobbies. We wanted the residents to put a face to our virtual service. I was mingling with the tenants at one of these events when I couldn't help but hear a woman with a Fran Drescher voice. Even though she seemed young, she was already Botoxed and collagened to death. Her hair was platinum blond and her eyebrows were tattooed. *Well,* I thought, *she's either in fashion, or she's an entrepreneur of some sort.*

"That must be Michael!" she said. "Oh, they're so fabulous. I have to introduce myself. Hi! I'm Michelle from apartment 15F."

"Oh, of course," I said. "We see your name a lot. Thanks for using the service." She was always going out to restaurants and calling car service, and spending a lot of money in the process.

"Well, my assistant loves you."

"That's great. We're an assistant's best friend."

"Yeah, I'm between L.A. and New York. It's really such a luxury to have you."

"What do you do?" I asked her.

"I'm a student."

How could she have an assistant, be bicoastal, and go to school? I wondered. *She must be an heiress of some kind.* "Well, where's your family from?"

"They're from Midland, Texas."

Hmm, oil. "What do you study?"

"I go to New York Film Academy. I decided that I want to be behind the camera instead of in front of the camera."

"Oh! You're an *actress*."

"Yeah, I do adult movies. You probably don't know me because I don't think you like my 'type,' but I'm pretty famous." She pulled out her phone and started to show me extremely explicit pictures of herself. "Yeah, this is me. And that's me. I'm really big into medical fetish." I thought that meant she dressed like a nurse and played doctor. But no. She showed me the medical fetish picture next: there were about fifty of those vein clamps that doctors use during surgery—all attached to her genitals. She was photographed sitting in a chair, and with all of the clamps hanging down it looked like Edward Scissorhands.

Thanks to her Fran Drescher voice, everyone in the lobby couldn't help but listen to her. Michelle helpfully started showing her phone around, explaining to everyone what the medical fetish was and letting them know about her AVN award. Then she explained to everyone what the AVN award was. It was one big community.

Besides not meeting the residents, we also had a legal issue by being off-site. When we were hiring housekeepers or ordering items for people, we were acting as their agent in a legal sense. Since we didn't see the tenants in person anymore, we made them sign a contract acknowledging that they were asking us to do these things for them. They also agreed, in writing, to reimburse us for anything they requested—and they had to send us a copy of their credit card. I learned that the hard way after people got Belinda Carlisle tickets without giving us anything in writing; we never saw that money again. But once you signed the forms, you were on file and everything was done. It was a formality that took two seconds, and nobody really had a problem with it—until the one guy who *did* have a problem with it.

Katie, one of my newer hires, called me with the problem. "I don't know what to do," she said. "This guy Abe has his apartment cleaned four or five times a week, sometimes twice in a day. He's a good customer and he sounds important, but at the same time he's got a very aggressive attitude. I've tried to get him to sign the credit card forms, but he hasn't. He's been too busy traveling all over the world."

She had totally bought into his air of entitlement—but I'd been there, so I knew where she was coming from. When someone acts high and mighty, most people in service naturally buy into their persona and kiss their ass. It's not like he didn't have the money to pay for housekeeping. The building he was living in was really expensive.

Ostensibly, the housekeepers are supposed to come in and clean. But I assumed that Abe was using the service more like his personal housekeepers, having them running errands and get groceries. If he wanted to spend a thousand bucks a week on that, it was fine with me. It would be easier on the housekeepers, too, and they'd be getting paid just the same.

"I'll talk to him," I told Katie.

"Well, he's *really* rude," Katie told me.

"How rude is *really* rude?"

"He's constantly changing the schedule. He's had a housekeeper show up, and he's kept her waiting in the lobby for two hours. When I called to say that she was just sitting there, he told me he didn't care and that he wasn't ready for her. And, like, why was I bothering him with this *nonsense*."

Now I got a chip on my shoulder. True, he was spending a lot of money every week. Big deal! He shouldn't be mean to people. All he had to do was let the woman know how long she should wait. Yes, she was getting paid for her time, but we had to have *some* protocol. But we needed his charge forms signed or no one was getting paid. I called him up, not to scold or bother him, but just to get him to try and understand my position.

He never called back.

I called him again.

He never called back. He never called back four or five times.

I got a tiny bit pissed. I left him a message, very professional but still a bit sterner than usual. "I'm sorry to bother you," I said, "but we just have a little matter that we'd just like to tidy up. If you don't mind, it'll take two seconds. I'm sure we can remedy this easily. It'll make me so happy, and then you'll be happy, and we'll stop calling you."

A few hours later, Abe called me back. He was very young, and *very* pretentious, and those two elements always combine to create the most charming person imaginable. He was in his early twenties, and proceeded to tell me how he was much too busy to speak with me. "This is becoming *such* a bother! I don't understand why *you people* have to constantly harass me for some form. Of course I'm good for the housekeeping bills. Have I done *anything* counter?" To be fair, he did have a valid point. We'd been processing charges on his credit card with no problem. It's just that we had no contract. "Yes, I understand. I don't have time for this frivolousness, but I'll send over the charge authorization. Email it to me again."

I emailed him the charge authorization. But the form never came back, and he still kept hiring housekeeping to his apartment.

This was the uncomfortable thing about dealing with people who are affluent. At that level of wealth, things like several thousand dollars for housekeeping are really not substantial. These are people who don't pay their own bills, because they have business managers. It's often the case that the more money you have, the more aversion you have to handling it. There are people in the world who haven't been to a grocery store, and couldn't tell you how much a pint of milk is. It doesn't make them *bad*; it just makes them annoyingly clueless.

I figured Abe was that kind of person. If he valued money at all, he could have hired a domestic for the amount he was spending. He seemed like the type of guy who eats snacks out of the minibar at a hotel. It didn't matter that the pretzels were seven dollars; what mattered is that they were convenient.

I decided to call him one last time, and once again I left him a message. "I *hate* to do this," I told him, "but I just really need this form. Let's say that I need it by next Monday, or we're going to have to discontinue the housekeepers."

He didn't call back even after that. On Monday, I phoned the housekeeping company. "Look," I said, "I'm sorry. I know he's a great customer to you guys. But this is it. You can't go to there because we don't have any written commitment from him to guarantee that he will pay."

Now Abe called me back, on my cell to boot. "How *dare* you? Are you implying that I'm a thief? I am very busy. You probably don't understand, but I'm traveling *all* over the world, and I have commitments. I can't afford to come home to find out that I don't have access to this service!"

"I'm really sorry," I told him, "but we tried it the other way, and it wasn't working. I'm just really not willing to take a risk." I tried to placate him by playing into his ego. "You might not understand because you're a very affluent man, but if something happened and I lost this money, it would be devastating."

"Well, I don't need you people. I'll find other services." Then he hung up on me.

A month went by, and I didn't hear a peep out of him. To no surprise, I then got a letter from American Express. Abe claimed he did not authorize any of the charges. I *knew* the procedure, and I *knew* you can't break the rules for people; this is the inevitable result. But it was still hard to believe that someone with all that financial substance was going to screw me over what was, to him, nothing. For someone like Abe, $3,000 is the equivalent of dropping twenty dollars on the street. Yes, you'd *notice* it—but you'd just go to the ATM and get more.

I spent time getting all of the entry records from the doorman; every time the housekeeper came, they'd had to sign in. I was able to prove that housekeeping had been there *dozens* of times—but it didn't matter at all. Abe didn't sign his consent, and he had only verbally given us his American Express number. I wasn't going to see a red cent—and I was *fuming*.

I called Abe and got his voicemail—again!—and left him message after message. "Look, you know what you did, and I know what you did. Let's just be real about this. This is not a nice game to play."

No response.

A couple of months later, Katie and I were talking and Abe's name came up for some reason. "What an *asshole*," she said. "He was so horrible. I wonder what he does. Where does he make his money?" She got on her computer and started searching around the Web for him. "Oh, look! I think I found him. He owns a graphics company. He must be extremely successful."

She showed me his website. He had billed himself as a graphic artist, but there was an awful lot of photography and a lack of any actual *graphics* on the site. The way he'd laid it out reminded me of looking through dirty magazines to find escorts. *Graphics, shmaphics,* I thought. *He's probably some spoiled kid who designs dirty DVD boxes for his father's porn company and calls himself an "artist."*

I went on my computer and started searching for him online as well—except I added the word "porn" after his name to my search. *Pay dirt.* There were pages and pages of results, all of him starring in different movies. Back in my hotel days, I'd been tipped off by somebody who worked in porn that adult stars earned a lot of their money for hire. They usually do strip shows or escorting on the side. Knowing that, and learning that he's a *gay* porn star, I knew for sure that he was a hustler—a hustler whose cell phone number I had.

"How much for a party?" I texted him from my friend's phone.

I hadn't even put down the phone before he responded. "Three seventy-five for an hour; fifteen hundred for overnight; five thousand for a week."

I started getting a little more graphic, trying to see where his boundaries were. He was "cool with a group," as well as spitting and verbal abuse. Frankly it got difficult to think of something he *wouldn't* be open to doing ("Choking?"). And yes, Abe assured me, all those amenities were included in his fee.

The next day I emailed him so that he'd know that it had been me. "This is one final attempt to give you the opportunity to correct what you've done," I wrote. "I understand the hectic schedule that you must have—and not to mention how difficult it must be to coordinate an entire group in your apartment. Looking at your housekeeping schedule, you apparently haven't been successful enough to book many full weeks. So if you *are* able to book one overnight this week, and you give just half of the money to me, then I'll forgive the balance of your debt."

Sadly, I never really got vindicated. But we did have fun in the office circulating pictures of his underwhelming anatomy. The thing was, it was very easy for difficult or wacky clients to earn a reputation in the office. People are more open with concierges—and we are *very* open with one another.

Affluent, wealthy, established people assign concierges some sort of intellectual credibility that they don't assign to servants. It's kind of like we're their confidant. It often becomes us versus them, me and the rich guy against other service people. It's kind of awkward because they confide their own prejudices. They're often predisposed to judge the intelligence of other people in service, especially when it comes to jobs like dog walking, housekeeping, or limo driving—in other words, the people they would never be bothered to speak with directly.

Todd Nybakken was that type of guy. He lived in a very fancy building on Central Park South, where the apartments started at $4 million. He also had a complete hang-up when it came to hiring a housekeeper, to the point where I felt like a hostage negotiator trying to send someone in. "They're not going to break anything, are they?" he demanded. "Do they steal?"

Obviously he would never ask a maid to her face if she stole. But the concierge is so blessed that we are permitted to interact with the masters directly. "We only work with professionals," I replied, trying to elevate his understanding. It wouldn't dawn on him that being a housekeeper can be a great job: It's not an enormous time commitment and if you took pride in your work you could do really well. You have a flexible schedule and you don't have to wake up that early. The pay is pretty good—good enough that you don't have to supplement it by stealing from rich people's drawers.

"Well, where are you finding these maids?" he said, as if we were throwing up random ads on Craigslist.

"They all come from reputable agencies, who often work with the same people for years. If there was *ever* any problem, we'd be sure to know about it." I wished I was a doctor. No one went to their doctor and challenged them on their way to a cure. But in service, every conversation is one question away from an interrogation.

Todd's housekeeping calls—plural—went on for forty-five minutes at a time. "Do they have insurance? How long do they take? Do they bring their own supplies? Do they do other people in your building? I don't want anybody who does anybody else in the building!"

Because you don't want them to tell your neighbors that you have body parts in your freezer, I thought.

"I really would feel comfortable with an in-writing breakdown of what they do," he insisted.

After a week of back-and-forth, he was finally comfortable enough to trust our recommendation for a housekeeper. But before we could make that call, he made very, very, very specific instructions regarding his place. Some people just close one bedroom and tell the maid not to bother. For Todd, it reached a whole other level: "There are two stacks of papers on the brown desk with the white chair. The right-hand stack must not be touched, and by 'right-handed' I mean from the perspective of the chair." Todd also had a wet bar in his living room and, apparently, there was an Emmy award displayed on its shelves. "Under no circumstances are they to touch the Emmy!!!! Under no circumstances are they to *move* the Emmy!!!! Do not even clean that shelf."

The day that the housekeeper was supposed to come, he called me in the morning to confirm that I got his instructions. "Did you tell her not to touch the Emmy?" he asked me.

"She knows not to touch the Emmy," I told him. *Everyone* knew: the owner of the company knew, I knew, Abbie knew, Daria knew, the maid knew. We all got the memo—*literally.*

"Are you *sure* that the same maid who you told about not touching the Emmy is the same one who's coming to my house? Maybe one of them got sick."

"Yes, I am sure."

"Well, all right," he said. "Just so long as you're *sure.*"

That afternoon, I got a call from Daria. "You're not going to believe what happened," she told me. "Remember the Emmy guy?"

"Of course I remember the Emmy guy!"

"The maid got caught with the Emmy."

"What?" I said, starting to laugh. It was almost like a self-fulfilling prophecy. Of *course* she forgot. He was so uncomfortable with the maid that he felt he had to spy on her. She was probably just trying to help him by finally cleaning his dusty Emmy.

"He'd come back to the apartment," Daria went on, "and the housekeeper was standing on a chair, at the wet bar, holding the Emmy and dusting the shelf. He walked in on her red-handed. He probably thought she was giving some imaginary acceptance speech." Now Daria started to laugh as well, but we were also a little scared.

"Don't worry. It's going to be fine."

"It's going to be fine? This is his worst fear, realized."

"Wait, so what happened? Did he tell her to leave?"

"Oh, no! He told *me* to call the maid service company. They paged the housekeeper and told her to get her out of the apartment *immediately.*"

Alarms were going off in the city: The maid had touched the Emmy. Mayor Bloomberg has been called, and Commissioner Gordon has lit the Bat-Signal. The Emmy has been touched. *This is not a drill.*

"Let him know that we won't charge him," I told Daria. "I'll eat the two hundred dollars or whatever it costs to clean his huge apartment. He's probably one of those people where you can just void the fee and he'll be fine . . . I *hope* he's one of those people."

"That's not going to work," she said. "He says that she damaged the statue." He probably thought the maid germs were eating away at the area of rubbing.

"Well, what is he saying happened to it?" I asked her. "Is it chipped? Is it rotting?"

"It's *scratched*. He believes that she had jewelry on, and her ring left marks."

Just to be on the safe side, we debriefed the housekeeper. "Walk me through it," I told her. "What did you do, specifically? What kind of rag was it? Was it Pledge? Windex? Fantastik?"

"I didn't do anything!" she insisted. "I didn't drop anything. I was just cleaning the bar, and there was a bunch of shelves, and they were glass shelves, and they were dusty. I lifted it and was dusting under it, and that's when he came in. I didn't drop it. I only picked it up. He saw. He saw me. All I did was pick it up. I didn't drop it!"

The funny thing is, this poor housekeeper probably didn't even know what an Emmy *was*. To her, it was some tacky gold statue. She would've held a piece of Lladró pottery with more regard than his precious, allegedly damaged Emmy.

I couldn't call Todd back myself, since I would've gotten the company into a lot of legal hot water if I said the wrong thing. Abigail Michaels had represented that the maid wouldn't touch the Emmy and, goddamnit, she touched the Emmy. We were the ones ultimately responsible for any kind of damages—not the housekeeping company.

Out of curiosity, I searched online to find out what Todd had won the Emmy for—and I couldn't find his name on any site that listed past Emmy winners. He'd probably bought it at an auction. Maybe some former lover won it, and the statue was important to Todd because it was all that he had left.

Poor Daria was beside herself. "I don't know what to do," she told me. "When he first called me, he said he was okay and that he understood that things happen. Now he's going on about how it's completely unacceptable, it is absolutely damaged, and how he's not going to sit by."

"You know what?" I said. "He's not going to be happy unless we make this very official, so I'll contact the Emmy people."

And I did. I reached out to the Academy of Television Arts & Sciences in Studio City. I told the story to many people, making my way up the chain until I could speak to someone in the Emmy repair department—the *nonexistent* Emmy repair department. I was telling it like a comic story. I didn't try to depict him as a lunatic, but as an absurd chain of events. I wanted them to be invested in helping me.

"You know what?" someone finally said. "Just send the statue to me. I'll take a look at it, and we can redip it. If it's that big of a deal, we'll just have it redipped."

"Oh my God. How much is that going to cost?"

"I don't know. Let me see what I can do."

Daria let Todd know that the Emmy was being taken care of through official Emmy channels. To be sure that he was mollified, we hired an air courier to ship it to Los Angeles. It required, literally, a courier coming to his apartment, putting the Emmy in a box, wrapping it in Styrofoam, and taking it directly to a waiting airplane. In other words, it was pretty much the same process that they use to handle human organs for transplant.

Our whole week was about the Emmy. Where's the Emmy? Did the Emmy get to Los Angeles? Now who's got it? Who signed for it? Has the Emmy dipper examined it and offered his appraisal of the damage?

After a week, Todd called Daria back. "This is *crazy*," he told her with a straight face. "I didn't think it was going to take this long. I need it back by Tuesday because I'm having a dinner party. Enough is enough!"

The Emmy guy in Los Angeles was as nice as can be, but he wasn't sure when he'd get around to it. I just made an executive decision that Todd was the kind of person who was his own worst enemy. He was much more interested in having "his" Emmy treated with reverence and respect than in having it actually redipped. "Just tell him it's done," I said to Daria, "and get them to reship it back to his house."

I don't even know if it was ever taken out of the box. They simply returned it to our office, box and all. Part of me wanted to see if there was any damage, but I was certain after talking to the maid that absolutely nothing had happened to it. We messengered it to Todd's big Central Park South apartment in time for his dinner party—and we never heard a peep out of him again.

WEALTHY-TO-ENGLISH DICTIONARY

Fantastic: Has replaced "terrific" and "fabulous."

Bespoke: Custom-made. It cries out "I'm special. This was made JUST for me."

Bootblack: Shoe shine or shoe repair.

Nothing precious: "We don't want to spend too much." You would never want to say, "We want something cheap."

Plebey: Rich people love to mix with "the people" from time to time. Plebey means "low brow," like a diner or a bowling alley.

Salad: Code for "nothing too expensive," but it also implies "we're really tight with our money." It's a big lady's term. "We want a really fantastic restaurant that does creative salads" means that if the entrées are thirty dollars, they'll just split a salad—but they want it to be gigantic and very filling with lots of stuff. There *are* places that specialize in just this, like the Cheesecake Factory and Planet Hollywood.

Artisanal: Technically it means "handmade," but it's a marketing term used to connote unique and special. It's such a new term that most computer software thinks it's a typo.

Girl: Housekeeper. "My girl is *so* great at windows."

continued

Man: Anyone within reach who looks like they can lift something heavier than a nine iron. "Ask the man to hang the picture."

Boy: A male who is needed to do something that doesn't require as much skill as hanging a picture. "The boy will collect my luggage."

Cellular: Rich people stick with the formal term "cellular" for their cell phones.

Nice to see you: The new "nice to meet you." This implies that one is so well traveled in social circles that they assume they've met everyone. It also provides insurance against saying "nice to meet you" to someone you have already met.

Marvelous: You have to be seventy years old to use this term, but it's the right one if you enjoy a bespoke lifestyle.

18.
Wake-up Calls

Out of the blue, I got a call from Whoopi's right-hand man Tom. "Whoopi is doing a radio show," he told me, "and she and I are moving to New York. I'm coming out there in a few weeks to look at apartments. Do you think you can get me a good rate at your hotel?"

"I'm not at the hotel anymore," I told him. "I have my own company now. But I can definitely set you up."

"Oh, that's great. What kind of business is it?"

"It's providing concierge service to luxury apartment buildings."

"Really? Well, that sounds interesting. We should get together. It'd be great to reconnect."

I got us some reservations at a really hip seafood restaurant. It was definitely the kind of place that I thought Tom would find impressive. It was cool in and of itself, but the TriBeCa vibe would make it seem even cooler after coming from L.A. I explained to him that, despite the help of Whoopi and all the other celebrities, the hotel business was still really hurting. It had seemed like the time to move on.

When dinner was over, I asked the waiter for the check. "There's no check," he told me. "This is compliments of the owner. Thank you for referring so much business, and congratulations on your company."

"Thank *you* so much!" I said, doing somersaults inside. They were doing me a favor by even seating us, so eating our bill was a double bonus—not to mention the fact that the waiter announced it to the whole table, instead of just taking me aside to let me know.

Tom looked at me, and he got this strange expression on his face. I had gotten him 50 percent off on his hotel room, and now I got a $200 dinner comped without even asking for it. He was witnessing the magic behind being a concierge.

From then on out, Tom and I spoke all the time. "What did you do today?" he'd ask. "Tell me about your job. This is *crazy*. How was this week? What happened?"

My wheeling and dealing really struck a chord with him, because he told me he wanted me to be a guest on Whoopi's show the week of its launch. Obviously I was thrilled at the opportunity—but terrified at the same time.

"Our producer is going to call you this afternoon," Tom said. "He just wants to preinterview you."

Oh my God, I thought. *This is weird. I'm going to be on a national radio show. I've never been interviewed live before. I've only been interviewed in articles.*

The producer was nice and normal and funny, and we had this ten-minute conversation about my job. I told him about some funny clients and a few techniques I used to help me with my work. Just like that, I was going to be on the air the next day.

I obsessed over how to act, and I obsessed about what I was going to say, and I obsessed about what I should wear right up until it was time for the show. It was kind of fun heading to the radio station, being on the list, and passing through security. They took me down a hall of studios, glass windows everywhere, until I saw the red ON

AIR sign. I walked up and paused right before the window into Whoopi's studio. I tried to calm myself down and act nonchalant, like I'd known Whoopi for years—even though we'd never met and I'd only spoke to her on the phone twice.

Do I just stand here until they're ready for me? I wondered. *No, they probably need to know that I'm here.* I channeled the outgoing side of me, the Michael who can walk into Penn Station and demand entry for a string quartet, and stepped forward with a big smile and a wave.

"Hold on," Whoopi said, over the air. "Michael Fazio's here! *The* concierge extraordinaire is here with me. Tune back in right after this commercial break and you're going to meet my friend Michael."

I came into the room and instantly some of my anxiety dissipated. It was like I was connecting with a friend that I hadn't seen in years. "Tommy told me what happened at the restaurant!" Whoopi said. Tommy had told her this and Tommy had told her that. "I *love* your job. I should've been a concierge. I'd be so good at it!" She was right; she *would* have been good at it. She definitely knows her stuff.

She interviewed me for a bit, and I shared some funny war stories about the profession. "Michael's going to come back on Friday, and he's going to take your phone calls." *I am?* "So if there's anything you want to ask him, you call back on Friday."

I scrambled to think of any more stories that I could offer, so there wouldn't be any dead air.

"This is going to be great," she insisted. "I want you to come back and we'll take some calls, and maybe you can fulfill some requests for the listeners."

Yes, Ms. Goldberg. Whatever you say, Ms. Goldberg. Right away, Ms. Goldberg!

I returned to the show on Friday with my notepad at the ready. I expected some Tiffany to be calling from Las Vegas, dying to go to Pure and asking for my tips on how to get in.

"If you want Michael to do something," Whoopi said, "don't ask him to do it for *you*. Ask him to do it for somebody that you want to help."

The very first call came from Ohio. "My best friend's brother is really, really into the wrestling, and the WWE is having a big show in Columbus. He would just love to meet the stars."

"Okay," I said. "That's great. What's his passion about wrestling?"

"He has cerebral palsy and he's in a wheelchair. He just loves the theatrics. They're like superheroes. I want to get tickets for him, but I really want to be able to make it super-special. Like front row seats or something."

"Stay tuned," I said. "My job is all about front row seats. Let's see what we can do and we'll report the results back here next week." It wouldn't be *that* hard, I figured, but we had to elongate the suspense.

It turned out that there was nothing available; the WWE really did have a big following. I knew every backdoor trick to getting front row center—and it was usually accompanied by a big price tag. But did it work the same way in Ohio? Was I going to be stumped on a national radio show by a Midwest wrestling match?

Wait a minute, I thought. *I'm on a national radio show hosted by Whoopi Goldberg.* It's not like I needed the tickets for Alan Chiles. My usual strategy would have started with the venue. Then I'd move on to a broker. Then I'd track down the wrestlers' reps. Cutting to the chase, I knew I just needed to go straight to the top.

I can find anyone anywhere, and in a few clicks of the mouse, I had a direct name and number for the person who handled all PR for the WWE. "I'm working on Whoopi Goldberg's radio show," I told them, "and we have a listener who's a huge fan. Can we take this over the top? Can he actually go backstage? What can you do?"

They vetted the guy's story—and then they rolled out the red carpet for him. They arranged for him to come during the day when they do all of their rehearsals. There was a preshow dinner backstage, which he was welcome to stay for. The wrestlers took tons of pictures with him, even ones sitting in his wheelchair. They went all out and over the top, as wrestlers are wont to do.

The original caller contacted Whoopi's show next week, absolutely beside himself. "I'm going to put my friend on the phone."

The friend was so excited that it was hard to understand him at first, but it was very easy to make out the "thank you"s and the word "awesome" that he must have said ten times. The thrill of what he got to experience was palpable. But it still felt a little awkward, because I figured any intern could have accomplished the same thing with the power of Whoopi's show behind them. But maybe I did have something special. After all, I knew *how* to ask, I knew *who* to ask, and I got it done quickly.

I looked at Whoopi while she was talking to him on air. She winked at me. It wasn't a scene from a Lifetime TV movie. It was just her and me enjoying a little private acknowledgment that we gave this guy a little lift.

As Whoopi wrapped it up to go to commercial, the guy said, "I love you Whoopi, and I will be listening to you every morning."

Her voice cracked as she signed off. It was a pretty great radio moment.

"That was wonderful!" the producer told me after the segment. "We're going to make an experiment. We're going to take requests on Wednesday and pay them off on Friday so there's not this lapse. Can you come back?"

"When?" I asked him, not believing what I was hearing.

"Every Wednesday and Friday?"

"I'd love to."

The next time I was there, the caller had a similarly touching story. "My son-in-law and daughter have been married for six weeks," she told us. "He was deployed to Iraq, and his twin brother was just killed last month. He's coming back for four days in three weeks. We live in San Diego. I don't know where to send them. Could you just tell me what I could do to make for a really magical evening? Anything, just so they can have a memorable night out. I don't even know what to plan for them."

"What do they like?" I asked her. "Tell me a little bit about them."

"He's all about the water. He loves fishing and he loves sailing; things like that are really his favorite."

"All right," I said. "I have a couple of ideas."

I remembered researching the $300,000 yacht I got for Zinovy's client. A little homework revealed that Royal Caribbean had a few short cruises from California to Mexico. It was a pretty generic itinerary, but it would be on their brand-new ship. Another few minutes of snooping scored the executive list for the company. I called the company, and once again it couldn't have been easier. I was Michael "the concierge expert," calling from a national radio show starring Whoopi Goldberg.

The young couple got the captain's suite. It was as if they stepped into an episode of *Lifestyles of the Rich and Famous,* with every decadent amenity possible on their three-day cruise to Mexico.

The radio show became all about "queen for a day," and what I could make happen for people. The calls got sappier and sappier over the course of a year, and the callers almost started to compete as to who had the saddest story—and therefore deserved the most free stuff.

"Listen!" Whoopi eventually said. "You can call for liver but you *can't* call him for *a* liver. Michael's the kind of guy who can find the best liver for you—but not *a* liver for you."

Then I got a call in Abigail Michaels office from Adam Farris. Adam was a developer who owned a couple of apartment buildings in the city. He was toying with hiring Abigail Michaels to provide concierge service in some of his developments. "Let's see how good you are," he said, like I was on some sort of audition.

"Try me." I couldn't stand people who started their communication with such a cliché challenge.

"I want you to get me a PlayStation for my son."

The PlayStation was *the* toy of the season. If he had asked me months before, it probably wouldn't have been a big deal. But he asked me three days before it was coming out. People were already camping out in front of the stores.

In other words, it was the kind of challenge that stirred up a lot in me. I was completely over *having* to prove myself. But I knew that I was wired to wow people, and I thrived on doing it anyway.

Who do I know at Sony? I thought. *Who do I know at Best Buy? Who do I know at Circuit City?* I started doing my networking calls, putting my request out to every possible resource. The response was universally negative. "Oh my God," a typical contact told me. "I don't know. The waiting list is a mile long with names like Steven Spielberg and Tom Cruise."

"Oh, I know," I said. "I know you can't—but you will for *me*, right? I know it's impossible. It's only my whole company's face that rests on this one request. The thing is, Adam's so great. He's *such* a nice guy." *Why am I still being so old school and begging?* I wondered. *Would it be considered bad if I used my new trump card? Or is that just a new part of my concierge craftiness that I have in my arsenal?*

All right, maybe I was being a *little* bad.

I wasn't getting real concrete evidence that anyone was going to come through. Finally, I pulled my trump card with a publicist. "Hi," I told her. "I do segments twice a week on the nationally syndicated radio show *Wake Up with Whoopi!*"

"How funny. I listen to her show all the time. You're that concierge guy?"

"Yes," I replied. I made it clear to her that it wasn't for Whoopi herself. But for the first time, I was acting like a "celebrity concierge" who can make things happen—rather than pleading for a client because my ass was on the line. "It's not like you need extra exposure, but it would be such good radio if I could announce to somebody that I got them a PlayStation. And it's a nice message for Sony, don't you think?"

"I don't know," the publicist said. "I'd have to get clearance. Let me see what I can do."

"Thanks. This would mean so much."

I still kept uncovering and reaching out to every contact I could. If you enlist twenty people, four of them will actually try to help you. In the rare event that two of them come through, you might be left with egg on your face—but I wouldn't hold my breath. Rarely, it *does* happen.

A few days later, the radio station called to tell me that I had a box there. I had it messengered to my office—and opened it up to find a PlayStation and half a dozen games with it. That same day, my Sony contact called to let me know that he had scored a PlayStation for me as well.

I took one of them and gave it away on the air, for free, to one lucky listener and made his day. I took the other one of them and gave it to Adam, for a lot of money, and made his son's day. True to his word, he ended up signing Abigail Michaels for his buildings. I considered it my reward for having done what concierges live for: helping the wealthy get things they don't really deserve.

CUTTING THE VELVET ROPE

I never did get a call from Tiffany in Las Vegas, dying to go to Pure and asking for my tips on how to get in. But if I had, I would have told her my plan that almost always pays off and yet no one ever thinks to try.

After September 11, Homeland Security agents were staked out in all the New York hotels. They were mostly undercover, but after seeing the same guy for two weeks in the lobby you could put two and two together. The agent heard all my exchanges with guests, and eventually he approached me and broke the ice. "Wow, where did they end up going?" he wanted to know. "What's that place like?"

We got to talking, and he became intrigued by what I did and how I did it. Then he gave me a "cop's friend" card. "My buddy's in the Nineteenth Precinct," he told me. "If you ever need something at the clubs over there, I can hook you up."

Ding! The lightbulb went off in my head: *Cops. Nightclubs. Liquor licenses. Legal issues. I bet the cops know everything about the clubs.* Of course the cops know all the doormen to the clubs. The doorman's outside all night, while the cop is casing the place to make sure that he's carding people. If a cop sent you to a club, the doorman can't let you inside fast enough.

The other thing people might not realize is that the police really are fraternal—if you knew one, you knew them all. Once I was in with my guy, I could call any precinct. Yes, it took nerve, but I could still pull it off. "I'm the concierge for the InterContinental Hotel," I'd tell them. "Who's working tonight in this area?"

Granted, the reaction was *never* friendly. They always vetted me. "You're the *what*? Hold on. Wait. What are you looking for?"

At that point I'd play dumb—and name-drop. "Oh, I'm sorry. Officer Lucas always helps me out on 54th Street. I thought somebody who did 14th Street could help me."

continued

Instantly, the tone changed. "Well, what do you need?"

"Do you guys know the people over at Lotus? Because I'm really having a tough time getting in there, and I just wanted to know if someone could help me. I know this is crazy." If I were doing this now, I'd throw in an aside that this was a one-time thing, and I'm doing someone else a favor. "My friend is having her birthday and she's been dying to go there. She's a really sweet girl and it would mean so much to her."

Let them take down your number. Never pressure them. "Here's what I need. Ask around. Think about it. If you think that you can help me, here's how to get in touch with me."

If it's a club you want to frequent regularly, make sure you go back to the precinct and thank them. Bring them cookies or some treat. Yes, they'll think you're crazy. But they'll also think of you as this crazy—but sweet—person, and they'll remember you and take your call. Then they can show off their power by getting you into the place.

If the cops are a dead end, find out the managing company that owns the property. Chances are no one asks them to show off, either, and this is *their* opportunity to be a big shot as well.

Just don't tell them Michael sent you!

19.
Get Up and Go

There was a wave of development, when big companies bought up every piece of land they could and then built brand-new structures. The next wave was of people buying historical sites and converting them into landmark buildings. That's when the unbelievable happened: The Plaza Hotel was going to turn condo. It's everyone's fantasy of romanticized New York. Located right on Central Park, staffed by doormen in top hats and surrounded by horse-and-carriages, it is elegance straight out of a movie. The Plaza was where Barbra played with Robert Redford's hair in *The Way We Were*.

Servicing the Plaza would be the absolute pinnacle. Thankfully Abigail Michaels had built up our brand enough that we were known in Manhattan real estate circles. With some of our first buildings, what we couldn't get in dollars we bartered for in publicity. We conceded pretty significantly on money, but our contract stated that the developers must use our name in all of their ads.

This was a time when the Sunday *New York Times* real estate section was around forty-five pages long. It was to New York what the Sunday *L.A. Times* movie section is to Los Angeles. But instead of there being a two-page ad for a movie, developers were taking a two-page spread for their new projects. There would be full-color photos of the building with a list of all the included features: billiard room, indoor pools, Pilates, closets—and Abigail Michaels Concierge.

We got an appointment with the Plaza, and we pitched to them that we'd be perfect because of our hotel background. We knew everything there was to know, and we could anticipate requests. The meeting went well, and we waited to hear back. Then we waited, and then we waited some more. Finally, Abbie and I found out that they gave the account to a company called Concierge Direct.

I was devastated. The worst part was that I'd never even heard of the firm. *Where the hell did they come from?* I wondered. I thought back to my days with Glennis, how she's instilled in me the need to dissect every possible opportunity. I started looking around online, and I learned that Concierge Direct was basically a function on a Crestron screen. The Crestron was a little device that you could carry around your house to perform many functions, like turning your stereo on or adjusting the lights. It happened to have a button on it for restaurant reservations. *I bet that button doesn't go anywhere,* I thought. *They may have built the technology, but they aren't really a concierge service. Where did this come from and who answers those requests?*

Trying to track down Concierge Direct really meant tracking down the company that invented the technology. I wound up calling Crestron in Stockholm. "What's your company?" the Crestron sales rep said. "What's your business? What are you doing?"

"I want to get to the people who are fulfilling the actual concierge request in this Concierge Direct model."

"I don't know who that is, but let me get you in touch."

Now I got a call from Steve from Concierge Direct. I think he realized that we could potentially be the source to fulfill that concierge button. I also think he realized I knew that button was presently empty, that it would be like dialing 911 but getting a dial tone. While we were feeling each other out, he must have recommended us to the developers, because Peter, a partner in a big conglomerate that owns Cooper Square Realty, gave me a call soon thereafter.

"I'm somewhat familiar with Cooper Square," I said carefully, "but can you tell me more?"

"Oh, we're going to be managing the Plaza. We're interested in talking to your company. You're very intriguing and we'd like to speak with you about providing service across our brand."

I did my homework before the meeting—and found out that Cooper Square managed around 250,000 apartments in New York. "This is crazy," I told Abbie. "We don't want the Plaza; we want Cooper Square. We want every single one of those apartments."

Instead of thinking of each building as an individual project, I started working out a whole model for a community of apartment complexes. I did a very detailed spreadsheet and got ready to present this big dissertation about how Abigail Michaels could upgrade Cooper Square's offerings.

We met in their conference room, with that classic long business table. Everything in the room was very fancy, all mahogany and gold leaf. The owner of Cooper Square kept challenging us on our business model. "Other than a fee," he wanted to know, "how do you make your money?"

"We get commissions from people," I said. "It's complicated."

"Well, let's see if we can simplify things. Do you handle dry cleaning? Can you pick it up and deliver?"

"Of course," I told him. "We do that all the time."

"Do you book massages?"

"Of course we book massages!" Abbie said.

"Well, do *they* pay you a commission?"

"It depends on if you get a happy ending or not," she quipped. There was something about her timing and her brassy personality that melted all the ice in the room. Everyone started cracking up, and it went from a formal business meeting to a sense of camaraderie.

They had us put together proposed models based on different scenarios, like whether we'd be more cost effective at 250,000 units or at 500,000. I bought beginner business books so I could really give him the information he wanted, in the format that he was used to. "It works at twenty dollars a unit," he told me, after looking over the numbers. "So really, it *is* scalable."

"Great!" I said. "What's the next step?"

"Would you be interested in being bought?"

"What?" *Being bought?* I understood what it meant when Delta airlines got bought by Northwest. But what that meant for us, I had no idea.

"Cooper Square is owned by a larger entity," he explained. "We love your concept and we think that this is scalable in a much larger fashion than what you're trying to do. Why don't you think about putting together a proposal for how you could service a million units? We'd like you to come to present that in Florida on Monday. Get it together and then call us. What's your EBITDA, by the way?"

I had no idea of what to tell him. *Our EBITDA is great. On a scale of one to ten, it's a ten!* "Let me first think about all of the other things we discussed, and then I'll let you know what our EBITDA is." *And what an EBITDA is to begin with.*

On the plane ride to Florida, Abbie and I rehearsed all my new-found business jargon. "Okay, EBITDA is Earnings Before Interest, Taxes, Depreciation, and Amortization. What's our cost per unit? What's our retail price per unit? What's our payroll expense? How do we derive our gross revenue?"

When we got to the Florida offices, I felt like an actor feels when going for a screen test at 20th Century Fox. It wasn't exactly a glamorous place, but it was *buzzing.* The office in Florida was one story, but it was expansive—about two blocks long. When we walked in past the reception area, there was pool after pool of people. In 20th Century Fox you'd walk past all the movie posters; here, it was poster after poster of beautiful buildings. *Oh my God,* I thought, *we've arrived.*

"This is what we want to do with you," they told us after our presentation. "We think that you're super-creative, but you don't know how to grow your business and we do. We employ twenty-five thousand people and we're almost a three-billion-dollar company."

I was as excited as somebody can get about business. Then the negotiations started. A business's purchase price is based on multiplying the EBITDA by whatever multiple is an industry standard. I looked online about purchasing real estate companies, and the standard multiple was anywhere between eight and twelve. Granted, our accountant was me and Microsoft Excel, but it still seemed like an amazing amount of money—*too* amazing.

Whenever any of our clients called for service, I looked up their email addresses. If they were @GoldmanSachs.com, I started asking them questions. "Hi! How was dinner last night? That's great. Listen, I've got a crazy question about EBITDA for you."

It became another form of promoting Abigail Michaels. Clients in the financial industry were impressed that we were getting an offer from a public company. They weren't as impressed, however, with my research skills. "A multiple of *ten?*" one client said. "Or even a multiple of eight? Forget it!"

"But I asked Jeeves." (Further confirmation that the site is useless.)

"That was like ten years ago! A multiple of around four is good."

It came down to the back and forth negotiating, and I got us a little bit more than they originally offered. They gave us a big, fat check and officially bought Abigail Michaels. I took the money and paid off every debt that the business had incurred. I stopped wearing the same suit all the time and bought myself another one. Finally, I bought a house in the Hamptons. It seemed like a really great place to network, since it was full of the kind of people that would be my clients—or that I would aspire to have as my clients, at least.

"We don't understand your business," our new owners told us after looking over our information, "but clearly you do. So what do you need from us?"

We went ahead and hired a slew of people. We got a new office space, and we got a website—not a homemade Michael website, but a real one that cost real money. Abigail Michaels started getting more and more accounts. It was full steam ahead, all luxury all the way.

Just like the *Titanic*.

The housing market crashed, and kept crashing. All of a sudden, new development stopped. There were no more projects, no more holes in the ground that were going to be luxury apartments. Nobody was buying landmark buildings and turning them into anything. Everything started to become sad and scary, and we had to start laying people off.

I got a sense of creativity through desperation. I started reinventing our business model. *Where is the next opportunity?* I wondered. I knew that people were always going to need service. I'd learned that, ever since Pharaoh, rich people stayed rich; they just had different *levels* of rich. They might cut back on how many necklaces they bought, but they wouldn't cut back on how many people were stroking them and helping them. They can do with one less pair of shoes, but not one less pair of hands.

I knew that Goldman Sachs wasn't going to be as frivolous, sending fifteen executives and fifty clients to see Beyoncé in the front row. That was definitely not a priority. But New York is a global destination. It's all about people coming here from other countries, especially while we had the weakest dollar ever. For foreign tourists, luxuries were now affordable. How could I reach those people? I could reach them in a hotel. I'd been reaching them since 1994, so I guessed I needed to reach back.

The Clefs d'Or had lost its luster and the usual players didn't seem to be keeping current. Maybe I needed to bring sexy back to the hospitality industry. I knew that the hotels were underestimating the value of what we provided. From a purely accounting standpoint, it was like having a thousand rooms—yet only thirty-five people using the concierge. I got that they wanted to save money and didn't want to have a full-fledged concierge. But it's part of the fabric that makes the thing work. How many people use the bathrobe? They put *two* of them in every room, which cost a fortune to clean. I suspected they wouldn't mind having a call center in midtown Manhattan that was staffed by concierges.

As these ideas were percolating in my head, I went to a dinner party in the Hamptons. When I got to the house, the weather turned to a torrential rain. The plan had been for everyone to eat outdoors, but now we had to bring everything inside. There really wasn't room to seat all fifty of us. We started putting trays and temporary tables up all over the place. One of these tables went upstairs into a bedroom, so I went up there to eat by myself.

Two minutes later, a guy named Rob walked into the room. He was around fifty years old, with salt-and-pepper hair and nice-looking glasses. He was clearly a Wall Street type. I might have been intimidated if I ran into him downtown, but here he just had a fun vibe about him.

We introduced ourselves and made small talk, and soon I was telling him what it was that I did. "How did you come up with that?" he asked me.

"Well, I worked at the InterContinental for a hundred years. So what do you do?"

"I build hotels."

"Oh, wow! That's *crazy*. Any hotel that I would know?" I asked, thinking he was going to tell me about some new Marriott Courtyard off Exit 26.

"The InterContinental."

"You work with InterContinental?"

"No, I work with Tishman Hotel Group. We're the developer of hotels, and we're partners with them on the brand-new InterContinental in Times Square."

One of the things I learned from Dolores was to keep things from getting intense. After it was clear that we had something in common—he worked in hotels, and I wanted to return to hotels—I changed the subject to something frivolous. I emailed Rob when I came back to the city on Monday, hoping to explore what we talked about.

I went to his office, and we had a meeting about the new Inter-Continental. It was going to be a complete departure from their usual model: They're almost always in business districts and Times Square is touristy. But their vision was basically that, even if you *stay* at the InterContinental, you wind up doing half of what you do near Times Square anyway. So why *not* bring the InterContinental to Times Square? They even brought in Jeffrey Beers, an architect known for designing cool, trendy places. They were branching out of their comfort zone—and thinking that it's hard to figure out the concierge piece.

I told Rob's team what Abigail Michaels could do for them, and they agreed to our offer. It's the same role that I'd filled for years, but somewhat in reverse. Yes, there definitely will be a uniform involved. But, much like everything else I get, I'll be getting it for someone else.

MY BEST SECRETS

The key to being a concierge is knowledge; knowing your client, knowing your city, and knowing how to gain access. But the best places are often free and open to the public—you just have to know about them.

And now you do, too.

Dogmatic (East 17th Street): A play on a hot dog stand. Delicious gourmet sausages served in a hollowed-out baguette with AMAZ-ING sauces.

Ace Hotel Lobby Bar (West 29th Street): It feels like a college library at the University of Hipster. It also helps that Stumptown coffee is practically a drug.

Second Cemetery of the Spanish and Portuguese Synagogue (72–76 West 11th Street): The headstones are almost completely eroded except for faint shadows of Hebrew on the twenty sites. A calming detour on crazy days.

Plexi-Craft (West 24th Street): A supplier and showroom for Lucite furniture. It's a bit of a journey back to shop class.

Jamali (West 28th Street): A florist supply store in New York "flower district," which is just one block long. Prop central for any-time I'm putting together a party or in need of anything visual— from nautilus shells to bamboo trays to colored LED lights that you can drop in cocktails for a disco effect.

Bookmarks, the Rooftop Lounge at the Library Hotel (Madison Avenue): A secret little atrium room on the roof of a prewar and very chic hotel.

CB I Hate Perfume (Williamsburg, Brooklyn): A "scent gallery" that sells perfumes which smell like real things and evoke a time and place. Try "Burning Leaves" or "In the Library."

continued

PDT (St. Marks Place) This is mixology, not bartending. It stands for Please Don't Tell. I wouldn't have told, but it's two years old now, so I imagine the secret is out.

The Roger Williams Hotel (Madison Avenue): The second-floor terrace bar is always empty, and is my favorite quiet meeting place. Very European.

Baked by Melissa (14th Street): Barbie-size cupcakes from a Barbie-size storefront.

Economy Candy (Rivington Street): Hundred-dollar chocolate truffles are great. But sometimes you just want to have Pop Rocks or Pez or all the great old-fashioned candy from the past.

Pulino's (Bowery): Breakfast pizza. Need I say more?

Per Se (Columbus Circle): Hardly a secret, it will normally set you back $350 per person. However, you can go for a drink and just nibble on truffle oil popcorn. (It's the most delicious thing I've ever had.)

Food Trucks (newyorktreats.com): LOJACK technology on gourmet food trucks makes it completely possible to find the most geographically desirable chicken briochette or ginger slush or artisanal ice cream.

Waterside Plaza: I'm really not sure I should say anything, but this is the *best* place to see the fireworks on July Fourth. They're not great at keeping it "residents only" so just blend in with the crowd. (It's rent-subsidized, so don't wear your Lilly Pulitzer coordinates.)

St. Francis Xavier Church (West 16th Street): One of the most beautiful, original, historical churches in the city. They have a soup kitchen that feeds the homeless and there's something peaceful about going inside the chapel. It's like a museum in Rome, but you would never know from the outside.

continued

Lady Mendl's (Irving Place): A little spot of tea? Pardon me while I sing "I'm an Englishman in New York."

Clic Gallery (Lafayette Street): A great place for interesting coffee table books that you won't find everywhere. They also have great art exhibits that are very high style, but not crazy expensive. My favorite part is the French lady who owns it. *Trust.*

You don't have to be rich or fancy to visit any of these places. And best of all, you don't have to worry about telling them that Michael sent you or giving me a tip.

This one's on the house.

Acknowledgments

What I intended as a temporary job became the best professional adventure of my life, and I had great help along the way. My cherished friend, Tom Leonardis, discovered that my crazy profession was interesting enough for the radio. Whoopi Goldberg shared her enthusiasm about me with many, many people. The two of them brought me to a place where I began to truly love and appreciate my job, and the public began to see the bigger picture of what I do.

My amazingly smart and funny collaborator, Michael Malice, patiently coaxed the good dirt out of me and then put it all together in a way that makes sense. Your intelligent talent and razor-sharp wit made this process flawlessly professional and great fun. In my wildest dreams, I never imagined that I would get to work with an editor as amazing as Elizabeth Beier. Thank you for directing this with your intelligent sense of humor and integrity. Kirby Kim is the perfect agent. I admired the fact that he never cut me from his call list, and I am truly thankful that he connected all the dots to make this happen.

Cara Stein, Suzy Unger, Scott Lonker, Glenn Meehan, Stu Sigel, Tony Tackaberry, and Adam Steinman were generous enough to entertain my concept in all of its incarnations. I hope they know that I don't take their time and energy for granted. Rob Weisbach encouraged me to put pencil to paper and connected me with a great writing coach, David Groff. Richard Abate listened to my thirty-second elevator pitch and said, "Yes, there's a book here." Call me anytime you need a table anywhere.

For eight healing years of therapy, Jack Tuchman deserves credit for talking me down from the edge when I thought that selling widgets would be a healthier career choice.

It was the early adopters who gave Abigail Michaels Concierge a chance to prove that people value good service: Jay Hennick, David Epstein, Michael Mendillo, David Kuperberg, Gene Gomberg, Peter Gordon, Frank Peditto, Josh Creel, Kamran Hakim, Steve Kass, Wendy Bosalovege, and Steven Charno. Special thanks to my business partner, Abbie Newman—it's a great journey to share with you. There is so much that has become possible because I have an amazing team of concierges at Abigail Michaels Concierge. I respect and admire each of you, and I'm so grateful that you bring such passion and talent to what you do. Daria Dooling, you are the glue and so much more.

Once upon a time, I dreamed of being a famous singer. Thank you, Dad, for being my collaborator of dreams and then supporting my change in plans. Thank you, Mom, for sewing those amazing sequined shirts—and for becoming a master of Salesforce and Excel and for being our honorary CFO. Thanks to my brother and three sisters for being so interested in all my crazy ideas. Selma Brody: If it ever becomes legal, you will be my mother-in-law. And Uncle Joe: You were right to advise me to focus on writing.

For someone who claims not to have dreams, Jeffrey Brody has certainly made mine come true.

—MICHAEL FAZIO

Acknowledgments

I wouldn't be where I am without Harvey Pekar.

I would also like to thank Elizabeth Beier, Kirby Kim, and of course, Michael Fazio. Warm thanks as well to Team Hughes/Moore/Adams/Chiles.

You need a mess of help to stand alone. I had Stephie Russell, Harjit Jaiswal, Andrea Jamison, Lux Alptraum, Beth Arzy, Dashiell Bennett, David Buer, Jerry Chu, Dave Cirilli, Molly Crabapple, L. B. Deyo, Katelan Foisy, John Girgus, Nadine Haobsh, Dax Herrera, Scooter Honig, Annette Knezevic, Paul Kodila, Lefty Leibowitz, Lauren Leto, Dave Lucas, Maddox, Judy McGuire, Scott Nybakken, Lisa Qiu, Lisa Ronson, Jeremie Ruby-Strauss, Heidi Schmid, Todd Seavey, Caitlin Sheehan, Rachel Shukert, Rachel Sklar, Mandy Stadtmiller, Corynne Steindler, Flora Stepansky, Alexis Tirado, and Kiki Valentine.

Finally I want to thank Asbeel, whose story remains untold.

—MICHAEL MALICE